RUSSIA AT THE POLLS

Voters, Elections, and Democratization

Christopher Marsh
Baylor University

CQ PRESS

A Division of Congressional Quarterly Inc.
Washington, D.C.

CQ Press
A Division of Congressional Quarterly Inc.
1255 22nd Street, N.W., Suite 400
Washington, D.C. 20037

(202) 822-1475; (800) 638-1710

www.cqpress.com

∞ The paper used in this publication meets the minimum requirements of the American National Standard for Information Sciences—Permanence of Paper for Printed Library Materials, ANSI Z39.48-1992.

Printed and bound in the United States of America

05 04 03 02 01   5 4 3 2 1

Designed and typeset by Auburn Associates, Inc., Baltimore, Maryland
Cover design: Karen Doody

Library of Congress Cataloging-in-Publication Data

Marsh, Christopher
      Russia at the polls : voters, elections, and democratization / Christopher Marsh.
            p. cm.
      Includes bibliographical references and index.
      ISBN 1-56802-629-3 (alk. paper)
      1. Voting—Russia (Federation)   2. Elections—Russia (Federation)
3. Political participation—Russia (Federation)   4. Democratization—Russia (Federation)   5. Voting—Russia—History.
I. Title.
      JN6699.A5 M27 2001
      324.947'086—dc21

                                                                                    2001003689

To my loving wife, Melissa,
for her encouragement, support,
and understanding

Contents

List of Boxes, Tables and Figures

Boxes

Tables

Figures

Preface

Francis Fukuyama's *The End of History and the Last Man* was one of the most influential books of the 1990s. That this book on the inevitability of Western-style liberal democracies appeared shortly after the collapse of the Soviet Union is no coincidence. The thesis is certainly appealing, but, as more than a decade of democratic reforms has made abundantly clear, Russia's history is far from over. The establishment of democracy in Russia was not completed with the introduction of competitive elections in 1989 or even with the independence of the Soviet successor states in the final days of 1991. Quite the contrary, these events only marked the beginning of the process. These societies now face the daunting task of making democracy work. As they quickly realized, much more is involved in the effective functioning of democracy than simply holding elections on a regular basis. Practically overnight, denizens must be transformed into citizens who can protect society against the overarching power of the state, and some of them must come forward to compete for positions of leadership and govern in the interests of the people. *Russia at the Polls* is therefore meant to survey Russia's experience with voting and elections and to assess the role they will play in the country's further democratization.

Given the centrality of elections and voting to Russian politics, the topic has not gone without serious scholarly attention. In fact, there is a burgeoning body of literature on the topic. Some of the more noteworthy studies include Colton and Hough's *Growing Pains: Russian Democracy and the Election of 1993*, Belin and Orttung's *The Russian Parliamentary Elections of 1995: The Battle for the Duma*, and McFaul's *Russia's 1996 Presidential Election: The End of Polarized Politics*. Also noteworthy is Hough, Davidheiser, and Lehmann's *The 1996 Russian Presidential Election*, which briefly summarizes the elections of 1993 and 1995 and provides a strong foundation for understanding the presidential elections of 1996, although it was published prior to those elections. Mention must also be made of the diligent work done by Clem and Craumer, who have contributed significantly to our understanding of the spatial dimension of voting in Russia with their insightful analyses of every national election in the post-Soviet period. This list could also include the many significant article-length studies on the subject. The reader will find that I rely heavily upon the work of all of these scholars throughout this book.

The list of works that analyze Russian elections and voting patterns over several elections is much shorter than that of books focusing on a single election. Noteworthy contributions include White, Rose, and McAllister's *How Russia Votes;* Wyman, White, and Oates's *Elections and Voters in Post-Communist Russia;* and Colton's *Transitional Citizens: Voters and What Influences Them in the New Russia.* None of the existing texts, however, presents concise descriptions and systematic analyses of all the major elections in a clear and accessible way, nor do they permit the kind of broad assessment of the subject that becomes possible only with a comprehensive account. *Russia at the Polls,* therefore, is intended to be a study that surveys all of these elections, provides detailed discussions of each while tracking the changes from one election to the next, and does so in a single volume of a manageable size.

This book is the result of many years of study of Russian electoral politics and is based on extensive field research, including the observation of the 1999 Duma elections and the 2000 presidential elections. My hope is that the book makes a significant contribution to the scholarly literature, but it is also intended to introduce readers to the subject of elections and voting. My impetus for writing it was my belief that a book was needed that will teach a wide variety of students about Russian electoral politics in an accessible manner. It is intended, therefore, to be used in courses ranging from those devoted primarily to the study of Russian politics or that include country studies of Russia to courses more specifically focusing on voting and elections from a comparative perspective. It was also my intention to make the book accessible to students with diverse educational backgrounds.

Chapter 1 provides a short introduction to the topic and includes a brief primer on the Russian Federation. This section may prove useful for those readers who have little or no knowledge of the Russian political system and will help them place into context the subject matter of the following chapters. The study of Russian electoral politics begins in chapter 2 with a discussion of institutions such as the *Boyarskaya Duma, veche, Zemskii Sobor,* and the *zemstvos,* as well as of the election of Tsar Mikhail Romanov. Detailed consideration is given to the constitutional reforms of 1905, the elections to Russia's first dumas, and the elections to the Constituent Assembly in 1917. This chapter provides a historical overview of Russia's electoral traditions and gives the reader the necessary context for understanding contemporary issues.

Chapter 3 begins by considering the theoretical issues involving elections in a communist society, how the "typical" Soviet-style election came to be, and what the function of elections was during the Soviet period. The remainder of the chapter focuses on the introduction of competitive elections in the late Soviet period, including reviews of the elections to the Congress of People's Deputies in 1989, the Russian Parliamentary elections of 1990, and the Russian presidential election of 1991.

Following a brief discussion of Russia's experience during its early days of independence, chapter 4 focuses on the turbulent year 1993, which began with a referendum on the Yeltsin administration and concluded with a new constitution, electoral system, and founding elections. Chapter 5 is a detailed examination of the 1995 and 1999 Russian parliamentary elections, with consideration given to issues of continuity, party development, and electoral coordination. In chapter 6 the focus turns to the 1996 and 2000 elections for the Russian presidency. Among the topics discussed are the issues of continuity and change between the elections of 1996 and 2000, specifically changes in the bases of support and the conduct of the electoral campaigns. Chapter 7, which surveys the various elections to positions in local and regional government, including republic president, regional governor, and mayor, is supplemented with an in-depth look at the 1998 elections to the St. Petersburg Legislative Assembly.

Chapter 8, the conclusion, is a more detailed look at the many difficulties facing the future development of Russian electoral politics. Here the focus is on the development of political parties, the problems of electoral coordination, and the nature of Russian political culture. The chapter includes an examination of some of the most influential factors involved in the process of Russian democratic consolidation, including civic engagement, electoral reform, and system legitimacy.

Several pedagogical features are incorporated into the text to facilitate its use in the classroom, including tables of electoral statistics. Readers will find tables of national-level returns for all the post-Soviet elections. References to statistical analyses, such as correlation coefficients and regressions, were kept to a minimum and have been placed in the endnotes where deemed appropriate. Statistical information is also displayed in figures to make the data visual and more accessible to students. Sidebars are used throughout the book to present interesting facts and trends without breaking the flow of the text. Following each chapter is a list of suggested readings to facilitate research on related topics. A chronology of major events in Russian history, particularly events related to elections and voting, appears as an appendix. This is intended to help students follow along as the book journeys throughout Russia's more than one-thousand-year history of voting in its various forms.

Instructors and students are also invited to visit a Web site devoted to the book at http://www.baylor.edu/~Chris_Marsh/. The Web site contains links to many sites devoted to the study of Russia and Russian electoral politics that may facilitate further research in this area.

Acknowledgments

In writing a book of this nature, which is meant to survey the entire electoral history of a country, it is necessary to rely upon the work done by numerous other scholars who have gone before. In this case, I relied particularly upon the work done by certain scholars, and I would like to acknowledge my debt to them. This list includes, but is certainly not limited to, Vladimir Brovkin, Ralph Clem, Peter Craumer, Terence Emmons, Theodore Friedgut, J. Arch Getty, Maxime Kovalevsky, Michael McFaul, Max Mote, Nicolai Petro, Nikolai Petrov, Oliver Radkey, Richard Rose, Richard Sakwa, Michael Urban, and Stephen White. This book is possible only because I was able to rely upon the excellent research already done (and in some cases in progress) by these and other scholars.

I also thank many colleagues who helped me in numerous ways during the research and writing. In Russia, I received invaluable assistance from Georgy Bovt at *Izvestiya*, Grigory Kljutcharev at the Russian Independent Institute for Social and Nationalities Problems, Anatoly Leonov and Aleksandr Slinko at Voronezh State University, and Valerii Patsiorkovskii at the Russian Academy of Sciences. I am also indebted to Andrei Parmekhin, who assisted me greatly in acquiring various sources, including leaflets, fliers, and ballots.

At Baylor University, many of my colleagues assisted me in ways they probably do not even realize, but I am in their debt. They include Jim Curry, Don Greco, Mike Long, Bill Mitchell, and Tom Myers. I am especially grateful to Nikolas Gvosdev for always being willing to lend an ear and answering questions as they arose and to Wallace Daniel for his continued support and encouragement. Thanks also to the International Research and Exchange Board and the University Research Committee at Baylor for providing grants to support research in Russia during important elections.

Thanks go to the students in my Politics of Russia and the Successor States class during spring 2001, who "test drove" the text in draft form. In particular, thanks to Cole Bucy, Lee Fletcher, John-Paul Hayworth, Julia Kralka, Kristine Logsdon, Chris Newton, and Natalie Tapken for their helpful comments, suggestions, and careful reading. Finally, a special word of thanks is due to Sean Callahan, Jim Marshall, and Justin Miller, who each helped me in important ways.

My deepest gratitude goes to the many people who reviewed the manuscript in its various forms, including William A. Clark of Louisiana State University, Ralph Clem of Florida International University, Nicolai N. Petro of the University of Rhode Island, and James W. Warhola of the University of Maine. In addition, Justin Miller and Bill Seekamp each read the manuscript carefully and provided invaluable comments and suggestions.

Finally, at CQ Press, thanks to James Headley, who encouraged me to tackle the project, to Tom Roche, who did an excellent job editing the text, and to Charisse Kiino, who walked me through the steps (at a brisk pace!) and made the whole experience an enjoyable one.

1

Introduction

The election of Vladimir Putin as president of Russia in March 2000 held deeper significance than an ordinary election of a chief executive. In many ways, this was a critical juncture in the development of Russia's post-Soviet political system. On the one hand, it marked the culmination of more than a decade of competitive elections and attempts at democratic reform in Russia. It was in March of 1989 that competitive elections to the Soviet Union's legislative bodies had been introduced, a tremendous stride in implementing Gorbachev's policy of *demokratizatsiya* (democratization), although Gorbachev himself did not stand for popular election. Shortly thereafter, the newly elected representatives set a course that led to the disintegration of the union within a brief two years. Following these events, Russia and the other republics gained their independence and continued along the long and arduous path toward democracy, a journey that they would all have to make separately.

Perhaps more definitively, Putin's election marked the end of the Yeltsin era, a period during which there was much speculation over whether Yeltsin would try to remain in power beyond the constitutionally limited period of two terms. With this threat on the horizon, many had seen the study of democracy and democratic institutions in Russia as perhaps little more than a passing fad, and Yeltsin as nothing more than a populist dictator similar to third world dictators. Yeltsin's terms in office were primarily characterized by a tremendous weakening of the state, the prevalence of disorder, and the rise of alternative centers of power, with the major beneficiaries being local political bosses and a small group of elites, known as the oligarchs, who were able to gain tremendous financial advantages from Russia's transition from Communism.

Although the Yeltsin era is over, it remains unclear what attributes will come to characterize the Russian political system under Putin's leadership. In the realm of foreign policy, one increasingly apparent development is the resumption of Russian national pride, complete with a revamped set of national symbols, and perhaps coupled with a more adversarial foreign policy. This is only one aspect of the larger process of strengthening the Russian state, as Putin seeks to replace the disorder of the Yeltsin period with order and stability. A primary component of Putin's policy of strengthening vertical power in Russia is the reeling in of the power of the oligarchs and local bosses, which is being accomplished by the creation of seven federal districts and increasing state control of the media. Elections and voting can serve as either a bulwark against authoritarian rule or a facade of democracy, and the role they will play in the new Russia remains unclear. But electoral politics will play an important role in any course of events, for this is where the difference between the form and substance of democracy is most fundamentally determined.

The Study of Russian Electoral Politics

In the past decade, the electoral landscape of the new Russia has taken shape. Although it has faced numerous obstacles to its political development, some of which have led to violence, the country has been able to hold itself together and retain a competitive political system. These events—from the standoff between the president and the legislature in the fall of 1993, which was followed by a referendum on the new constitution, to the wars in Chechnya, which influenced the 1996 and 2000 presidential elections—have had an important influence on the electoral process itself.

Russians went to the polls many times in the 1990s to express their opinions in referenda and to elect officials at all levels of government, from local town officials to the national legislature and the president himself. Some may view these developments as alien to Russia's traditions and historical experience, but an examination of Russia's electoral heritage shows surprising continuity with contemporary electoral politics. This similarity has not gone unnoticed by the Russians themselves. The restoration of pre-Soviet traditions has even been identified as a key to the success of post-Soviet programs of political development.[1] Whatever the specific mechanism by which historical traditions affect contemporary developments may be, even a cursory look at modern Russian politics illustrates that history is not forgotten or irrelevant.

Competitive elections have become the most legitimate means—in the opinion of both the populace and the political leaders themselves—for gaining a position of political leadership in the government and for transferring power from one set of leaders to another. The process of the institutionalization of the Russian electoral system is still under way, but this only adds to the importance of studying the evolution of elections and voting in Russia.

The primary purpose of this book is to help readers understand elections in Russia and the historical, structural, and cultural factors that influence them. The completion of a full decade of major electoral developments presents us with an ideal opportunity to reflect on this experience and assess its successes and failures. To achieve this study's objectives, I apply to Russian electoral politics an eclectic mix of techniques and theories, including statistical analysis and institutional theory. Additionally, the subject matter of the study is a mix of electoral politics and voting behavior, as I focus as much on campaigns and media coverage as on electoral rules and voting patterns. The purpose of this approach is not to test the veracity of specific social science theories or to weigh in on one side or another in any methodological debate. Rather, the purpose is to illuminate the complex subject of Russian electoral politics.

The primary method of investigation I use is to survey some of the many elections that have taken place in Russia, both historically and more recently. The survey focuses on Russia's presidential, parliamentary, and regional elections, from the introduction of competitive elections in the late-Soviet period to the gubernatorial elections of 2000. Specifically, the book is organized in the following way. First, chapter 2 introduces the reader to Russia's rich electoral heritage, and chapter 3 completes this process by bringing the discussion up to the final days of the Soviet Union. Chapter 4 then focuses on the many events that brought Russians to the polls in 1993, including a referendum, constitutional plebiscite, and legislative elections. After applying this chronological approach, I then switch in later chapters to comparative analysis of specific types of elections, focusing on the 1995 and 1999 legislative elections in chapter 5 and the 1996 and 2000 presidential elections in chapter 6. Gubernatorial and regional legislative elections are similarly discussed in chapter 7. The organization may seem confusing at first, but it proves very useful for at least two reasons. First, it allows detailed consideration of elections that are similar. Second, it is conducive to examining continuity and change between elections.

A Primer on the Russian Federation

Some readers may be quite familiar with the Russian political system and developments in contemporary Russian politics, but others may be relatively unacquainted with the subject matter under investigation. This section is intended to introduce the latter readers to the basic facts of the Russian political system, to help them better understand the detailed analyses that follow. It is by no means intended to be a comprehensive account of Russian politics. Readers seeking more detailed accounts of the subject should consult texts listed in the *For Further Reading* section at the end of this chapter.

Any introduction to Russia must begin by considering the country's immense size. Russia stretches across eleven time zones, bordering Finland and Poland in the west and China in the east. Russia reaches into the Arctic Circle in the north, and along its southern perimeter it borders Georgia and Kazakhstan, two fellow members of the Commonwealth of Independent States. Within its borders reside approximately 149 million people, among whom the unemployment rate exceeds 12 percent, and approximately 40 percent of whom live below the poverty line. Life expectancy for men is a mere fifty-nine years, and although women can expect to live to age seventy-two, the population is experiencing a negative rate of growth.

Russia is home to great diversity, and its population is made up of more than 128 different ethnic groups, although 80 percent of the population is ethnically Russian. It is also religiously diverse, and although more than three-quarters of the population are Russian Orthodox, there are significant populations of Christians of other denominations, Jews, Muslims, Buddhists, and even animists. Given its great size, Russia is also geographically diverse. Some parts of the country have natural resources such as oil, minerals, or mineral-rich soil, and others almost entirely lack a natural resource endowment. The country is highly urbanized and is home to ten cities with populations of more than one million, but the vast majority of the territory is relatively uninhabited, particularly in Siberia and the Russian Far East.

The Russian Federation is composed of eighty-nine political divisions, properly known as the subjects of the federation (*see Figure 1.1*). In comparison to the United States, the subjects of the federation are roughly analogous to the fifty states plus the District of Columbia, Puerto Rico, and Indian reservations. Of Russia's eighty-nine subjects, there are twenty-one republics, six krais, forty-nine oblasts, two administratively autonomous cities (Moscow and St. Petersburg), and eleven autonomous areas (ten autonomous okrugs and the Jewish Autonomous Oblast). The most critical difference between these regions is the ethno-territorial principle in thirty-one of them—the twenty-one republics and the ten autonomous okrugs (the status of the Jewish Autonomous Oblast is not based on any ethnic tie to the area). The different ethnic groups in the republics and autonomous okrugs are given some recognition of their ethnic identity through varying degrees of autonomy within the federation. The cities of Moscow and St. Petersburg have special status (similar to the District of Columbia), and the oblasts and krais may simply be thought of as ordinary regions.

The differences between Russia's constituent parts are not limited to their nomenclature, or even to their varying degrees of autonomy in relation to Moscow. The country's diversity has a strong regional component. For example, some regions have Muslim majorities, and others are predominantly Russian; some regions have a strong agricultural base, and others are more industrial. These regional patterns manifest themselves in Russian politics. As the rest of the book will show, different parts of Russia exhibit different political orientations and trends. For instance, Moscow and St. Petersburg are the most reform-oriented, some of the Muslim republics exhibit neo-authoritarian tendencies, and the blackearth region (in southwest Russia) has traditionally been a stronghold of the Communist Party. Geographic patterns, although not always so simple, are certainly discernable across the country.[2] This vast land, although it has faced challenges to its territorial integrity, is held together by a common history and identity.

Following the collapse of the Soviet Union in December 1991, Russia was left as the largest successor state and continued on its own along the path toward democracy, a journey begun under Gorbachev's leadership several years earlier. The path has not been an easy one, and one of the most difficult issues has been the balance of power between the executive and legislative branches of government. This problem culminated in an armed stand-off

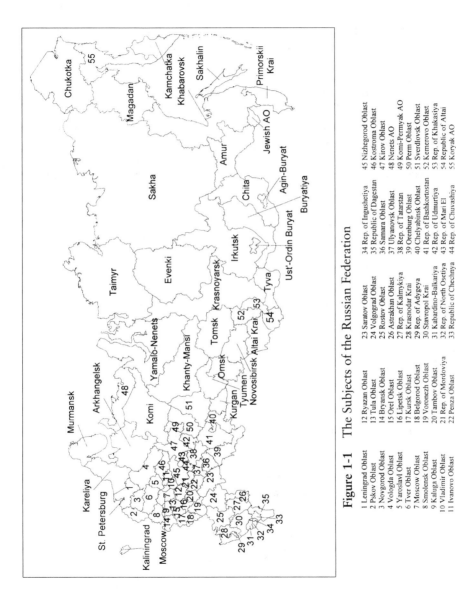

Figure 1-1 The Subjects of the Russian Federation

1 Leningrad Oblast
2 Pskov Oblast
3 Novgorod Oblast
4 Vologda Oblast
5 Yaroslavl Oblast
6 Tver Oblast
7 Moscow Oblast
8 Smolensk Oblast
9 Kaluga Oblast
10 Vladimir Oblast
11 Ivanovo Oblast

12 Ryazan Oblast
13 Tula Oblast
14 Bryansk Oblast
15 Orel Oblast
16 Lipetsk Oblast
17 Kursk Oblast
18 Belgorod Oblast
19 Voronezh Oblast
20 Tambov Oblast
21 Rep. of Mordoviya
22 Penza Oblast

23 Saratov Oblast
24 Volgograd Oblast
25 Rostov Oblast
26 Astrakhan Oblast
27 Rep. of Kalmykiya
28 Krasnodar Krai
29 Rep. of Adygeya
30 Stavropol Krai
31 Kabardino-Balkariya
32 Rep. of North Osetiya
33 Republic of Chechnya

34 Rep. of Ingushetiya
35 Republic of Dagestan
36 Samara Oblast
37 Ulyanovsk Oblast
38 Rep. of Tatarstan
39 Orenburg Oblast
40 Chelyabinsk Oblast
41 Rep. of Bashkortostan
42 Rep. of Udmurtiya
43 Rep. of Mari El
44 Rep. of Chuvashiya

45 Nizhegorod Oblast
46 Kostroma Oblast
47 Kirov Oblast
48 Nenets AO
49 Komi-Permyak AO
50 Perm Oblast
51 Sverdlovsk Oblast
52 Kemerovo Oblast
53 Rep. of Khakasiya
54 Republic of Altai
55 Koryak AO

between Boris Yeltsin and the Supreme Soviet in October 1993. After the resolution of this conflict, Russia adopted a new constitution and political structure. The basic framework of the political system, which is still very much a work in progress, centers on the country's eighty-nine regions and the Federal Assembly, the country's bicameral legislature. The lower house of the legislature, the State Duma, is composed of 450 representatives. Half of the deputies in the Duma are elected in district races, and half are assigned on the basis of proportional representation, using party lists. Voters cast two votes in the parliamentary elections, one for the candidate of their choice in their local single-member district and one for the party of their choice. Parties that receive 5 percent or more of the party-list vote receive seats in the Duma in proportion to the percentage of the vote they received nationally, with the votes that were cast for parties that failed to receive 5 percent of the vote—and were thereby wasted—being redistributed equally to the parties that did.

The upper house of the national legislature, the Council of the Federation, is composed of two representatives from each of Russia's eighty-nine subjects of the federation. These officials were originally elected, but the original system was changed under Yeltsin to a system whereby the executive and legislative heads of each region held seats in this body ex officio. This system is currently undergoing a process of amendment that will likely result in an arrangement whereby the executive and legislative branches of the regions will each appoint one representative to the Federation Council.

As democratic institutions and elected positions have been established in the new Russian political system, it has, of course, been necessary to conduct elections on a regular basis to select representatives to fill these posts. Russia has held elections for thousands of positions, from town council members and city mayors to national legislators and the president. The election of leaders and representatives in Russia, as I will show, is not new but instead dates back to the medieval period. Since current developments in Russian electoral politics necessarily take place against the backdrop of the nation's rich electoral heritage, it is only proper to begin our investigation with this topic.

For Further Reading

Bater, James. *Russia and the Post-Soviet Scene: A Geographical Perspective*. London and New York: Arnold, 1996.

Colton, Timothy. *Transitional Citizens: Voters and What Influences Them in the New Russia*. Cambridge: Harvard Univ. Press, 2000.

Hough, Jerry. *Democratization and Revolution in the USSR, 1985–1991*. Washington, D.C.: Brookings Institution Press, 1997.

Marsh, Christopher. *Making Russian Democracy Work: Social Capital, Economic Development, and Democratization*. Lewiston, N.Y.: Edwin Mellen Press, 2000.

Petro, Nicolai. *The Rebirth of Russian Democracy: An Interpretation of Political Culture*. Cambridge: Harvard Univ. Press, 1995.

Remington, Thomas. *Politics in Russia*. Reading, Mass.: Longman, 1999.

Remnick, David. *Resurrection: The Struggle for a New Russia*. New York: Random House, 1997.

Rose, Richard, ed. *International Encyclopedia of Elections*. Washington, D.C.: CQ Press, 2000.
Sakwa, Richard. *Russian Politics and Society*. London: Routledge, 1996.

Notes

1. Sergei Ryzhenkov and Galina Liukhterkhandt-Mikhaleva, eds., *Politika i Kul'tura v Rossiiskoi Provintsii* (Moscow: Mezhdunarodnii Institut Gumanitarno-Politicheskikh Issledovanii, 2001).
2. See the many articles written by Ralph Clem and Peter Craumer referenced in the *For Further Reading* sections following each chapter.

2

Russia's Electoral Heritage

Contrary to popular perception, Russia has a long and rich electoral heritage that dates from the medieval period. Elections in medieval Europe of course differed greatly from the modern electoral institutions with which scholars of electoral politics usually are concerned. Russia's history and cultural traditions, however, do affect the current process of democratization in the post-Communist states of Russia and Eastern Europe, if only as a source of symbols and a "usable history" upon which opinion leaders and politicians can draw as they seek to place the process of democratization into a domestic context. Although the direct impact of Russia's electoral heritage on contemporary developments may be slight, it is enlightening in its own right and provides a valuable context for Russia's current experience with electoral institutions and voting.

A study of Russian electoral politics must consider the introduction of competitive elections during the late Soviet period, but to properly understand the later developments one should also review the electoral traditions rooted deeper in Russia's history. Russia's electoral heritage is as important a context for the study of contemporary Russian electoral politics as are Athenian democracy and the Magna Carta to the study of modern democratic systems the world over. Russia's early elected bodies were of course weak in relation to the tsar. Some scholars have maintained that they are therefore not worth investigating, but such cursory dismissals seem wrong on at least two accounts.[1] First, as documented by many sources, electoral bodies in medieval Russia, particularly in Novgorod, often effectively checked the power of princes.[2] Even if these institutions became weak under the tsar in later periods, the question of how this occurred is itself worth investigating. Second, Russia's electoral traditions are of interest as a means of better understanding the process of voting in Russia, regardless of the strength of the legislative institutions themselves. These traditions, especially the elections held in the early twentieth century, have something important to tell us.

This chapter presents an historical overview of Russia's electoral heritage from medieval times to the elections to the Constituent Assembly in 1917. It begins with a discussion of the role of voting and elections in medieval Russia, focusing on the ancient political institutions of the duma and the veche—participatory bodies that existed more than a thousand years ago—and the customary right of the people to choose a monarch when the need arose. It then discusses important political bodies that were established later in Russia's history, such as the zemskii sobor, the Governing Senate, and the zemstvos. It then turns to the modern era, as we consider in detail the constitutional reforms of 1905, the resurrection of the Duma, and the series of elections held to that body. Next, we examine the elections to the Constituent Assembly in 1917, before reflecting on Russia's electoral traditions and their common characteristics.

Elections and Voting in Medieval Russia

Russia has a long history of voting and of electing representatives and leaders, using various procedures, at all levels of society. We now think of elections as events that take place at regular intervals, with citizens going to a polling station to cast a ballot in one manner or another, whether by dropping a slip into a box or using a voting machine. But voting and elections have a long and varied history, as all across the world elections have for centuries been held in a variety of ways and for various reasons. Although today we think of elections as opportunities to choose our elected officials, they have been held for a variety of other purposes as well. For instance, clergy in Russia were elected for centuries (*see box, The Election of Archbishop Mantury, 1193*). To understand Russia's electoral heritage we must look back to its earliest documented beginnings. In medieval Russia, voting and elections primarily took place through two electoral and participatory institutions—the *veche*, or popular assembly, and the *duma*, or council of boyars.

The Veche

Before princes ruled over the Russian people, power was exercised collectively through the oldest known political institution in Russia—the veche. As early as the sixth century, Byzantine historian Procopius wrote that "the Slavs were known to live in democracies; they discussed their wants in popular assemblies."[3] The early existence of the veche is well documented, and the institution actually predates princely rule in Russia. Once princes arrived on the scene, they occupied key positions in both justice and administration, although the veche was able to exercise various degrees of control over the princes at different times in Russia's history.

The word *veche* is derived from the root *vet-* and *vech-* meaning "to speak" or "to say," and it is related to the modern words so*veshchatsya*, "to deliberate, to consult" and so*vet*, "advice, council."[4] The veche, which functioned in a manner similar to direct democracy, was a town assembly akin to the assemblies of freemen that existed at about the same time in the West.[5] All male heads of households were eligible to participate in it, and the original veches were probably based on tribal or clan divisions. No children, slaves, or convicts could take part, but peasants and the lower classes were represented equally with other classes. The assemblies could be convened by anyone at

---

The Election of Archbishop Mantury, 1193

The archbishop of Novgorod, Gabriel, passed away on May 24th, the day of our holy Father St. Simon. And he was solemnly buried in the porch of the Cathedral of St. Sophia next to his brother whose name was George after he took holy vows. And then the people of Novgorod, the abbots, the Chapter of St. Sophia, and the clergy began their deliberations as to who should be the new archbishop. Some wanted to elect Mitrofan, while others wanted to elect Mantury, and still others wanted Grichina in this office. There was a great feud among them, and they decided to cast lots after High Mass in the Cathedral of St. Sophia. And they prepared the lots, and after service they sent for a blind man and he was given to them by God. And with the help of Divine Grace the blind man cast, and Mantury was chosen. And they sent for Mantury and they brought him to the court of the Archbishop. And they announced his election to the Metropolitan of Kiev, and he sent for Mantury with great honors.

Source: "The Election of Archbishop Mantury, and Novgorod Wars against the Ugrians," *The Novgorodian Chronicle,* in *Medieval Russia's Epics, Chronicles, and Tales,* ed. Serge A. Zenkovsky (New York: Penguin, 1974), 81–82.

---

anytime simply by ringing the bell in the town square, where most veches were usually convened.[6] Climbing up on a podium, speakers and leaders would address all those that had gathered and lead the day's order of business.

The veches did not meet according to any regular schedule but were convened as often as necessary, whenever a question of public importance was raised. Groups of citizens could also convene the veche when dissatisfied with the prince's policies. The veche decided such issues as war and peace, the confirmation or rejection of laws offered by the prince, and taxation. In Novgorod the veche elected, and could remove, the chief judge of the early court.[7] In many towns the veche also elected mayors and other city officials. The veches were also involved in the resolution of conflicts between citizens and their prince and between rivaling princes. One of the most important functions of the veche was the election and dethroning of princes. In early times, the veche was able to choose a prince from among the various members of the royal family, which was the house of Riurik. In later periods succession by primogeniture became established, but when a succession crisis arose it was still customary for an elected assembly to choose the successor.

In contrast to proto-democratic institutions in other parts of the world, decisions in the veche could only be made by a unanimous vote. The veche was not a majoritarian institution, in which a majority could legitimately rule in the name of all the people. Instead, its decisions had to be unanimous. Of course,

---

Voting, Unanimity, and a Dip in the Volkhov

If unanimity could not be arrived at, the minority was forced to acquiesce in the decision of the greater number, unless it could persuade the members of the majority that they were wrong in their opinion. In both cases the veches passed whole days in debating the same subjects, the only interruptions being free fights in the street. At Novgorod, these fights took place on the bridge across the Volkhov, and the stronger party sometimes threw their adversaries into the river beneath. A considerable minority very often succeeded in suspending the measure already voted by the veche, but if the minority was small, its will had soon to yield to open force.

Source: Maxime Kovalevsky, *Modern Customs and Ancient Laws of Russia* (London: David Nutt, 1891), lecture 4.

---

it was not always easy to arrive at a consensus, since, then as now, people are often bitterly divided on political issues. When differences of opinion arose and neither side could convince the other, the majority would force the minority into submission. When the members in the minority would not agree to vote for the majority position, fights would break out and members of the minority would be beaten with rods (*see box, Voting, Unanimity, and a Dip in the Volkhov*). If any still remained opposed, their property could be taken and even burned.[8] We will see in later chapters that the strong emphasis on unanimity and the belief that decisions arrived at by assemblies are binding upon all members of society are traditions that survived in various forms through the Soviet period.

The veche existed all across Russia, and similar bodies existed in other Slavic lands, including Bohemia, Croatia, Poland, and Serbia. According to one historical source, the *Suzdal Chronicle,* the inhabitants of the great cities of Kiev, Novgorod, and Smolensk, and of all the principalities of Russia, met in veches. Veches existed on at least two levels, that of the city and the borough, and most likely at the level of the principality as well. In the case of the cities and boroughs, the cities would meet first, and the boroughs would then deliberate on the promulgations of the city. The boroughs did not have to agree with the city, but, as with disagreements within a veche, disagreements between a city and a borough often led to violence. Throughout their history, the veches were genuine popular assemblies at the grassroots level that provided the people with a voice on political matters.

The Duma

Another electoral body in early Russia was the *duma,* or council of boyars. The term *duma* is related to the modern Russian verb *dumat,* "to think," and evolved from an old Russian verb that meant "to deliberate," especially about affairs of state. The duma was a forum for consultations between the prince and his closest advisers, and its members participated in the drafting of legislation and the codification of laws. The body could also act as a supreme court. It was headed by a group of the tsar's closest advisers, known as the *druzhina,* who functioned as a cabinet of sorts. The duma existed above the veche and was clearly an aristocratic body, being composed of various levels of noble and princely families.[9] The boyars were at the top of the duma's hierarchy, followed by smaller princely families and dukes, with lesser nobles being summoned only on certain occasions. The different estates that were represented during the larger council meetings, including the lesser nobles, each gave a separate decision on the matters under consideration.

The boyar duma varied in size from 30 members in its early existence to 167 near the end of the seventeenth century. Although the duma was a permanent institution, it was based on custom rather than law and thus met sporadically. Under some rulers the duma met very frequently, even daily, and under others decades would pass without its being convened. The duma at this early stage could not be considered a parliament, but it played an important role as the constant adviser and collaborator of the prince. There are cases when the senior druzhina refused to follow a prince because he had failed to consult the duma before taking an action. The higher nobility were thus able to limit the tsar's power to a certain extent. At this early stage the duma was not composed of elected representatives, but its membership was meant to give representation to the nobility as a class, and decisionmaking within the duma was undertaken according to votes cast by its members.

The Zemskii Sobor

As the Mongol yoke was slowly lifted from Russia's shoulders and Moscow began the gradual process of the gathering of the Russian lands, the relationship between the princes and representative bodies changed. The prince assumed a more dominant position, the duma lost its ability to effectively circumscribe the ruler's authority, and, finally, the veche ceased to exist. This did not mark the end of the electoral principle and representative organs of government in Russian politics, however. During the first half of the reign of Ivan IV (1533–84), commonly known as Ivan the Terrible, Russia's most famous tyrant implemented several significant reforms. Foremost among them was the convocation of the first full *zemskii sobor,* or landed assembly, in 1549. The zemskii sobors were sporadic gatherings convened by the tsar to discuss an important issue, similar to the gathering of representatives of estates in other parts of Europe. Unlike the veche, which functioned as a participatory democracy, and the duma, which represented only the nobility, the zemskii sobor was a representative body composed of society's disparate elements. Although the zemskii sobor was similar in some respects to the Estates General in Western Europe, it did not serve as a representative assembly as the term was understood in the medieval West, since it did not limit the tsar's power but only aided and supported the tsar. It did serve an important consultative function, however, and influenced most important matters of state, such as succession to the throne, war and peace, and state finances. Moreover, that it was allowed such a role indicated a desire on the part of the elites to spread the responsibility for state authority beyond the tsar's immediate court.

Also during the reign of Ivan IV, a new legal code and reforms in local government were enacted. The local government reform allowed for popular participation in local affairs, and in certain areas locally elected officials replaced centrally appointed governors. Where governors remained, the people could elect assessors to check the activities of the governors and impeach them when necessary. Unfortunately, the enlightened period of Ivan IV's reign was followed by a reactionary period, during which he became a bloodthirsty tyrant, and for which he received his appellation. Many of his liberal reforms were rescinded during this period, but they would leave an indelible mark on Russia's history.

Electing a Monarch

Russia's electoral heritage from the medieval times included more than various representative institutions. Russian monarchs themselves had also traditionally been subject to popular election. Succession to the Russian throne had been regulated according to two principles, genealogical seniority and popular election, with the latter remaining dormant as long as the former functioned smoothly. Traditionally, it was the responsibility of the veche to elect the country's ruler, and the veche also had the right to replace him if he led the country to disaster or offended the people. An individual ruler could be replaced because the Russian throne did not belong to any one ruler but to the royal family, the house of Riurik, which had held it from the beginning of the Russian state.

The royal bloodline died out in 1598, however, with the death of Tsar Theodore. To complicate the process of choosing a successor, the veche, which was responsible for choosing rulers when the need arose, was at this time no longer in existence. It was understood, however, that the responsibility of choosing a new tsar, and thus a new royal family, rested with the people. One of the tsar's closest advisers, Boris Godunov, sought to ascend the throne himself upon Theodore's death rather than leave the decision to an elected assembly. Godunov himself recognized the right of an elected assembly to choose the new tsar, and in order to legitimize his usurpation of power, he called together a zemskii sobor to formally place him on the throne. The sobor he convened was not truly representative of the country, with the vast majority of its 457 members coming from the bureaucracy and nobility. It unanimously elected Godunov as Russia's new tsar in what amounted to a coup d'état. This episode led Russia into a period in its history known as the Time of Troubles, during which the country was invaded by Poland and Sweden and several people tried to seize the throne.[10] The end to this dark period would only come with the election of a new tsar.

In 1606 a sobor was convened under circumstances similar to those surrounding Godunov's assembly, only this time it was packed with boyars. It elected another tsar, Vasilii Shuiskii, and, as required by the ancient custom of acclamation, its choice was sanctioned by a crowd of commoners and other people who had assembled outside of the Kremlin. Another zemskii sobor met in 1610, only this time to take the crown away from Shuiskii.

Perhaps the best example of the customary right of an elected body to select a monarch, however, was the concluding event of the Time of Troubles. Once the enemy had been successfully defeated and peace had finally been brought to the country, the first aim of the victors was to convene an assembly to elect a new tsar who would be able to lead a legitimate government. Prince Dmitrii Pozharskii, one of the military commanders who had freed Moscow from foreign occupation, himself called together the zemskii sobor charged with the task of selecting the new tsar. Unlike the sham sobor that had been convened to elect Godunov, this one was genuine. Pozharskii sent instructions for representatives to be elected from all corners of the country, with each electoral district (roughly comprising a city and its surrounding areas) electing one or two men from the clergy, two from the nobility (boyars), and two from the city residents.

When the zemskii sobor met in 1613, it consisted of between 500 and 700 members drawn from all segments of society, including the clergy, the boyars, the gentry, the townspeople, and even some representatives of the peasants. The assembled representatives drew up a list of possible candidates, including Ivan Golitsyn, Dmitrii Trubetskoi, and Dmitrii Cherkasskii; Pozharskii himself was even mentioned as a possible candidate. Given the power and privilege that hinged on the choice, the affair was inevitably surrounded by intrigue and quarrels. After almost a month of deliberation, the nomination of the young Mikhail Romanov (only sixteen years old at the time) began to gain support. Once the nomination was announced to the assembled crowds outside the Kremlin, the people voiced their support for the young man. Special emissaries were then sent to all the corners of the realm to sound local opinion, which strongly favored Mikhail as well. The sobor then announced its decision, and the Romanov dynasty, which would rule Russia until 1917, was thus brought to power by the people and the Time of Troubles came to an end.

Electoral Institutions in Imperial Russia

Russia entered the imperial period of its history upon the ascension of Peter the Great (ruled 1682–1725) to the throne. Throughout his reign, Russia's Westernizing tsar attempted radical administrative reforms, although many of his reforms either were not implemented or faced major problems upon being implemented. Peter the Great was an autocrat and a firm believer in enlightened despotism, borrowing his conception of autocracy and of the relationship between ruler and subject from the Swedish monarchy. He had a high regard for the law, however, and considered himself the first servant of the state. The zemskii sobor and boyar duma found no place in Peter the Great's reformed empire. The zemskii sobor had fallen into decline beginning in the mid-seventeenth century, and the duma had lost much of its significance by the start of the eighteenth century, finally being left to die out after Peter ceased to make new appointments to it.

With the decline of these institutions, however, elections and elected representatives did not cease to be a feature of the Russian political landscape. There remained thousands of elected representatives in positions of local government during the imperial period. Citizens chose elected representatives to fill various posts in local government, which rested between the state bureaucracy and Russian society at large. These officials performed such functions as managing public funds, serving in customs houses, and even collecting taxes.[11] Assembling in guilds according to one's position in society, citizens elected representatives to hold posts in the *magistrat* (or the *ratusha*, in smaller towns), a communal body consisting of a president and a small number of councilors and deputies, depending on the size of the town. By one account, these elected officials numbered approximately fifteen thousand in the mid-eighteenth century.[12]

The Governing Senate

Peter's plan to Westernize Russia allowed no place for the traditional institutions of the zemskii sobor and duma, which fell into decline as Peter focused his attention on the establishment of a Western-style parliament, the Governing Senate. Peter created the Governing Senate in 1711 as the highest agency of the state and gave it the responsibility of administering the affairs of state while the emperor was away and engaged in military endeavors.[13] It would eventually become a permanent body charged with the supervision of judicial, financial, and administrative affairs, although it continued to play no role in foreign policy (except for trade) or military affairs. Another important function of the Senate was the appointment and confirmation of many officials in the state administration, which was done according to an elaborate system of secret ballot, apparently devised by Peter himself.

Originally composed of nine senators, the Senate had a membership of twenty-one by 1762. The senators had to participate in all matters under discussion, and their decisions were meant to be unanimous, evidence that the ideal of unanimity was alive and well in the imperial period. The Senate served as a forum for the settlement of differences among lower-level agencies, and its primary goal was to reach consensus on major issues of domestic policy. The position of procurator general was created to act as an intermediary between the Senate and the tsar, since the latter rarely participated in the Senate's meetings. The Senate communicated with the tsar by issuing reports and orders through the procurator general, who thus performed a role not unlike that of a modern prime minister.

The Legislative Commission

A further stage in the evolution of Russia's electoral institutions came with the ascension to the throne of another influential Westernizer, Catherine the Great (1762–96). Heavily influenced by the writings of the French *philosophes,* such as Voltaire and Montesquieu, Catherine introduced the Enlightenment to Russia and took the first steps toward liberalism. In 1766 she called a Legislative Commission to codify Russia's laws and thus work toward modernizing Russian society. The convocation of the Legislative Commission was an important development in allowing for popular participation in the legislative process. It consisted of 564 deputies, 536 of whom were elected (the other 28 were appointees representing state institutions such as the Senate). The deputies represented different segments of the population, such as the landed gentry, townspeople, peasants, and Cossacks and national minorities. Although the Legislative Commission met for a year and a half and held 203 sessions, it accomplished little, as the members split along class lines, with the gentry, merchant, and peasant delegates divided over serfdom and trade.

Catherine the Great also presented a charter called the *Nakaz,* or Instruction, to the Legislative Commission for its consideration. The *Nakaz* took two years to compose and contained 655 articles, about four-fifths of which were based on Montesquieu's *The Spirit of the Laws,* although some of the ideas had been modified or even distorted in order to "adapt" them to the Russian context.[14] The *Nakaz* was considered a liberal document, although what was considered liberal at that time differs drastically from our current conception. For instance, rather than abolishing serfdom, the *Nakaz* contained a provision suggesting that lords not use excessive physical force against their serfs. The *Nakaz* fell short of truly limiting autocracy in Russia, but the convocation of the Legislative Commission was an important step toward popular participation in the legislative process.

The Zemstvo

During the reign of Alexander II (1855–81), Russia underwent its most far-reaching reforms since Peter the Great. In addition to abolishing serfdom in 1861, Alexander II reformed local government by establishing a new organ of local self-government known as the *zemskii sobranie* (estate assembly), or zemstvo, in 1864. The zemstvo system combined aspects of bureaucratic management with popular participation, and it represented a modernization and democratization of local government. These institutions of self-government were introduced at both the district and provincial levels, originally in 34 provinces containing a total of 359 districts.[15] Each level of government contained an assembly (*sobranie*) and an executive council, with the former constituting decisionmaking bodies and the latter serving as executive organs.

The assemblies were composed of deputies elected by three separate and distinct groups of voters, with the divisions based on property qualifications. No other qualifications existed, although foreigners, those under twenty-five, and persons under criminal investigation or on trial were excluded from either voting or serving. Voters were grouped into three electoral *curiae* (Latin for council), based on the type of property they held, whether rural, urban, or village communal property. The three groups met separately to vote on their deputies, who would serve three-year terms. Candidates were voted on individually and in alphabetical order, with a majority of the votes constituting election. The number of deputies elected in the district assemblies ranged from as many as ninety-six to as few as twelve. The district zemstvos, in turn, then elected deputies to the provincial zemstvos from among their own ranks.

Before long the principles of the zemstvo were applied to town government by the municipal reforms of 1870. The reforms reorganized town governments, which were to consist of town councils and a town administrative board that was elected by the town council. The town council itself was elected by all property owners or taxpayers based on a three-tier system, with the group that paid the top third of all taxes electing a third of the delegates, the group that paid the second third electing another third of the delegates, and the group that paid the bottom third electing the remaining delegates.

Reform, Counter-Reform, and Revolution

To this point we have only considered reforms initiated by the government, but the impetus to reform also periodically came from groups within Russian society itself. A prime example of a populist call for greater participation in the political process is the Decembrist Uprising of 1825, during which a revolutionary group of military officers took advantage of the opportunity afforded by the coronation of Alexander I's successor to stage a mutiny. Their plan was to march on the Senate and prohibit the coronation of the new tsar until he signed a manifesto limiting his power. Such an agreement would not have been without precedent, as many Russian monarchs had been forced to sign agreements upon their ascension to the throne, including Mikhail Romanov. Among the provisions specifically mentioned in the manifesto were the abolition of serfdom and censorship, the equalizing all classes before the law, freedom of religion, a fair and open trial system, the introduction of elections at all levels of government, and the convention of a "Great Council" (*Velikii sobor*) that would determine the most appropriate form of government for Russia.[16] This event shows that despite the existence of autocracy, there was support among the ruling classes for a transition to a more constitutionally limited form of government based on the election of the country's leaders.

The Decembrist Uprising was put down, as the troops refused to follow their officers, but Russia would again find itself faced with calls for reform.

As the twentieth century began, the country was in turmoil, strikes were spreading throughout, and student protests and disturbances had become frequent occurrences from 1898 on. In November 1904 a zemstvo congress even demanded a representative assembly and civil liberties.

The intense calls for reform would eventually have to be addressed, one way or another. Unfortunately, the impetus to reform would not come without a cost. On January 22, 1905, a peaceful procession of demonstrators converging on the Winter Palace, carrying icons and portraits of the tsar, was fired upon by the capital police, with 130 people killed and several hundred wounded. The people had assembled as the tsar's loyal subjects to beg for redress and aid; yet, unbeknownst to them, but emblematic of Russia's opaqueness of governance, Nicholas had not even been present. Following this incident, which came to be known as "Bloody Sunday," strikes and protests spread throughout the country, and many of those who had remained loyal to the tsar now joined the forces of the opposition and demanded reform.

Shortly thereafter, in March, Nicholas declared his intention to convoke a consultative assembly. This was not enough to quell the opposition, however, and throughout the summer of 1905 the revolutionary tide continued to swell, with strikes, peasant uprisings, military rebellions, and revolutionary movements among national minorities. On August 19 an elective Duma, having consultative powers only, was created by one of Nicholas' decrees, with elections scheduled for January 1906. According to the accompanying electoral law, however, large segments of society were to remain without a voice, as industrial workers, small private landowners, and the mass of the urban population (which included the bulk of the intelligentsia) were not given the right to vote. This gesture was not enough to placate the people, and revolutionary activity continued.

In late October the social and economic unrest culminated in what has been described as "the greatest, most thoroughly carried out, and most successful strike in history."[17] Nicholas II finally capitulated and issued the October Manifesto, announcing that the Duma was to be elected by all classes of adult males and would have true legislative functions in the passing and rejection of law. Furthermore, civil liberties, such as freedom of conscience, speech, assembly, and association, would be guaranteed. Quite simply, Russia was to be a constitutional monarchy.

The Resurrection of the Duma

The resurrection of the Duma as a national legislature was perhaps the most significant event in Russia's political development since the establishment of the zemstvo system. It would provide large-scale opportunities for the country's citizens to participate in the political process. The electoral system established following the October Manifesto was not based on the principle of "one person, one vote." Rather, as with the zemstvo system and other electoral bodies in existence at that time in Russia, it was a complicated system made up of curiae, electoral assemblies, and electors. For our purposes, we can think of the system as based on electoral colleges and indirect election. Under this electoral scheme, the electorate was divided into four curiae, one each for the landowners, urban residents, peasants, and workers, with a special fifth curia for Cossacks and other national minorities. The members of these curiae chose electors, who constituted the electoral colleges at the provincial and city levels. These electors then chose the 524 deputies who would make up the State Duma.

This arrangement was essentially the same as the one established by the August 1905 electoral law, except that property qualifications had been effectively eliminated and a separate workers' curia had been created. Although most of the population would now have the chance to vote in at least some way for the legislature, many were still excluded. The excluded people were primarily women and servants, and approximately four million workers were also still excluded (such as construction workers, day laborers, and workers at small enterprises). Nevertheless, the resurrection of the Duma and the establishment of popular election of its members were significant developments in the establishment of electoral institutions in Russia.

In addition to unequal access to the franchise, there also remained inequality among those groups included in the electoral process. First, the different curia did not have equal representation in the electoral college. The urban curia were accorded slightly more than 40 percent of the total number of electors, the peasants 32 percent, the landowners 25 percent, and the workers only 2.7 percent. This disparity becomes even more apparent when one considers the relative populations of the different groups represented by the curia. The peasants were by far the largest segment of the population (approximately 75 percent), the workers were the second largest (21 percent), and the landowners (who chose 25 percent of the electors) were only 4 percent of the population. Just how different the levels of representation were can be seen by comparing the number of people represented by one elector. Whereas one elector for the landowners' curia represented only 2,000 landowners, an elector for each of the other curiae represented many more people: 4,000 urban residents, 30,000 peasants, and 90,000 workers, respectively.[18]

The first national elections to the Duma saw high levels of participation, with more than 50 percent of the eligible electorate casting ballots. The 524-member Duma they chose was dominated by peasants and the nobility, who were represented by 231 and 180 deputies, respectively. Also among the deputies were members of the intelligentsia, tradesmen and industrial workers, salaried employees, and clergy. In terms of ethnic composition, about 60 percent were ethnic Russians, with another 14 percent being Ukrainian and 11 percent Polish.

The political orientation of the deputies is difficult to determine, since during the First Duma the political parties were in the early stages of formation and thus still in a state of flux.[19] The three main party factions to emerge from the Duma were the Constitutional Democrats, the Trudoviks, and the

Octobrists. The Constitutional Democrats (or Kadets), who were represented by 170 deputies, favored the extension of political liberties and the establishment of a constitutional order; in short, they supported the establishment of a liberal democracy. The Trudoviks were a left-leaning labor faction made up of 90 deputies, mostly of peasant origins. Finally, with only 16 deputies, the Octobrists were a rightist, pro-regime party that favored a constitutional monarchy with a consultative assembly. This party was strongly favored by the regime. The remaining deputies were members of other smaller factions or of a nonparty faction.

Compromise and consensus were not easy to achieve among this unruly bunch of legislators. Nevertheless, the First Duma made staunch demands, ranging from radical land redistribution to the abdication of the tsar. The Basic Law of 1906, which established the legal framework of the new system, left the emperor with tremendous powers, including the power to appoint the government of his choice, to issue emergency decrees with the power of law, and even to dissolve the Duma at his discretion. With these powers in his hands, and facing opposition from the Duma, Nicholas II dissolved the First Duma after seventy-three days in session, rather than put up with the sharp dissent coming from Russia's new legislature.

This was not the end of the Duma as an institution, however, as elections to the Second Duma were almost immediately set for February 1907. The elections were held under the same electoral rules as the previous year, and turnout was up slightly, to approximately 55 percent. The deputies of the Second Duma were somewhat younger and less well educated than those of the First Duma, and as a whole the Second Duma was certainly more radical. As a result of the process of party development that had begun with the First Duma, the party affiliations of the deputies changed substantially from the First to the Second Duma. The Kadets remained the largest single faction with 123 deputies, which represented a decrease from the previous year. With the Kadets' decline in support, support correspondingly increased for the Trudoviks (97), the Social Democrats and Socialist Revolutionaries (83), and even a slight gain by the Octobrists (18). Finally, the number of nonparty deputies decreased from 112 to only 21, further evidence that party formation was progressing rapidly.

This somewhat better organized group of deputies brought two major issues to the fore. The first was the agrarian question and resulted in a radical land reform program to which the government was staunchly opposed. The second was the national minorities question, an issue that was inextricably linked to the agrarian question, since the Polish delegation had supported the land reform program in exchange for support on the national minorities issue. Although it was certainly not a smooth-running legislature, the Second Duma was better able to negotiate, compromise, and draft policy proposals—some of which worked against the interests of the tsar and his government. Rather than facing such dangerous and unacceptable policy initiatives, Nicholas II once again resorted to dissolving the legislature on June 3, 1907, a move that was seen as a coup d'état.

Rewriting the Rules of the Game

Nicholas had again resorted to dissolving the Duma, but not with the purpose of permanently ending the legislature's existence. Instead, he sought to make it more compliant. Perhaps the most effective way to alter the composition of an elected body is to change the method by which its members are selected, that is, to change the electoral law. Nicholas, therefore, in violation of the constitution, rewrote the electoral law so as to diminish the representation of troublesome groups while simultaneously giving an advantage to the landed gentry and other pro-regime factions. He did so by radically changing the number of seats assigned to the different curiae. The representation of the landowners' curia increased dramatically, as it became the largest curia, and the peasants' curia was halved, so that it became even smaller than the urban curia, which had been slightly increased. The workers' curia remained roughly the same size. Diminishing the strength of the peasants was not Nicholas's only objective, however, since the national minorities were also proving troublesome. In order to make the Duma more "Russian in spirit," therefore, he substantially diminished the number of deputies elected from the border regions (home to many national minorities), which also decreased the total number of deputies in the Duma, from 524 to 442. In this way the representation of the two groups that had caused him the most difficulty was reduced.

The changes had their desired effect. The Third Duma was dominated by the landowning nobility, who accounted for 40 percent of the deputies, and the number of peasants and national minorities had been greatly reduced. Moreover, the number of opposition deputies had been halved, from approximately two-thirds to less than one-third.[20] An opposition remained, but only in much smaller (and more manageable) proportions. The Octobrists became the leading political force, with 150 deputies, and they joined forces with Prime Minister Peter Stolypin. They would remain the leading faction for the rest of the Duma's history, despite the party's splintering in later years. In short, the Third Duma proved much more compliant to the tsar's wishes, and it served out its five-year term.

Electoral turnout for the elections to the Third Duma was only 19 percent, compared to 55 percent turnout for the election to the Second Duma earlier that year. The drastic decline in turnout could be at least partially attributed to the people's discouragement with the entire process, and it perhaps reflected their understanding that their electoral voice had been effectively muted by the rewriting of the electoral law.

Imperial Russia's Fourth Duma, which would be its final Duma, was elected in 1912. The Octobrists remained the largest single faction in the

Duma, although their numbers decreased by sixty deputies. Parties to the left and right of the Octobrists seem to have gained seats at their expense. Whereas the Fourth Duma was more divided and less stable than the Third Duma, this was not the cause of its downfall, as it lasted until being swept away in the turmoil of the revolutions of 1917.

Elections to the Constituent Assembly

The imperial regime fell abruptly in March 1917, amid riots and demonstrations in the capital over shortages of bread and coal. The regime had proven utterly unable to contain the situation, and troops who had been sent to suppress the rioters joined them instead. Significantly, the people turned to the Duma for leadership during the crisis, evincing trust and hope in this elected body. A committee of Duma members was shortly brought together, and it created the Provisional Government. A few days later, Nicholas II abdicated the throne in favor of his brother, who in turn abdicated in favor of a Constituent Assembly. In this ignominious manner the Romanov dynasty came to an abrupt end.

The Provisional Government repeatedly delayed convoking the Constituent Assembly, which was to be charged with drafting a new political system for the country. By the time the elections to the Constituent Assembly were finally held in November 1917, the Bolsheviks had already seized control. On the night of November 7 (October 25 according to the old style calendar, hence the October Revolution), Bolshevik-led troops had occupied several strategic points throughout the capital and prepared to seize control of the country by storming the Winter Palace, the headquarters of the Provisional Government. The Bolsheviks faced little opposition, and the Provisional Government was effectively eliminated. As the Bolsheviks attempted to spread their control over the rest of the country, elections to the Constituent Assembly were being held. The elections were eagerly awaited by many who considered the Assembly the legitimate and definitive authority in the country.

The elections to the Constituent Assembly in November 1917 were significantly more democratic than any previous elections in Russia. With all men and women aged twenty and over eligible to participate, the franchise was even broader than in national elections in either the United States or the United Kingdom at the time.[21] All told, 44 million voters cast ballots in the election, for a turnout of around 55 percent.[22] Turnout rates as high as 70 percent in the cities and even higher in rural areas were reported—up to 97 percent in some villages.

Despite their enthusiasm, the people showed signs that they lacked political maturity. For instance, some villages voted en masse, with everyone casting their votes for the same party. This practice has been criticized as indicating poor understanding of the electoral process, but it can perhaps be more properly understood as reflecting the tradition of consensus and unanimity in Russian political culture.

The elections also had other irregularities. For instance, the Bolsheviks threatened voters in several districts, although the threats remained just that and did not escalate into actual violence. In other areas the Bolsheviks themselves were the victims of repression, with agitators taking Bolshevik ballots from voters and threatening them with violence if they did not vote for the Socialist Revolutionary Party. No one group was more effective at intimidating voters than another. The many acts of intimidation are well documented, but they were by no means the general rule, and in most places the elections went quite smoothly and without any question as to their validity. Overall, the elections should be considered relatively free and fair, even the conduct of the Bolsheviks; after all, the fact that the Bolsheviks did so poorly shows that they did not make a concerted effort to falsify the vote.[23]

In contrast to the elaborate system used for selecting deputies for the Duma, the delegates to the Constituent Assembly were elected according to a party-list system, whereby voters cast their ballots for parties and the parties received seats in the Assembly in proportion to the percentage of the vote they had received. The parties would then assign delegates to the seats according to their party lists, on which party members are ranked with the party leader at the top.

More than thirty parties competed in the Constituent Assembly elections, including the Kadets, the Socialist Revolutionaries, and two parties to emerge from the old Social Democratic Party—the Bolsheviks and the Mensheviks. In addition to these socialist-leaning parties, other parties covered the entire political spectrum, from the Cossack, Landowner, and various nationalist parties (including Ukrainian, Armenian, and Polish parties) to Orthodox and Muslim parties. Although some parties, such as the Kadets and the Bolsheviks, had existed for a while, others had been formed specifically to participate in the elections to the Constituent Assembly.

The Socialist Revolutionaries (SRs) were the clear winners of the election, garnering 40 percent of the vote nationwide. The Bolsheviks were second and not far behind, with 23.9 percent. The Kadets received just below 5 percent, and the Mensheviks barely surpassed 2 percent. The SRs found relatively stable support across the country, although their support diminished in inverse proportion to the greater support shown for local parties of choice, such as nationalist parties in various regions, and the support shown for the Bolsheviks in their strongholds, for example, Petrograd (the renamed St. Petersburg), Moscow, and the blackearth region. Other smaller parties also found pockets of support and accounted for the remaining 30 percent of the votes cast.

Although the results show that there was strong socialist sympathy among the electorate, the Bolsheviks did not win a majority, or even a plurality, of the vote, indicating at least two things. First, the Bolsheviks were not supported by a majority of the population. At the time the elections were held this was not in doubt, and the Soviet regime would later explain it as caused by the lack of workers' self-consciousness. Secondly, the Bolsheviks' relatively poor showing, despite the party's position of advantage (at least in comparison with the Socialist Revolutionaries), attests to the probable accuracy of the elections in providing a reliable representation of the political preferences of the Russian people.

When the Constituent Assembly met in January 1918, the Socialist Revolutionary Party held an absolute majority of the seats, and the Bolsheviks occupied only 170 of the 707 seats. As this put the Bolsheviks at a great disadvantage, Lenin had no use for the Assembly, and he had it disbanded by force. The anti-Bolshevik forces, or the Whites, resisted this move and sought to reestablish either the Provisional Government or the monarchy itself. As a sign of resistance to the Bolsheviks' closure of the Assembly, some right-wing Mensheviks and Socialist Revolutionaries set up a rump Constituent Assembly in Samara. The struggle between the Red and White forces led to a Civil War that ravaged Russia from 1918 to 1921, the battle lines of which were uncannily similar to the lines of support demarcated in the Constituent Assembly election.

The greatest scholar on the election to the Constituent Assembly, Oliver Radkey, maintained that it was "the one real election in the experience of the Russian people—real, that is, in the sense that it was a fundamentally free election, contested by definitely organized and sharply divergent parties, on the basis of universal, equal, direct, and secret suffrage."[24] It was certainly Russia's one true election before the democratic reforms of the Soviet political system in the late 1980s discussed in the next chapter, and it remains significant today, if only as evidence that the Russian polity had been evolving toward free and competitive elections at the turn of the century.

The Significance of Russia's Electoral Heritage

In their earliest recorded form, elections in medieval Russia were based on popular and direct participation in community affairs. Following the introduction of princely power, even princes remained accountable to the proto-democratic veche and the aristocratic duma. As the power of the princes increased, however, and eventually reached the point at which the grand prince (and later tsar and emperor) assumed a position of *primus inter pares,* the veche slowly died out, and the duma was able to persist only a short while longer. Slowly and incrementally, Russia's proto-democracy gave way to autocracy. Nevertheless, although Russian autocracy left little role for popular participation in the country's affairs, aspects of its earlier democratic traditions lingered on in the form of institutions such as the zemskii sobor, the zemstvo, and later the resurrected duma.

By the twentieth century, however, Russia's democratic traditions had been considerably altered. Institutions such as the veche, which had allowed for direct participation, had given way to more modern, representative forms—the election of local officials and elections to representative bodies such as the zemskii sobor, the zemstvo, and the duma. In a sense, however, even the participatory traditions had always contained a representative element. The veche, for example, was not based on universal participation but relied on heads of households to represent the best interests of their families. It was always, however, very close to the people and accountable to them.

Many manifestations of Russia's rich electoral heritage can be discerned in the events of the Soviet period and even today. Perhaps foremost among them is the emphasis placed on unanimity and *soglasie* (concord or harmony). From veches that voted by acclamation to villages that voted as one during the Constituent Assembly elections of 1917, in political matters Russians have tried to speak with one voice.[25] Unfortunately, but perhaps necessarily, this tradition of concord is closely intertwined with a great distaste for discord, which manifests itself in the idea that the opposition is illegitimate. This idea is also deeply rooted in Russian political culture, from the early practice of beating the opposition into submission to attempts to force neighbors to vote for a certain party, as was done in the Constituent Assembly elections. As discussed in the next chapter, even the Soviet policy of democratic centralism contains strong elements of these traditions.

Much of Russia's electoral heritage is based on institutions that were subject to the tsar's whim. Study of it still can show that elections and accountability in Russia are not merely Western imports but instead are based on ideas that have a history in Russia that is very long indeed. No matter how autocratic Russia was at various points in its history, the autocracy always existed against a backdrop of elites who sought to check the power of the tsar in order to protect their own interests. Moreover, Russians have for long believed that the monarch was obligated to serve in the best interests of the people and that the people had a right to seek redress from their leader. These beliefs manifested themselves in such practices as electing a monarch when succession was in dispute and having the monarch sign a manifesto upon his or her coronation. Russians were not, therefore, merely loyal, passive subjects, and the practice of voting thus becomes an important expression of the people's will, an opportunity to voice one's concerns and have them addressed by those in positions of authority. These were not traditions that could be easily eradicated, even by a regime as bent on altering political behavior as the Soviet Union.

For Further Reading

Billington, James. *The Icon and the Axe: An Interpretive History of Russian Culture.* New York: Vintage Books, 1970.

Emmons, Terrence. *The Formation of Political Parties and the First National Elections in Russia.* Cambridge: Harvard Univ. Press, 1983.

Emmons, Terrence, and Wayne Vucinich, eds. *The Zemstvo in Russia: An Experiment in Local Self-Government.* Cambridge: Cambridge Univ. Press, 1982.

Gvosdev, Nikolas. *Emperors and Elections: Reconciling the Orthodox Tradition with Modern Politics.* Huntington, N.Y.: Troitsa Books, 2000.

Kovalevsky, Maxime. *Modern Customs and Ancient Laws of Russia.* London: David Nutt, 1891.

Petro, Nicolai. *The Rebirth of Russian Democracy: An Interpretation of Political Culture.* Cambridge: Harvard Univ. Press, 1995.

Radkey, Oliver. *Russia Goes to the Polls: The Election to the All-Russian Constituent Assembly, 1917.* Ithaca: Cornell Univ. Press, 1989.
Zenkovsky, Serge A., ed. *Medieval Russia's Epics, Chronicles, and Tales.* New York: Penguin, 1974.

Notes

1. Matthew Wyman, Stephen White, and Sarah Oates, eds., *Elections and Voters in Post-Communist Russia* (Northhampton, Mass.: Edward Elgar Pub., 1998), 1.
2. Maxime Kovalevsky, *Modern Customs and Ancient Laws of Russia* (London: David Nutt, 1891), lecture 4; Nicholas Riasanovsky, *A History of Russia* (New York: Oxford Univ. Press, 1984), 50–51.
3. Kovalevsky, *Modern Customs and Ancient Laws of Russia,* lecture 4.
4. George Patrick, *Roots of the Russian Language* (Lincolnwood, Ill.: Passport, 1992), 41.
5. Robert Dahl, *On Democracy* (New Haven: Yale Univ. Press, 1998), 18–21.
6. George Vernadsky, *Kievan Russia* (New Haven: Yale Univ. Press, 1976), 185.
7. Kovalevsky, *Modern Customs and Ancient Laws of Russia,* lecture 4.
8. The option of paying a sum of money, determined by the person's social rank, was also available. See ibid.
9. Vernadsky, *Kievan Russia,* 182–85.
10. Perhaps the best account in English of this period is Ruslan Skrynnikov, *Time of Troubles: Russia in Crisis, 1604–1618* (Gulf Breeze, Fla.: Academic International Press, 1988).
11. John LeDonne, *Ruling Russia: Politics and Administration in the Age of Absolutism, 1762–1796* (Princeton: Princeton Univ. Press, 1984), 49–56.
12. Ibid., 51.
13. *Decrees on the Duties of the Senate,* in Basil Dmytryshyn, ed., *Imperial Russia: A Source Book, 1700–1917* (New York: Holt, Rinehart and Winston, 1967), 15.
14. *The Nakaz, or Instruction, of Catherine II to the Legislative Commission of 1767–1768,* in Dmytryshyn, *Imperial Russia,* 67–94.
15. Terence Emmons and Wayne Vucinich, eds., *The Zemstvo in Russia: An Experiment in Local Self-Government* (Cambridge: Cambridge Univ. Press, 1982), 33.
16. Nicolai Petro, *The Rebirth of Russian Democracy: An Interpretation of Political Culture* (Cambridge: Harvard Univ. Press, 1995), 40.
17. Riasanovsky, *A History of Russia,* 407.
18. Terence Emmons, *The Formation of Political Parties and the First National Elections in Russia* (Cambridge: Harvard Univ. Press, 1983), 239.
19. Ibid., 353–55.
20. Ibid., 374.
21. Women were not eligible to participate in national elections in the United States until 1920 (with passage of the Nineteenth Amendment) and in the United Kingdom until 1928.
22. These statistics are based on the revised and updated estimate offered by Oliver Radkey in *Russia Goes to the Polls: The Election to the All-Russian Constituent Assembly, 1917* (Ithaca: Cornell Univ. Press, 1989), 99.
23. Ibid., 48.
24. Ibid., 3.
25. For more on the democratic traditions of Russian political culture, see Petro, *The Rebirth of Russian Democracy.* For an account of how Russia's religious traditions affect elections and democracy today, see Nikolas Gvosdev, *Emperors and Elections: Reconciling the Orthodox Tradition with Modern Politics* (Huntington, N.Y.: Troitsa Books, 2000).

3

Elections during the Soviet Period: From Democratic Centralism to *Demokratizatsiya*

The Bolshevik's seizure of power meant that the Constituent Assembly's historic opportunity to craft a democratic political system for Russia would not be realized. The new regime did not bring an end to the conduct of elections, and although the elections it held would be noncompetitive for decades, they were a central component of the Soviet political system and served important functions for the regime. This all changed in March 1989, when after decades of noncompetitive elections, competitive elections were introduced as an aspect of Gorbachev's reformist policy of *demokratizatsiya*. Instead of repairing the system's problems, however, competitive elections facilitated the Soviet regime's collapse, as they brought to power leaders bent on radical reform. Within a brief two years, the Soviet Union's newly elected representatives set a course that eventually led to the disintegration of the union and the independence of Russia and the other republics, who were then left to face the long and arduous journey toward democratization alone.

This chapter discusses the elections that were held during the Soviet period and assesses their role in bringing about the Soviet Union's collapse. The first half considers the function, conduct, and meaning of elections during various phases of Soviet history. The second half turns to the introduction of competitive elections in the late Soviet period and continues with reviews and analyses of the elections to the Soviet Union's Congress of People's Deputies (CPD) in 1989, the Russian parliamentary elections of 1990, and the Russian presidential election of 1991.

The Function, Conduct, and Effects of Soviet Elections

The use of noncompetitive elections in the Soviet Union was not a foregone conclusion due to anything implicit in Marxist theory, but several factors worked to ensure that the new regime would not institute competitive elections. First among these was the Bolsheviks' experience during the elections to the Constituent Assembly in 1917, which had taught them that they had little support among the masses. Their experience with elections to the soviets indicated that their support among the workers was no stronger. They were thus acutely aware that they lacked popular support. Second, the early years were marked by revolution and civil war, conditions hardly conducive to contested and universal elections. Elections could not just be eliminated altogether, however, since they were a potential source of legitimacy for the new regime and the people continued to demand electoral participation. In order to continue to hold elections while guaranteeing favorable outcomes, the regime undertook several measures. It denied the right to vote to the groups most likely to oppose it, such as the White Guards, kulaks (wealthy peasants), and priests, who were considered "class-alien elements." It instituted voting by a show of hands instead of by secret ballot, since this would likely increase support for those conducting the elections. Finally, it introduced indirect elections, thus putting greater distance between the people and their leaders and providing more opportunities to manipulate outcomes. Although these policies were mostly pragmatic during the Soviet Union's early years, they would later prove difficult to change without threatening the existence of the regime itself.

Marxism, Leninism, and Democratic Centralism

Contrary to popular conception, Marxism itself does not preclude competitive elections, as can be seen in *The Civil War in France,* for example, where Marx extols the principles of universal suffrage, direct representation, and recall of representatives.[1] In Marxist theory as understood by communist theorist, Karl Kautsky, the dictatorship of the proletariat was in essence to be majority rule by the working class through democratically elected parliamentary institutions.[2] Although this position was sharply rejected by Lenin, the main debate among Marxists regarding elections was over using electoral institutions as a means of coming to power.[3] Kautsky argued that free and competitive elections were a means whereby communist parties could come to power, but his opponents argued that the chances for this seemed slim so long as suffrage remained limited, which of course it did for much of the nineteenth century. Hence, Lenin advanced the policy of revolution led by a vanguard of the proletariat. Once a communist regime came to power, elections would be potentially powerful channels for expressing popular sovereignty during the phases of socialist construction and the transition to communism.

After Lenin and the Bolsheviks came to power in Russia through revolution, however, their first order of business was to dismiss the democratically elected Constituent Assembly. This move was deemed necessary because the people had not given the majority of their votes to the Bolsheviks, and an assembly led by the Socialist Revolutionaries would slow the transition to communism sought by the Bolsheviks. Although the Bolsheviks were perhaps dissatisfied with the situation, it made perfect sense to them that they had not received a majority of the votes, since the country lacked widespread class-consciousness, and people therefore had not voted for the party that would best serve their interests. The dismissal of the Constituent Assembly, moreover, did not imply that elections were no longer a legitimate means of choosing representatives. In fact, the Bolsheviks continued to function through a system of elected bodies, the workers' and soldiers' soviets.

After the Constituent Assembly was shut down, the town and rural soviets remained the only electoral institutions in operation in the country. The soviets were councils composed of elected representatives chosen by the workers at their factories or by soldiers in their units. These representatives would then meet at groupings of factories or units and would elect representatives from among themselves to serve on executive committees and to fill various posts within the soviet. Elections to the soviets were not held on a regular schedule but were a continuing process, with elections held every few months or so, and with representatives subject to recall by one-quarter of the electorate during the interim.[4] The franchise was limited to individuals over eighteen who depended upon their own labor (or, in the case of women, their husband's) to earn a living, including members of the army and navy. Anyone who employed wage laborers or who lived off of unearned income, including priests, was not allowed to vote or to stand for election. The same was true for criminals and the clinically insane.

Unfortunately for the Bolsheviks, they were no more successful in the elections to the soviets than they had been in those to the Constituent Assembly. And in the spring of 1918, when opposition candidates won majorities in elections to local soviets across the country, the Bolsheviks showed no more tolerance toward the soviets than they had toward the Assembly. They arrested their opponents, changed the electoral rules, and reserved seats for themselves on the executive committees. When that did not work, they sometimes simply suspended elections altogether. The people, however, resented the Bolsheviks' attempt to wrest power from them, and uprisings spread. The Bolsheviks responded by banning demonstrations, shutting down opposition newspapers, and issuing curfews. The conditions under which multiparty elections to the soviets could be held were thus removed.

There still remained one forum within which electoral power could be exercised—the Bolshevik Party itself. Although the Bolsheviks would not rest until they had a monopoly on power, this did not mean that elections within the party would necessarily be undemocratic. After all, the workers might lack the class consciousness necessary to understand their own interests, but this was not a justification for denying members of the party the right to choose leaders from within its ranks. At the Tenth Party Congress of 1921, however, Lenin introduced two principles to the Bolshevik government that had been in practice within the party itself since 1903—democratic centralism and the ban on factions. Although they did not directly or immediately preclude competitive elections within the party, these two policies would strongly and adversely shape the function and efficacy of elections in the Soviet Union.

In theory, democratic centralism was a democratic form of organizing party operations, which was seen as desirable by the Bolshevik Party. As a clandestine revolutionary group hiding from the tsar's secret police, however, the Bolsheviks had needed strict party discipline—internal fighting or the failure to implement an agreed-upon action could lead to the destruction of the party and betrayal of the revolutionary cause. The democratic ideals of the early Bolsheviks, therefore, had to be compromised in order to maintain strict discipline.

As a policy, democratic centralism provided for debate on all issues until a decision was reached, at which point there would be no further discussion and all members were required to participate in implementing the decision. Once this policy was applied to party operations in the Soviet Union, debate would begin at the lowest level of the party and then continue on up the party hierarchy to the highest level of leadership. When a decision was reached at the apex of power, the lower bodies were then bound by it and obligated to carry it out. Since the decision had been arrived at through a democratic process, further debate was seen as unnecessary and would no longer be permitted. This policy is consonant with the value placed on unanimity so prevalent in Russian political culture, as discussed earlier.

The ban on organized factions was another measure meant to promote party unity and prevent internal division. Introduced by Lenin with a classic understatement, "I do not think it will be necessary for me to say much on this subject,"[5] it was meant to promote party consensus and prevent internal fighting. Although such a measure was perhaps necessary during the party's early days in power in order to consolidate control over the country, it would leave the party susceptible in later periods to being controlled by an authoritarian leader, because it essentially prevented opposition.

Democratic centralism and the ban on factions were both pragmatic policies meant to facilitate the party's ability to curb dissent and lead the country along the path to socialism. In making unanimity a centrally important party policy, however, both hindered the efficacy of electoral institutions. This was not their explicit intention, as they were simply responses to the circumstances of the time, but it was perhaps their most profound effect.

Elections and Voting in the Soviet Union

In the period of the dictatorship of the proletariat, the Bolsheviks could easily justify preventing class-alien elements from voting and nonparty candidates from standing for election. Once class enemies had been eliminated and the social classes destroyed (in theory, of course), so too was the ideological basis for noncompetitive and restrictive elections. As Stalin phrased it at the Seventeenth Party Congress in 1934, with the victory of socialism, "there is no one left to fight."[6] Theoretically, therefore, the dictatorship of the proletariat could thus be relaxed. In addition to the economic and social changes that could now be pursued, there was now little reason to prevent universal suffrage, direct elections, and secret ballots in the political realm. After all, Lenin's stated intention had been for the early restrictions on elections to be only temporary. It was in this context that the drafting of a new Soviet Constitution, with the promise of greater civil and democratic rights, was announced in 1935.

In the process of drafting the new constitution, the Soviet leadership took several steps that seemed to imply that direct, secret, and competitive elections would be introduced, even soliciting suggestions from citizens (*see box, Electrifying New Ideas on Voting*). Stalin and other members of the leadership also made moves that had the apparent aim of implementing competitive elections at almost all levels of the party, from local and regional party organs to the Supreme Soviet. These moves were made in the midst of the purges of the 1930s, however, which forces us to question whether the Soviet leadership truly intended to democratize the electoral process.[7] Most scholars discount the significance of such gestures, but some argue that these steps may have been taken in preparation for a revolution from below, in which Stalin and his circle would rid the party of undesirable elements through the voting booth. One scholar who belongs to the latter camp points out that Stalin would hardly have needed such an elaborate campaign to accomplish what he was already realizing with simple murder plots.[8] The debate over the true objectives of the electoral reforms will continue, but no one disputes the outcome—voters were given a limited slate of candidates to "choose" from, with the number of candidates equaling the number of positions up for election. The tale of how this occurred, however, is still revealing.

The electoral procedures introduced at this time called for polling to take place on Sundays, with multiple candidates competing for each post, and for voting to take place by secret ballot. Deputies could be recalled at any time, and elections would be held regularly, at least once every four years. Competition was introduced by allowing voters to cross out all names on the ballot except for the one candidate they wished to vote for. Finally, the franchise was to be extended to all classes. In the national discussion that took place over the provisions of the new constitution, many protested against extending suffrage to the class-alien elements, arguing instead that the franchise should continue to be limited to workers and peasants. Others argued that Bolshevik propaganda could be used to minimize the danger posed by allowing White Guards, kulaks, and priests to vote, and that this would prevent these undesirable elements from slipping into governing bodies.

Following the enactment of the Constitution in 1936, elections under the new procedures were scheduled for 1937. Elections to the newly created Supreme Soviet were scheduled for December, with an electoral campaign planned for October. Before these would be held, however, Andrei Zhdanov, the central committee secretary, in what seems an attempt to implement the policies within the Communist Party itself, scheduled party elections for the spring of 1937. These elections would be for lower party secretaries and committee members and were to take place at the lowest level of the party (primary party organization) all the way up to the regional level (oblast or krai), and they had to be held by May 20, 1937. Zhdanov also publicly announced

---

Electrifying New Ideas on Voting

During the drafting of the Soviet constitution of 1936, those involved promoted a national discussion on its various provisions and procedures and sought suggestions from the public. One of the most original suggestions had to be that by a Mr. G. I. Kurkov of Romny, who submitted an elaborate electrical voting scheme—complete with a diagram! According to Mr. Kurkov's plan, a voter would insert his or her hand into a machine that would be connected to every other voting machine in the country. The machines would then measure the total voltages generated in order to determine the winner.

Source: J. Arch Getty, "State and Society under Stalin: Constitutions and Elections in the 1930s," *Slavic Review* 50 (spring 1991): 19.

---

that these elections were not to be like those of the past, when there was "no debate on the various candidacies, and voting was in the open and by list; a 'mere formality.' "[9] Again, we should be careful about attaching too much significance to these statements, as in the Soviet Union a vast chasm often separated rhetoric from true intentions.

To a greater degree than previous Soviet elections, the party elections held in the spring of 1937 were free and competitive. Importantly, the elections were held by secret ballot. They began with a twelve-day publicity campaign and the nomination of candidates. In the Leningrad regional party organizations alone, some forty-one thousand candidates were nominated for slightly more than seven thousand posts. When the elections were held, there was almost complete participation by party members. Although powerful regional officials and party secretaries retained their posts, more than 50 percent of lower party secretaries and committee members were voted out of office.[10] Within some fifty-four thousand party organizations surveyed after the elections, 55 percent of committee leaders had been voted out of office, more than half of whom had been judged unsatisfactory in their work.[11]

Once the 1937 party elections were completed, the regulations and procedures for the elections to the Supreme Soviet were announced. They too, it seemed, were to be contested, and provisions had even been made for runoff elections between the top two contenders when no one received a majority of the vote. According to one interpretation, local and regional officials, who were by and large party members and were thus aware of the results of the May party elections, had learned a valuable lesson—their positions were in jeopardy.[12] They started to take measures, therefore, aimed at preserving their positions and undermining the elections, including restricting voting rights and falsifying voter lists. Local and regional party officials, according to this interpretation, understood the elections as part of the center's plan to effect a turnover of mid-level party and state personnel, using grassroots populism. The policy of holding free, contested, and secret elections in the Soviet Union never was actually implemented, but whether this was due to a reversal based on pressure from the regional bosses or was simply what had been intended all along is still a matter of debate.

Very quietly, without any of the fanfare that accompanied the introduction of the policy the previous year, the method of allowing voters to choose from among the candidates was replaced by that of choosing between, in the words of the party, "blocs of party and non-party elements." When voters arrived at the polling stations, they were still told to cross off the names of those they did not support, but now there was only one name on the ballot for each post. Although dissent was still possible, it would have meant either crossing off the names in the middle of the room or stepping into a voting booth where this could be done in secret. But why would anyone need to step into a voting booth unless they were going to cross off names? Such a move certainly came with great risk in the midst of Stalin's purges.

The Intended and Unintended Effects of Soviet Elections

The elections of 1937 established the pattern for subsequent elections throughout the Soviet period. Soviet elections were not a means of choosing between candidates but rather served a legitimizing function, as citizens were asked to demonstrate their support for the regime. Participation was made very easy. Voting day was a declared holiday and was always a Sunday, to minimize time lost from work. The process itself was simple: all one needed to do was receive a ballot and then drop it in the ballot box. Voting in Soviet elections was "manipulated unanimity . . . designed to create an illusion of representation and participation in public affairs."[13]

The manipulation, however, was not perfect. Although the regime had effectively eliminated voter choice by placing only one candidate on the ballot for each post, ballots still contained the instruction to "leave the name of the one candidate for whom you are voting, and strike out all the others."[14] Theoretically, then, the electorate retained the ability to vote *against* candidates, although to do so would have virtually no consequences. This option provided a potential opportunity for voters to voice their discontent with local officials, but this potential was unlikely to be realized unless the secret ballot was preserved. In fact, the electoral law stipulated that there had to be a voting booth in all polling stations for voters to exercise their right of the secret ballot. In accordance with this provision, a voting booth was almost always provided, and it was usually placed between the registration table and ballot box in order to make it convenient to use.[15] The significance of the voting booth was, of course, that within its narrow walls it was safest to cross out the names of candidates. Only about one in five voters even used them, however, which generated suspicion of those who did.[16] Again, why would someone need to visit the

voting booth except to cross off the names on the ballot? And why would anyone want to reject the bloc of party and nonparty candidates? According to
official statistics, very few people actually crossed off the names on the ballot.
From 1961 to 1975 only between 0.11 and 0.82 percent of the electorate,
reportedly, cast negative votes.[17] This figure does represent approximately one
million Soviet citizens, a considerable number to be participating in a blatant
form of anti-regime behavior. In fact, the actual number is probably much
closer to the 20 percent who visited the voting booth, since there was little reason for someone to visit a voting booth if he or she was simply going to drop
the ballot into the box as it was (*see box, Voting in the Soviet Union*).

The regime was not satisfied with artificially manipulating support
through electoral procedures, however; it also strived to attain 100 percent
participation in the electoral process. All people not only were given the right
to vote through the policy of universal suffrage but also were expected to turn
out to vote for the slate of official candidates. The Soviet Union's officially
reported turnout rate, however, which was usually about 99.98 percent, was
misleading for several reasons. First, people had the right to request a "certificate of right to vote elsewhere," which entitled them to vote at another
polling station upon presenting their certificate. Upon presentation of the certificate, their names would be removed from the voter list at the original station and therefore would not be calculated in that station's official turnout
statistics. Of course, if they never presented this certificate at another polling
station no one would ever know. Secondly, electoral commission officials
would often assume that comrade x, who did not show up to vote, must have
forgotten to request his certificate and would thus strike his name from the
list, further reducing in number the counted electorate. Estimates are that
about four million Soviet citizens were removed from the voting lists by both
methods.[18] A significant proportion of the country's voting-age population
thus participated in a dissident activity—failing to take part in the elections.
Although perhaps not as risky as visiting the voting booth to cross off the
names of candidates, their refusal to take part was nevertheless a significant
sign of discontent with the farcical electoral system.

The Soviet elections, although they were designed to perform a system
legitimizing function, thus also provided various avenues of protest against
the system. Their democratic guise, moreover, drew the ire and contempt of
many.[19] After all, Soviet citizens were smart enough to understand that there
was no choice at all. The regime did not ask a population of millions to go to
the polls and participate in "democratic" elections on a regular basis for
decades without any consequences. Instead of forgetting what free elections
were really about, Soviet citizens would be reminded of the truth every time
they went to the polls to drop their ballot in the box. An unintended effect of
regularly holding elections to various governmental bodies, therefore, may
have been the legitimization of the electoral process itself. As the Soviet
regime continually praised democratic elections but did not hold them, the
gap between the ideals the regime espoused and its actual policy was obvious

---

Voting in the Soviet Union

You get your ballot—everyone is looking at you. You pull a pencil out of your pocket—everyone can guess your intentions. Young Pioneers or poll attendants are standing by the polling booth. If you go into the booth, it's clear that you voted against the candidate. Those who don't want to vote against go straight to the ballot box. It's the same at plant trade union elections and party election conferences. You can't even go off into a corner by yourself before a curious eye is peering over your shoulder.

Source: Stephen White, Graeme Gill, and Darrell Slider, *The Politics of Transition: Shaping a Post-Soviet Future* (Cambridge, Eng.: Cambridge Univ. Press, 1992), 22.

---

to many. It would only be a matter of time before someone would seek to invest elections with true democratic content.

From *Glasnost* to *Golosovanie:* The Introduction of Competitive Elections

Before leaving for the meeting at which he was to be selected as the new general secretary of the Communist Party of the Soviet Union (CPSU), Mikhail Gorbachev said to his wife, "life can't be lived like this any longer."[20] Shortly after assuming the party's leading office in 1985, Gorbachev announced his intention to introduce sweeping reform into the Soviet system. Within two years, *glasnost* and *perestroika* would become household words the world over.

Gorbachev soon realized that minor reforms would not be enough to cure the Soviet Union's ills, and that complete restructuring, or *perestroika,* was necessary. At an address to the CPSU Central Committee in 1987, Gorbachev emphasized the seriousness of the social problems the Soviet Union faced and placed the blame for these conditions on the leading organs of the state and the party. Gorbachev's solution to the problems was to make party and state leaders more responsive to the people's needs by opening them up to criticism. Greater public criticism and access to information, therefore, would be permitted as part of the policy of *glasnost,* or openness. Public officials would also have to appear on radio and television programs to answer consumer complaints. Finally, party and state officials would be held personally accountable and have to stand for competitive elections. Beginning in 1987, positions within the Communist Party, trade unions, and Komsomol (Communist Youth Organization) would be filled through competitive, secret, and direct elections. In June 1987 a limited experiment was conducted in local soviet elections—5 percent of the deputies were elected in multimember districts in competitive elections. The democratic institutions and principles that had existed on paper for decades were thus beginning to be realized. Gorbachev's motivations for such measures of democratization were not, however, entirely beneficent or well-intentioned, as he expected that the new democratic procedures would increase his chances of defeating his conservative, anti-reform colleagues.[21] Nevertheless, once the reforms were implemented they took on a life of their own.

In December 1988 the Supreme Soviet adopted several amendments to its constitution, including one creating a new legislative body and another establishing a new electoral law. The country's new legislature was to be the Congress of People's Deputies (CPD), composed of 2,250 deputies. Once the Congress convened, it would then elect from among its ranks the 542 members of the Supreme Soviet, which was to be the supreme legislative body and would be responsible for managing the daily affairs of the legislature. The new electoral law stipulated that there could be "any number of candidates," meaning that elections should be contested. In addition, elections were not to be conducted as in the past, and there would be no more "passive voting"— voters were to make real decisions about who should lead the country. Voting booths had to be erected before the ballot box could even be placed in the room, and everyone had to enter the voting booth and make a choice, except for rare cases in which a seat was not being contested. The wording of the new laws did not differ drastically from previous Soviet electoral laws, but voters would now be offered a choice of candidates, and elections were to be free, fair, and secret. The voting rights that had been "guaranteed" in the past were now to be realized.

Electing the Congress of People's Deputies of the Soviet Union

The new rules called for the 2,250 members of the Congress of People's Deputies (CPD) to be chosen in three different ways. The first group of 750 deputies was to be elected in territorial districts, which were single-member districts divided on the basis of population size. The second group of 750 deputies was to be elected in national-territorial districts, which were electoral districts based on the titular nationality of certain territories. Both of these groups were to be elected by a majority vote in the given electoral district. The final 750 deputies were to be chosen by social organizations. The Communist Party and trade unions were each given 100 seats, and the Women's Committee, the Komsomol, and the Veterans' Committee were each given 75 seats, with the remaining 325 seats distributed among various organizations, some of which received only one seat. Some seats in the new parliament were thus reserved for the Communist Party, but the vast majority of representatives were to be chosen in democratic and contested elections.

The elaborate procedures for electing deputies seemed strange, not only to outside observers. Soviet citizens themselves found them confusing, and many had strong objections to them. For instance, why should certain groups, including cultural organizations and hobby clubs, have seats reserved specifically for them? In addition to their special representation, members of such organizations could also vote for deputies from their electoral district, as did everyone else. If the previous system, which had offered no choice among candidates, was illegitimate, the new system seemed to some not much better.

The selection of deputies was to take place in three stages. First would be the nomination of candidates, followed by the selection of the candidates who would be placed on the ballot. Finally, the people chose their representatives from the candidates listed on the ballot. To be placed on the ballot, potential candidates had to be nominated either by enterprise collectives, resident groups, or individual residents (in practice the last option was hardly ever attempted). To select nominees, resident groups had to gather the signatures of 500 residents and submit a petition to the Electoral Commission for a permit to hold a nominating meeting. Then, at least 500 residents had to be present during the meeting, with at least 51 percent of those present voting for the selected candidate. The process of gathering signatures and achieving the required turnout proved much more difficult for the resident groups than for enterprises, since they were not able to call general meetings that all employees would be required to attend, as could the enterprises.

The nomination process provided numerous opportunities for obstruction, as enterprise managers (and the local branch of the KGB) in many cases made sure that the candidate list contained only "approved" nominees. In one case seventeen candidates had been nominated by the workers in a factory in Minsk, but only three were placed on the list for the general meeting.[22] Apparently factory managers had taken it upon themselves to select nominees. Nominations made by citizen groups also ran into resistance by local authorities. Some clearly violated the electoral law, in many instances refusing to issue meeting permits to resident groups, and election officials in one district were even quoted as saying, "We do not need these novelties. The Electoral Commission will decide itself how many candidates will be left on the ballot."[23]

Once nominations had been made, the nominee lists then had to be approved by selection conferences in the district or social organization in which the candidate was seeking election. These selection meetings gave participants the opportunity to vote on the lists themselves and decide which nominees would be placed on the ballot as candidates in the March elections. These meetings were criticized for several reasons. First, the electoral law stipulated that at least 50 percent of those present had to be representatives from enterprises, which ensured that the enterprises would dominate the meetings. Additionally, since only a few hundred people were present at each meeting, a relatively small group of citizens would essentially decide for all the residents of an electoral district which candidates would be on the ballot. Finally, local officials used several techniques to control the outcomes of the meetings, including packing the meetings with reliable people, under-representing residents in the meetings, and intimidating candidates. When these techniques did not work, they often altered the decisions to suit their own interests.[24]

The nomination and selection process in the social organizations was different in several ways. Although the level of competition varied greatly among the various organizations, by and large nominees were not elected by the organization's membership but by the leadership structure of each group. Quite often, lists of candidates were drawn up in advance and then simply presented to the organization for approval. In the case of the Communist Party, the party leadership drew up its list of 100 candidates for its 100 seats and only faced slight opposition (although several party members did vote against Mikhail Gorbachev himself). In contrast, the Writers' Union selected its twelve candidates from a field of ninety-two nominees. Finally, the Academy of Sciences, in a strategy similar to that of the Communist Party, left several scientists whom its members supported off the list, including intellectual dissident and Nobel Prize for Peace winner Andrei Sakharov. To make their voices heard, a group of scientists from the Academy conducted a successful campaign to cross off all of the names on the lists and thus force a second round of voting. After such a display, Sakharov and others were put on the list.[25] While the process as a whole had begun with 912 nominees, on election day only 871 candidates were left to compete for the 750 seats allocated to the social organizations.

The nomination and selection process for the 1,500 seats allocated by territorial and national-territorial districts was much more competitive than that for the social organizations. In the first stage, 9,505 candidates were formally nominated, with 4,162 being approved by nominating committees. Following the selection meetings, that list was shortened to 2,850, with 1,431 candidates for the territorial districts and 1,419 candidates for the national-territorial districts.

Platforms and Campaigns

The policy platforms of the candidates that made it onto the ballot represented a great diversity of ideas and opinions, ranging from support for current government policy to open criticism of the Soviet system.[26] Many Communist Party candidates touted *perestroika* and *demokratizatsiya*, while others criticized Soviet economic policies, including the practice of not allowing enterprises to retain the profits they earned when they exceeded production targets. Discussion of such a possibility would have been considered taboo only months earlier, but other candidates raised even more contentious issues. Some spoke of the need to establish a free-market economy and a private sector, and others explicitly criticized the existing social, legal, and political order, including the monopolistic role of the Communist Party, and called for the establishment of a multiparty system. Outside political rallies, however, such views were not widely disseminated, for while moderate candidates received favorable coverage in the Soviet press, more radical candidates received scant attention.

One candidate joined the race at the urging of his colleagues at the Leningrad State University Institute of Law. Anatoly Sobchak, a little-known law professor who counted Vladimir Putin among his students, ran a modern campaign, even participating in televised debates between candidates, the first time such things had ever taken place in the Soviet Union.[27] Although he failed to win a first-round victory by a slim margin, he was able to win a seat in a runoff election. As a rule, all the stages of the electoral process tended to be freer and more open in the major cities, such as Leningrad and Moscow, and in the Baltic republics. In contrast, the Central Asian republics were the most restrictive, and regional leaders and party functionaries effectively controlled the process from start to finish.

The Elections

On March 26, 1989, almost 175 million citizens (or 89.8 percent of the electorate) went to the polls to participate in the Soviet Union's first free, multicandidate national elections. (One-third of the seats did remain reserved for certain organizations.) Voters were again allowed to cross off the names of the candidates they did not support, but now, as all voting was done in secret voting booths, they had the freedom to actually do so. Many voters took advantage of this option. In 195 districts in which only one or two candidates were on the ballot, in fact, a majority of the voters crossed out the names of the candidates offered to them, thus forcing repeat elections to be held within two months. This had been a regular phenomenon in previous Soviet elections, but probably never to such an extent (we do not know for sure, since during earlier periods electoral authorities regularly "corrected" such ballots). Also, in only three districts were repeat elections necessary due to an electoral turnout below 50 percent. Again, in the past election officials may have crossed off the names of those who had "forgotten" to request a certificate to vote elsewhere. In the final analysis, how different was the electorate's behavior during this election? Perhaps it was not as different as we think, and perhaps study of it can lend insight into electoral behavior in previous Soviet elections as well.

The level of competition varied widely from district to district. In 399 districts candidates ran unopposed, which attests to the strong role played by party secretaries in the nomination process. Two-thirds of the districts, however, did have competitive races, with two or more candidates competing for the seat. In 76 districts in which three or more candidates competed for the same seat, none secured an absolute majority. In such cases the electoral rules called for runoff elections between the top two contenders. A large number of candidates running in each district, therefore, did not have drastic consequences. In fact, the number of candidates competing against each other was as high as twelve in one Moscow district.

Moscow was also the site of one of the most heated electoral confrontations. In the Moscow national-territorial district number one (which encompassed all of Moscow), Communist Party candidate Yevgenii Brakov faced opposition leader Boris Yeltsin in a race that was important symbolically, in that it pitted the old party against the new opposition. Although Yeltsin was only able to appear on central television once, as party officials attempted to obstruct his campaign, he held successful rallies that drew large crowds.[28] Yeltsin used the opportunity to attack party privileges and demand improved living conditions. In one of the most glaring defeats for the Communist Party, Yeltsin won the contest with almost 90 percent of the vote.[29]

Mikhail Gorbachev and the Communist Party did gain a victory in important respects, however. A larger share of seats went to members of the Communist Party in the 1989 CPD elections than in previous Soviet elections. Although in the past 71.5 percent of seats customarily went to members of the Communist Party, with a balance between party and nonparty members meant to provide the illusion that the party did not monopolize politics, in the 1989 CPD elections 87 percent of the seats went to party members. Of the 191 party secretaries that were on the ballot, 153 won election. There is more to the story than this, as 120 of the party secretaries had won uncontested elections. Also, there were some grand defeats of major party leaders, including the prime ministers of Lithuania and Latvia and the president of Lithuania. Finally, despite the high percentage of Communist Party members winning election, 88 percent of the new deputies had been elected for the first time. The CPD would have a strong Communist Party representation, therefore, but it was not to be dominated by the old guard.

When the new Congress of People's Deputies met for the first time in late May, it elected from among its own ranks the 542 members who would compose the new Supreme Soviet. The Supreme Soviet, in turn, then elected Mikhail Gorbachev as its chairman. Although the initial stages of *demokratizatsiya* seemed to have gone off without a hitch, within one year things would change drastically. In February 1990, at Gorbachev's direction, the Supreme Soviet would vote in favor of amending Article 6 of the Soviet Constitution, which had guaranteed a political monopoly for the Communist Party. At its next session in March, the CPD ratified this decision and thus brought the Communist Party's monopoly on power to an end. The following day, the CPD elected Gorbachev the first president of the Soviet Union in an uncontested and indirect election. These two moves—the legalization of alternative political parties and the creation of a presidency—would affect the future course of action in the republics, which were about to undergo their first free and contested elections.

Electing the Congress of People's Deputies of the RSFSR

The creation of a competitively elected Congress of People's Deputies was a tremendous step forward in the democratization of the Soviet Union, but the balance of the Soviet system remained virtually unchanged. It soon became clear to observers and participants alike that true democratization would require elected bodies at all levels of government, including at the level of the republics. In the case of the Russian Soviet Federated Socialist Republic (RSFSR), which was the Soviet Union's largest constituent republic and home to the capital, Moscow, the first action republican leaders took was to create a Russian legislature to manage the republic's affairs. This set into motion a chain of events—including the creation of a Russian presidency and a declaration of sovereignty one year later—that saw Russia gain more autonomy from the Soviet Union and eventually independence in the wake of the Soviet Union's collapse.

The structure of the Russian Soviet Federated Socialist Republic's Congress of People's Deputies (RSFSR CPD) was based on the Soviet Union's CPD in many ways. It was made up of 1,068 deputies elected to five-year terms, with 900 deputies elected in single-member districts and 168 elected in national-territorial districts, but with no special representation afforded to social organizations. The CPD in turn elected the 252-member Supreme Soviet, with 126 deputies in the Council of the Republic and the other 126 in the Council of Nationalities.

The cumbersome and problematic nomination process, which had allowed local party officials to screen out undesirable candidates, was also discarded. Manipulation of the electoral process still took place, however, as local authorities refused to register some candidates, and the names of others were not even put on the ballot. In addition, even though all candidates were supposed to be given equal access to radio and television for advertising, Communist Party candidates and the favorites of local authorities received favorable coverage and preferential treatment. Finally, ballot stuffing and fraudulent counting took place. By most accounts, however, the process was freer than in the Soviet Union's CPD elections one year earlier.

The Communist Party was the only official party in the election, but it would not be accurate to view the election as dominated by a single party for several reasons. First, the Communist Party was internally divided, and party members competed vehemently against each other. In addition, due to their radical reformist views, many party members were as much a part of the opposition as they were members of the Communist Party itself. The candidates competing in the elections can be divided into four groups.[30] The first group was composed of Russian nationalists and neo-Stalinists and advocated maintaining the strength and territorial integrity of the Soviet Union. Although it would achieve only minimal success in this election, it began to emerge as a political force and would do better in subsequent contests. The second group was the traditional Communists, who still advocated Leninist ideals and supported the maintenance of one-party rule and a command economy. The third group, which we can call the reform Communists, advocated continuing Gorbachev's policies of perestroika and continued reform. Finally, the fourth group was the self-styled democrats, who included prominent public figures such as Boris Yeltsin and united under the umbrella of Democratic Russia (*Demrossiya*).

Although levels of participation were not as high as in previous elections, 77 percent of the electorate did turn out on March 4, 1990, to elect the 1,068 members of the first Russian CPD. The elections were in many ways more competitive than those of the previous year, with a total of 6,705 candidates competing against each other. There were more than three candidates competing against each other in 906 districts, and as many as twenty-eight candidates competed in one district. The number of candidates made it very difficult for a single candidate to receive 50 percent of the votes cast, as required by electoral law. Only 121 seats were filled in the first round of voting, and in 33 of these cases the candidates had actually stood unopposed. Voters had choices in many more districts than in 1989, but this in itself created difficulties. Almost 80 percent of the candidates had to go through runoff elections two weeks later. Low electoral turnout continued to pose a problem, however, and only 1,061 deputies were eventually elected, as seven districts again failed to attract the required 50 percent turnout.

The candidates who won in March 1990 tended to be engineers, managers, physicians, teachers, journalists, lawyers, poets, writers, and artists—in short, members of the intelligentsia. Members of the intelligentsia won 56 percent of the seats in the Russian CPD.[31] Although 86 percent of the deputies elected were members of the Communist Party, these deputies again represented diverse political positions. Whereas 35 to 40 percent of the deputies elected were conservative Communists, another 40 percent were reformers who supported rapid economic reform, with the remainder holding more centrist positions. The electoral returns also exhibited distinct regional patterns, with a rural-urban divide becoming evident. Russia's urban electorate tended to exhibit greater support for liberal and reformist candidates, and rural districts favored traditional Communist and nationalist candidates. This was the beginning of a geographical pattern that would become more pronounced as time went on.

Among the reformist-democrats elected was Boris Yeltsin, who won a stunning victory in his home district of Sverdlovsk with more than 80 percent of the vote. At the Russian CPD's first session in May, Yeltsin was elected chairman of the Supreme Soviet. He then used his popularity and influence to strengthen his position as Russia's chief executive and simultaneously pushed for the creation of a Russian presidency.

Russia Elects Its First President

As the Soviet Union began to come undone in the wake of the bloody suppression in January 1991 of Lithuania's drive for independence, Gorbachev held a referendum on March 17 on the preservation of the union. A total of 75 percent of Russia's electorate turned out to answer the question, "Do you consider necessary the preservation of the Union of Soviet Socialist

Republics as a renewed federation of equal sovereign republics, in which the rights and freedoms of the individual of any nationality will be fully guaranteed?" Armenia, Georgia, Moldova, and the Baltic republics boycotted the vote, but 71.3 percent of Russians who participated favored the preservation of the Soviet Union (*see box, Preserving the Soviet Union*). Also, 69 percent indicated that they favored the creation of a national presidency for Russia, in response to a question tacked on to the ballot at Yeltsin's direction. This percentage, however, did not amount to a two-thirds majority of the entire electorate, as was required for the implementation of any "constitutional matter." But the next day it was decided that establishing a presidency by referendum was not in fact a constitutional matter and could be accomplished by a simple majority of those casting ballots.[32] By May the Supreme Soviet and CPD had each voted in favor of a new law creating a presidency for Russia and setting the election date for June 12. According to its provisions, the president had to be between thirty-five and sixty-five years of age, could serve no more than two consecutive five-year terms, and, although retaining the right to appoint ministers and issue decrees, could not dissolve the parliament.

Although the Russian presidency had essentially been tailor-made for him, Yeltsin would still have to face the electorate and opponents before he could occupy the post. He enjoyed widespread popularity, but his opponents both within and outside government were continuing to grow in number, and they, too, would have the chance to run for the office. Yeltsin's opposition may have had no real chance in June, but the opportunity to deprive Yeltsin of a first-round victory and force a runoff was perhaps motivation enough for some to stand for election.

Candidates and Campaigns

Although the campaign officially kicked off on May 18, and thus would officially last only a little more than three weeks, it had actually been under way since the referendum itself was held back in March. A total of six candidates managed to get on the ballot, by either submitting petitions with at least 100,000 signatures or by winning the endorsement of a party or public organization with 20 percent of the deputies in the CPD among its membership.

Yeltsin, who had the backing of the Democratic Russia grouping, was easily able to collect the required signatures. Democratic Russia, a hybrid of a political party and mass movement that had taken shape during the previous year's legislative elections, was a revolutionary democratic group that called for the resignation of Gorbachev and the entire legislature and for the holding of new elections for a new, non-Communist state. Although Yeltsin had backed away from the group following his victory in the CPD elections, he found the organization and its resources useful for his presidential bid. With 150,000 mobilized members at its disposal, Democratic Russia was able to set up stations at metro stops and in town squares, pass out literature, can-

Preserving the Soviet Union: Citizens v. Leaders

On March 17, 1991, 147 million Soviet citizens (80 percent of those eligible) participated in a referendum on the preservation of the Soviet Union, with 112 million, or 76.4 percent of all citizens, voting in favor of preserving the union. Not all the republics participated in the referendum. Notably, Armenia, Estonia, Georgia, Latvia, Lithuania, and Moldova refused to participate.

This expression of the will of Soviet citizens did not exert any particular influence on the swiftly developing process of the country's disintegration. The Baltic republics had spearheaded the process, but, paradoxically, the role of catalyst in this process was played by those who wanted at any cost to preserve the Soviet Union, primarily the Communist bigwigs who formed the so-called State Emergency Situation Committee. Until August 1991 Moscow had managed—at least formally—to preserve the country's unity, but after the abortive putsch the Union leadership was compelled to recognize the independence of the three Baltic republics.

During the autumn and winter of 1991, attempts were undertaken to "modernize" the Soviet Union, but all of them proved futile, and when the CIS was formed, the very notion of a Soviet Union passed into oblivion. On December 25 of the same year, the first and only president of the Soviet Union, Mikhail Gorbachev, resigned as head of state. The former Union republics entered a new stage of development as sovereign states.

Source: Adapted from "Ten Years Ago Soviet Citizens Voted in Favor of Preserving the USSR," *Strana.ru,* March 17, 2001.

vass door to door, and arrange campaign rallies.[33] In short, the group ran Yeltsin's election campaign.

Yeltsin had no real campaign platform, however, other than a pledge to continue the policies he had begun as chairman of the Supreme Soviet. His political stance was centered on radical reform, including land reform and the privatization of state property. Also on his agenda was the continued devolution of Soviet power and greater autonomy for Russia and the other republics. To downplay the radical nature of his proposals, Yeltsin also touted the ideals of "peace and stability." To balance the ticket and attract more moderate voters, Yeltsin chose as his running mate military hero Aleksandr Rutskoi, a reform Communist who had broken with Gorbachev over the bloody crackdown in Vilnius but who had assumed a less radical political stance than Yeltsin. Rutskoi was more concerned than Yeltsin with military affairs and the country's deteriorating social conditions. It was hoped that Yeltsin and Rutskoi together could appeal to a large segment of the electorate.

A central tactic of the Yeltsin camp was to create the impression that he was too busy managing the affairs of the country to campaign like an ordinary politician. He even failed to take part in televised debates, whereas the other candidates had participated. Yeltsin instead took a series of trips to localities all across the country, during which he would meet local citizens and officials and listen to their complaints and suggestions. Not wanting to leave his potential supporters empty-handed, he frequently concluded special agreements with local authorities authorizing improvements for local conditions. Overall, Yeltsin did not campaign so much as he tried to project an image of himself as a statesman above petty politics.

Yeltsin's only serious competition was from former Soviet prime minister Nikolai Ryzhkov. Ryzhkov was the candidate of the political center and could count on support from the defense sector, state planners, and those in collectivized agriculture, all of whom were threatened by Yeltsin's proposed changes. Ryzhkov opposed the private ownership of land and the privatization of state property. Although he also opposed allowing prices to be determined by the free market, he publicly stated that he supported a market but not one "based on the deprivation and suffering of workers."[34] With his running mate, Boris Gromov, Ryzhkov assumed a position that was moderate but also critical of Gorbachev and his policies.

Another candidate, Vladimir Zhirinovskii, also criticized Gorbachev, but he assumed a nationalist position appealing to Russians' imperial ambitions and desire to maintain the Soviet empire, publicly stating, for example, that "Russia, Moscow, the center, and the USSR are all one."[35] Not all candidates took an anti-Gorbachev position, however. Vadim Bakatin, known for his liberal policies as minister of internal affairs, supported Gorbachev and was touted as the one candidate supported by Gorbachev himself. The two remaining candidates were Albert Makashov, a military conservative, and Aman Tuleev, a local politician from the Siberian region of Kemerovo.

Election and Results

When Russia's first presidential election was held on June 12, 1991, 74.66 percent of the electorate went to the polls, thus easily meeting the 50 percent electoral turnout required for the vote to be valid. Except for Tatarstan, where an attempted boycott led to a turnout of only 40 percent, turnout was consistently high across all regions of Russia, ranging from 65 percent in Moscow and St. Petersburg to a high of 85 percent in Kursk and Belgorod Oblasts.

There was little surprise when the ballots were counted and it was announced that Boris Yeltsin had received 57 percent of the votes cast and was awarded the Russian presidency in a first-round victory. (*See Table 3.1.*) Although almost 70 percent of the electorate had supported the creation of a Russian presidency back in March, it seems that not all of these voters had had Yeltsin in mind for the office. Yeltsin did garner considerable support, but

Table 3-1   Results of the 1991 Presidential Election

Candidate	Percentage of valid vote	Percentage of vote
Boris Yeltsin	45,552,041	57.20%
Nikolai Ryzhkov	13,395,335	16.85
Vladimir Zhirinovskii	6,211,007	7.81
Aman-Geldy Tuleev	5,417,464	6.81
Albert Makashov	2,969,511	3.74
Vadim Bakatin	2,719,757	3.42
Against all	1,525,410	1.92

Source: Tsentral'naya Izbiratel'naya Komissiya Rossiiskoi Federatsii, *Vybory Prezidenta RSFSR 12 Iiunya 1991 goda.* Available online at www.fci.ru/archive/vyb91.htm.

the Russian people were not so much endorsing Yeltsin's policies as seeking a savior. The path that lay ahead for Russia would require nothing less.

As expected, Nikolai Ryzhkov finished a distant second, though he did manage to garner nearly 17 percent of the vote. Zhirinovskii and Tuleev, who would become permanent features of the post-Soviet Russian political landscape, received slightly less than 8 and 7 percent, respectively. Makashov and Bakatin, who each received less than 3 percent, quickly vanished from the scene. The election results indicated not only that Yeltsin had widespread support but also that few supported the policies being pursued by Gorbachev (as evidenced by the weak support for Bakatin) or the alternative proffered by Ryzhkov and his fellow centrists.

Russia and the Path to Democracy

The creation of a Russian presidency and Yeltsin's election to the post put the Soviet Union in a precarious position. Although Gorbachev continued to search for solutions to the Soviet Union's many ills, the Russian presidency provided an alternative power structure, which Yeltsin used to continue his call for the sovereignty of Russia over the Soviet Union while encouraging the leaders of the other republics to do the same. Yeltsin pursued this strategy, moreover, despite the results of the March 17 referendum, which had demonstrated strong support among Soviet citizens for the preservation of some form of renewed union. As if the situation was not perilous enough, a group of Communist hardliners staged an attempted coup d'état on August 19, 1991, on the eve of the signing of a new Union Treaty that would have led to a looser union among the Soviet Union's republics and perhaps pacified the nationalist aspirations of the secession-minded republics. Once the coup attempt had been put down by Yeltsin and other liberal forces, the torch seemed to have been passed to Yeltsin, who, unlike Gorbachev, had stood up against the hardliners and who could claim a popular mandate based upon his electoral victory.

The coup attempt had sought to prevent the de jure weakening of the union, but, ironically, its failure resulted in its de facto demise. On December

25, 1991, Gorbachev resigned his post as president of the Soviet Union and the Russian parliament voted to withdraw from the Soviet Union, as prescribed by the Soviet Constitution, thus following the Baltics and Ukraine, which had already abandoned ship. The remaining republics quickly followed suit, and the Soviet Union was relegated to the dustbin of history.

One underlying reason why the Soviet Union ultimately failed in its attempt to reform, and instead collapsed in the process, may be that the Soviet system was in many ways alien to Russia and incongruent with the country's cultural heritage and traditional values. As one scholar cogently explains, Bolshevism was never deeply rooted in Russian political culture but was "rather a particular ideology whose popularity was directly tied to the fortunes of the Communist Party."[36] Moreover, "despite decades of trying, the Soviet regime ultimately failed in its effort to legitimize the rule of the Communist Party."[37] Another reason why the Soviet regime was unable to legitimize its rule may be that, while it had espoused democracy and marched its citizenry out on a regular basis to participate in staged elections, it had not allowed the people any real role in the political process. Its support for the forms of democracy, moreover, perhaps legitimized genuine elections and eventually led to calls from the people for true democracy.

Rather than serving as the culminating event of Soviet democratization, Gorbachev's policy of *demokratizatsiya* shattered the foundation of the Soviet Union itself and contributed to its eventual collapse. Before a new democratic foundation could be laid, however, Russia would have to overcome numerous obstacles, including a challenge to its own territorial integrity.

For Further Reading

Brovkin, Vladimir. "The Making of the Elections to the Congress of People's Deputies (CPD) in March 1989." *Russian Review* 49 (1990): 417–42.

Conquest, Robert. *The Great Terror: A Reassessment.* Oxford: Oxford Univ. Press, 1991.

Embree, Gregory. "RSFSR Election Results and Roll Call Votes." *Soviet Studies* 43 (1991): 1065–84.

Friedgut, Theodore H. *Political Participation in the USSR.* Princeton: Princeton Univ. Press, 1979.

Getty, J. Arch. "State and Society under Stalin: Constitutions and Elections in the 1930s." *Slavic Review* 50 (spring 1991): 18–35.

Gorbachev, Mikhail. *The August Coup: The Truth and Consequences.* New York: HarperCollins, 1991.

Lentini, Peter. "Reforming the Soviet Electoral System." In *Elections and Political Order in Russia: The Implications of the 1993 Elections to the Federal Assembly,* ed. Peter Lentini. Budapest: Central European Univ. Press, 1995, 36–59.

Mote, Max. *Soviet Local and Republic Elections.* Stanford: Hoover Institution Press, 1965.

Pravda, Alex. "Elections in Communist Party States." In *Communist Politics: A Reader,* ed. Stephen White and Daniel Nelson. London: Macmillan, 1986, 27–54.

Thatcher, Ian. "Elections in Russian and Early Soviet History." In *Elections and Political Order in Russia,* ed. Peter Lentini, 15–35.

Urban, Michael. "Boris El'tsin, Democratic Russia and the Campaign for the Presidency." *Soviet Studies* 44 (1992): 187–207.

Notes

1. Karl Marx and V. I. Lenin, *The Civil War in France: The Paris Commune* (New York: International Publishers, 1988).
2. Karl Kautsky, *The Dictatorship of the Proletariat* (1919; reprint, Ann Arbor: Greenwood, 1964).
3. Vladimir Lenin, "Kautsky and Dictatorship of the Proletariat," in *Lenin Anthology,* ed. Robert Tucker (New York: W.W. Norton, 1985).
4. Ian Thatcher, "Elections in Russian and Early Soviet History," in *Elections and Political Order in Russia,* ed. Peter Lentini (Budapest: Central European University Press, 1995), 25.
5. Quoted in Ronald Hill, "The CPSU: From Monolith to Pluralist?" *Soviet Studies* 43 (1991): 219.
6. Quoted in J. Arch Getty, "State and Society under Stalin: Constitutions and Elections in the 1930s," *Slavic Review* 50 (spring 1991): 19.
7. For more on Stalin's purges, see Robert Tucker, *The Great Terror: A Reassessment* (Oxford: Oxford Univ. Press, 1991).
8. J. Arch Getty, *Origins of the Great Purges: The Soviet Communist Party Reconsidered, 1933–1938* (Cambridge, Eng.: Cambridge Univ. Press, 1987), 252 n. 49.
9. Quoted in ibid., 142.
10. See ibid. for detailed figures of the electoral turnover rate for party secretaries and committee members (159–60) and for a detailed account of the party elections of 1937 (153–63).
11. All data cited here are from ibid.
12. Again, this is Getty's interpretation of the events.
13. Merle Fainsod, *How Russia Is Ruled* (Cambridge: Harvard Univ. Press, 1963), 382.
14. Max Mote, *Soviet Local and Republic Elections* (Stanford: Hoover Institution Press, 1965), 105, includes a printed copy of a ballot with this instruction on it.
15. Theodore H. Friedgut, *Political Participation in the USSR* (Princeton: Princeton Univ. Press, 1979), 111.
16. Ibid., 112. The figure cited here is given as an average of those cited.
17. Ibid., 120.
18. Ibid., 116–17.
19. Ibid., 75.
20. Mikhail Gorbachev, *Zhizn' i Reformy,* 2 vols. (Moscow: Novosti, 1995), vol. 1, 265.
21. The author would like to thank William Clark for helping clarify the presentation of this section.
22. Vladimir Brovkin, "The Making of the Elections to the Congress of People's Deputies (CPD) in March 1989," *Russian Review* 49 (1990): 421.
23. Ibid., 424.
24. Ibid., 431–436.
25. Jerry Hough, "The Politics of Successful Economic Reform," *Soviet Economy* 5 (1989): 17.
26. Brovkin, "The Making of the Elections to the Congress of People's Deputies (CPD) in March 1989," 427–31, contains the best discussion of the various platforms of the candidates.
27. Stephen White, Richard Rose, and Ian McAllister, *How Russia Votes* (Chatham, N.J.: Chatham House, 1997), 29.
28. Ibid., 26.

29. For more on Yeltsin's campaign and strategy, and that of other Moscow candidates, see Brendan Kiernan and Joseph Aistrup, "The 1989 Elections to the Congress of People's Deputies in Moscow," *Soviet Studies* 43 (1991): 1049–64.
30. Richard Sakwa, *Russian Politics and Society* (London: Routledge, 1996), 102.
31. Gregory Embree, "RSFSR Election Results and Roll Call Votes," *Soviet Studies* 43 (1991): 1065–68.
32. Michael Urban, "Boris El'tsin, Democratic Russia and the Campaign for the Presidency," *Soviet Studies* 44 (1992): 188.
33. Ibid., 193.
34. White, Rose, and McAllister, *How Russia Votes*, 37.
35. John Morrison, *Boris Yeltsin: From Bolshevik to Democrat* (New York: Dutton, 1991), 260.
36. Nicolai Petro, *The Rebirth of Russian Democracy: An Interpretation of Political Culture* (Cambridge: Harvard Univ. Press, 1995), 59.
37. Ibid.

4

Laying the Foundation of a New Russia:
The Referenda and
Founding Elections of 1993

Following the collapse of the Soviet Union, the Russian Republic faced the difficult task of governing a society in turmoil from within the altered remains of the Soviet system. The institutional framework in place was poorly suited to the task of governance, not to mention democratic development. After all, the Soviet system was never meant to function as a competitive democracy, in which leaders would be chosen through contested elections. Simply adding this fundamental component onto the existing system would not provide an adequate cure for the system's many ills. What was needed was a fresh start—a new constitution and a new set of institutions, based both on Russia's cultural heritage and the experience of modern democracy in other countries. The problem was how to accomplish this task in a country in great flux and undergoing spontaneous change from all directions.

This chapter focuses on the turbulent year of 1993, during which Russians went to the polls on two separate occasions to vote on a series of national issues. In April they participated in a referendum on Yeltsin's leadership and the issue of early elections, and then in December they voiced their opinions on a new constitution and chose members of the new parliament that it would establish. The chapter begins with a brief overview of the stalemate between the president and the Congress of People's Deputies (CPD) that precipitated the calling of the April referendum. Following an analysis of the referendum, it then turns to Yeltsin's decision to disband the CPD and offer a new constitution to the people in the December plebiscite, and to the elections to the State Duma that would be resurrected that same day.

The Executive-Legislative Impasse

Yeltsin had enjoyed the support of many of the reform-minded leaders when he was Speaker of the Supreme Soviet, but once he became president and his deputy Ruslan Khasbulatov took over his old post as speaker, a rift developed between the two that became a broader struggle between the executive and legislative branches.[1] The nascent Russian system was still unclear about the direction in which the balance of power between the executive and legislative swung, and both Yeltsin and Khasbulatov wanted it to swing in their direction. Unlike in the United States, where power is meant to be balanced among the judicial, legislative, and executive branches, Russia at this time had no provisions in its constitution that demarcated precisely where the power of one branch ended and that of another began. The resulting struggle between the executive and legislative leaders (with the judicial branch itself divided and weak in relation to the other two) would only be resolved with violence.

The struggle was not only over power, however, as Yeltsin and Khasbulatov and their respective camps had different views on what course the country should take. Khasbulatov opposed the rapid economic reforms being proffered by Yeltsin's deputy prime minister, Yegor Gaidar, and he used his position in the Supreme Soviet to block reform legislation. Under Khasbulatov's leadership, the Supreme Soviet refused to confirm Yeltsin's promotion of Gaidar from acting prime minister to prime minister in 1992. The parliament then requested that Yeltsin submit a slate of candidates from which they could chose a prime minister. When a vote was taken, Gaidar came in third, and Viktor Chernomyrdin, a less radical reformer and a former deputy prime minister, won. The choice was apparently amenable to Yeltsin, for he then appointed Chernomyrdin prime minister in December 1992.

Yeltsin and Khasbulatov continued to counter each other's moves, and neither was able to gain the upper hand for long. In January 1993 Yeltsin raised the possibility of holding a national referendum to settle the dispute. His proposal called for the people to speak out on whom they supported— the president or parliament. The parliament responded, however, with its own plan for a referendum, one that would put to the nation the issue of early elections to both the presidency and the parliament. A solution was then offered by the Constitutional Court, which set a date for the referendum, April 11, 1993. Shortly thereafter, the parliament voted to cancel the referendum. In response, Yeltsin gave a televised address saying that he would go ahead with it anyway. An emergency meeting of the parliament was then called to decide how to deal with the issue.

As soon as it met on March 26, the parliament attempted to impeach Yeltsin, ostensibly based upon his attempt to institute "temporary" presidential rule as a reaction against the CPD's refusal to grant him emergency powers. The vote fell short of the two-thirds majority required, but the CPD did agree that a referendum would be held on April 25, although on questions somewhat different from those proposed by Yeltsin, including whether to hold early presidential elections. Yeltsin was confident that a majority of the people supported him and his ideas, but he had not intended to stand for early reelection. After all, his term was not set to expire until June 1996—a full three years away. The issue of a national referendum, which ironically had been raised as a solution to the political impasse between the parliament and the president, thus was the subject of another battle between the two. Nevertheless, an agreement had finally been reached. The people would be asked whether they had confidence in Yeltsin and his reforms, and whether early presidential and legislative elections should be held.

The April 1993 Referendum

On April 25, 1993, the issues of leadership and reform were finally brought to the people in a national referendum. The referendum asked the people four questions: whether they supported Yeltsin and his government, whether they supported Yeltsin's social and economic policies, whether they favored early presidential elections, and whether they favored early parliamentary elections (*see Table 4.1*). The Constitutional Court had decided that the first two questions would have no formal legal status—that is, they would not require any formal action on the part of the president or his government. On the issue of early elections, however, the Court ruled that a decision reached by a majority of all eligible voters (not simply a majority of the electorate that turned out) would be binding and necessitate early elections.[2] The referendum was thus a gamble for both Yeltsin and the parliament. Yeltsin hoped to gain an advantage by winning a renewed mandate, but he was putting his own position in jeopardy at the same time. The parliament hoped to win a renewed mandate of its own and perhaps to rid itself of Yeltsin in the process.

In his campaign leading up to the referendum, Yeltsin and his supporters urged the country to vote "yes, yes, no, yes," to show their support for Yeltsin and his policies while at the same time calling for a new legislature. With the media largely on his side, Yeltsin promised grants for students, increased retirement benefits, and better salaries. The parliament and its supporters, meanwhile, urged the people to vote "no, no, yes, yes," showing its willingness to stand for election themselves, as long as there would also be elections for a new president.

The referendum had a relatively high turnout, with almost 65 percent of all eligible voters participating. This was a decline from the Soviet-era referendum of 1991, in which 80 percent of eligible voters had participated. The main reason for the decline in participation seems to have been feelings of alienation and apathy among the electorate. According to a public opinion survey conducted at the time, four-fifths of those who did not vote stayed home because they believed that the referendum would not make any difference to the outcome.[3]

Turnout ranged from a high of almost 79 percent in Ryazan to an unusually low 22 percent in Tatarstan (the only region in Russia in which turnout fell below 55 percent), and no voting took place in Chechnya. The European areas of Russia had the highest levels of participation, and the Russian Far East and the ethnic republics had among the lowest. Participation in a national referendum is one of the best indicators of the degree of civic engagement among a country's citizens, and the high level of participation indicates that Russians were indeed interested in their country's affairs and in following the path of reform. More illuminating, of course, are the specific views they expressed at the polls.

Yeltsin won a solid victory on the first question, as almost 59 percent of the electorate expressed its confidence in him personally. Only a slim ma-

Table 4-1   The Questions Posed in the Referendum of April 25, 1993

Question 1.	"Do you have confidence in the president of the Russian Federation, B. N. Yeltsin?"
Question 2.	"Do you approve of the social and economic policy conducted by the president of the Russian Federation and by the government of the Russian Federation since 1992?"
Question 3.	"Do you consider it necessary to hold an early election for president of the Russian Federation?"
Question 4.	"Do you consider it necessary to hold early elections for Russian Federation People's Deputies?"

Source: Ralph Clem and Peter Craumer, "The Geography of the April 25 (1993) Russian Referendum," *Post-Soviet Geography* 34 (1993): 481–96.

jority felt the same way about his economic and social policies, however, as only 53 percent approved of the policies he and his government were pursuing. A public opinion survey conducted at this time explored this issue more deeply by asking, "Do you support the policy that the president and government have pursued since 1992?"[4] Those who supported Yeltsin and his policies tended to support the new regime and dislike the Communist system. They also tended to believe that they had gained more freedoms over the previous several years, to hold negative views on the Soviet Union's socialist economy, and to be optimistic about the future. Finally, Yeltsin supporters tended to be urban residents, ethnically Russian, and religious adherents.

The geographical regions most supportive of Yeltsin and his policies, as indicated by the results to the actual referendum, included the Urals, Moscow City and Moscow Oblast, and regions in the Far North, Siberia, and the Russian Far East. The geographical patterns of support for questions one and two largely mirror each other, although in four cases (Buryatiya, Kurgan, Orenburg, and Saratov) a majority of voters approved of Yeltsin while disapproving of his economic policies.[5]

On the issue of early elections, as posed in questions three and four, the electorate gave its clearest message. Although the people were almost evenly divided on the issue of early presidential elections, a secure majority of those who voted—67.2 percent—favored holding early parliamentary elections (*see Table 4.2*). The majority equaled only 43.1 percent of all eligible voters, and however, did not mandate new elections, according to the requirement handed down by the Constitutional Court. But the results did show quite clearly that Yeltsin had more support than the legislature he was battling.

The regions that were the most supportive of Yeltsin and his policies (as determined by "yes" votes in questions one and two) tended, as a corollary, to be the least supportive of holding early presidential elections. This is not surprising, as confidence in Yeltsin and his policies can be interpreted as support for his leadership, making early elections unnecessary. These Yeltsin strongholds, moreover, were the most supportive of holding early parliamen-

Table 4-2   The Results of the Referendum of April 25, 1993

	Question 1	Question 2	Question 3	Question 4
Percentage voting "Yes"	58.7%	53.0%	49.5%	67.2%
Percentage voting "No"	39.2	44.6	48.3	31.0
Turnout of eligible voters	64.2	64.1	64.1	64.1

Source: Ralph Clem and Peter Craumer, "The Geography of the April 25 (1993) Russian Referendum," *Post-Soviet Geography* 34 (1993): 481–96.

tary elections, again as one would expect given the adversarial nature of Yeltsin's relations with the parliament at this time.

With solid majorities expressing their support for him and his policies, the referendum was in many ways a victory for Yeltsin. First, he had gained a renewed mandate and could claim popular support, both for himself personally and for his reforms, all without having to stand for early reelection. In addition, the voters' support for early parliamentary elections, although not legally binding, gave Yeltsin an ace in his pocket, for the results indicated that a majority of voters would probably support Yeltsin over his opponents in future elections. This was a card he would hold onto until an opportune time presented itself.

The Battle of the Constitutions

Despite the small margin of support the referendum had given him (after all, almost half of those who voted supported an early election for president), Yeltsin could at least claim to be governing with the consent of the people, which gave him an edge over Khasbulatov. But the relationship between the parliament and the president remained strained. Faced with a legislature hostile to his policy initiatives, Yeltsin resorted to ruling by decree in order to carry through his reforms. The country did not have many options available to it. One was to rewrite the political system entirely from scratch, beginning with a new constitution. This was the solution James Madison and others had proposed, following the United States' difficulty in governing itself under the Articles of Confederation. As had the United States, Russia almost certainly needed a new constitution. The country's law was a hodge-podge of documents, from the Soviet constitution of 1978 to the decrees that had created the Russian parliament and presidency, and was riddled with ambiguity and contradiction. Although these amendments in fact had created a new political system, they failed to clearly define the roles of the presidency and the parliament, issues which would become "a bone of contention between the federal branches of legislative and executive power."[6] Yeltsin was no Madison, however, and instead of leaving the task to a constitutional convention, he had a group of close advisers begin work on a draft constitution that would create a strong presidential system.

Yeltsin and his advisers were not the first to recognize the need for a new constitution, or the first to begin working on a draft that would create powers favorable to those drafting it. The first attempt at creating a new constitution had begun in 1989, when the Soviet Union's CPD agreed to begin drafting a new Soviet constitution. The Russian CPD had done the same in June 1990, with Yeltsin himself as the chair of the constitutional commission. The commission completed its first draft by August of that year, but successive drafts were to come with almost each new session of the congress, in what was to be a continuing process of drafting, reconsideration, and revision.

By the time the referendum was held in the spring of 1993, two distinct drafts had emerged. The first was the version that had been drawn up by the constitutional commission of the CPD, which had by this time gone through several drafts. The other was the draft that Yeltsin and his team had been working on, which favored a strong presidency. As White, Rose, and MacAllister point out,

> The two drafts had a good deal in common. They agreed that the new Russia should be a presidential republic based on a separation of powers and with human rights defined in terms of the "generally recognized principles and norms of international law." In both cases the president was to be chosen by a popular election for a maximum of two five-year terms; he was to take a leading role in foreign affairs and would head the armed forces and make appointments to key positions. In both drafts the prime minister was to be nominated by the president but confirmed by parliament; the president could submit draft legislation, but the Russian government, that is, the premier [prime minister] and departmental ministers, were to be the main originators of policy.[7]

There were several significant differences between the two drafts as well. They differed on who should have the authority to call referenda, with the president and parliament each wanting this power, and on the position of vice president, which the parliament's draft included and Yeltsin's draft did not. The most contentious point, however, was the tremendous power that Yeltsin's draft gave to the president, whose power the parliament sought to hold in check. In particular, Yeltsin's draft provided that the president could dissolve the parliament if that body rejected his nomination for prime minister on three consecutive occasions. The parliament recognized the significance of this power, which Yeltsin would later use to push through his appointment of Sergei Kirienko as prime minister in March 1998.

Following the April referendum, Yeltsin decided to take advantage of his popular support to call a constitutional conference, perhaps hoping that the opposition would now agree on his version. After initial hesitation, the parliament agreed to participate, although it fought to have its version used as the working draft. The conference began on June 5, 1993, with 762 representatives participating. Shortly after the conference began, several deputies, including Khasbulatov, left after they came to view it as nothing more than an occasion for Yeltsin to add an air of legitimacy to his constitution. The remaining members agreed on June 26 to a significantly revised version of Yeltsin's draft, and on July 12 it was formally approved by the conference. But the Supreme Soviet, at Khasbulatov's insistence, refused to endorse the conference's version and began work on another draft of its own. Moreover, important issues, such as how to properly ratify a constitution, still remained to be addressed.

In the summer of 1787 Madison and the other delegates in Philadelphia had learned that crafting a political system is a contentious process, and that the only way to reach agreement is through compromise, no matter how much certain groups may be against one provision or another. In the U.S. Constitutional Convention, two points of contention were the importation of slaves and the method of representation in Congress. In both cases the convention was sharply divided, and many delegates on both sides left the convention feeling that they had lost crucial battles. Whereas the delegates in Philadelphia compromised on these issues in order to reach a consensus, however, the battle of the constitutions in Russia would not have such a peaceful resolution.

With Yeltsin proffering a constitution with a strong presidency, the parliament favoring stronger checks and balances against the president's power, and the two groups refusing to settle even on the means of arriving at a compromise, the process of changing the outdated constitution itself fell victim to the executive-legislative impasse. The only way to extricate the country from this stalemate, therefore, would be for one side either to give in or to unconstitutionally exert its dominance. Unfortunately, the latter is what occurred.

Russia's Engineered Founding Elections

To bring an end to the stalemate, Yeltsin issued the infamous Decree No. 1400 on September 21, 1993, which dissolved the legislature. He also issued a decree calling for elections to a new parliament to be held on December 11 and 12, 1993 (with the date later changed to only December 12). Yeltsin apparently believed that once the new legislature—whose structure and powers were outlined in his draft constitution—was elected and convened, it would be amenable to ratifying his constitution. Khasbulatov and Rutskoi, however, refused to accept Yeltsin's unconstitutional move. Considering themselves defenders of parliament and the law, they barricaded themselves in the White House, and then they themselves made several unconstitutional moves. Rutskoi had himself declared acting president and urged the crowd outside the White House to march on the Kremlin. Later an anti-Yeltsin mob attempted to seize the Moscow City Administration building and the Ostankino television tower. For nearly two weeks the country stood in a deadlock and crowds amassed outside the barricaded White House, some in support and others in defiance. Finally, on October 4, the military took action and began blasting the building. Rutskoi, Khasbulatov, and their supporters soon conceded defeat and were arrested. Using these "October Events" (as they had become known) as a pretext, Yeltsin pushed ahead with his plans to craft a new political system with more clearly defined functions and powers and a strong presidency. Russia would have its founding election, but it would be, in the words of Timothy Colton, an "engineered founding election."[8]

During the standoff Yeltsin had publicly expressed his willingness to stand for reelection, and on September 24 he had issued a decree calling for a presidential election to be held on June 12, 1994. The defiant parliamentary leaders were not satisfied with this gesture, however, and the negotiations continued. A settlement was nearly reached whereby both legislative and presidential elections would be held in early 1994, and the issue of the constitution would be postponed temporarily. Having successfully taken a military option, and with his detractors under arrest and the defiant parliament disbanded, Yeltsin announced that the legislative elections, which had earlier been scheduled for December 12, would be held as planned, along with a plebiscite on the new constitution. Since his opponents were out of the way (or behind bars), there was also no longer a need for Yeltsin to stand for early reelection, and he announced on November 6 that he would finish out his term, which was not due to expire until June 1996.

When the Russian voters finally went to the polls on December 12, 1993, to have their say on the future order, they had the opportunity to cast at least five votes (and in some cases more, as several regions scheduled local elections to coincide with the national voting): a vote on the constitution, a vote for the party of their choice, a vote for a candidate from their local single-member district, and finally a vote for each of their region's two members of the Federation Council, which was to be the new upper house of the parliament. The elections to the Federation Council would be by the majoritarian method in two-member districts, whereby each voter casts two votes and the top two finishers each receive a seat.

Only 489 candidates ran for the 176 available seats in the Federation Council (2 seats were allowed for each of the eighty-eight regions participating, with no elections being held in Chechnya), and on average only two or three candidates for each available seat. When the returns were counted, only 171 candidates had been elected. In Tatarstan repeat elections were necessary due to low voter turnout, and in Chelyabinsk a shortage of candidates also forced repeat elections. Finally, in the Yamalo-Nenets Autonomous Okrug (A.O.) only one delegate was elected, because of low turnout. Overall, independent candidates—those not affiliated with any party or group—were the largest group of winners. The Federation Council elections thus told little about the political preferences of the electorate, with the most significant characteristic of the deputies elected being the strong presence of members of the various regional administrative elites. The remainder of this chapter, therefore, focuses on the results of the constitutional plebiscite and the elections to the State Duma.

Turnout was much lower than in previous years, with only 54.8 percent of eligible voters participating, an all-time low. Considering that the issues on the agenda were as important as the ratification of a new constitution and elections to a new parliament, it seems surprising that turnout was so much lower than in April of that year, when 64 percent of the electorate participated in the referendum. One reason may be feelings of indifference among the electorate. When asked if they thought that the new constitution would help to establish a lawful and democratic Russian state, only 14 percent agreed, and 30 percent disagreed.[9]

Overall participation was low, but some regions had lower levels of participation than others. Tatarstan again had the lowest level of turnout—it essentially boycotted the elections, with only 13.9 percent of its electorate participating. Excluding Tatarstan, regional variation ranged from a low of 39.7 percent in Khanty-Mansi to a high of 70.3 percent in Karachaevo-Cherkessiya. Although turnout had declined following the April referendum, the geographical pattern of the vote was very consistent with the pattern established at that time.[10]

Russia Gets a New Constitution

After nearly four years of debating the issue, the Russian people were finally given the opportunity to voice their opinion on the new constitution. It would be wrong to say that they were given a real choice, however, since the ballot papers simply asked, "Do you approve of the constitution of the Russian Federation?" Disapproval meant that gridlock under the old constitution would continue, and that the other votes being cast that day to fill the seats in the new parliament would be wasted. It would have been possible, of course, to give the people a choice between competing drafts of the constitution, and indeed this was on the agenda of some leaders. Whether this would have been practical, however, is another matter. After all, constitutions are long, detailed, and complicated documents that the average citizen would have great difficulty understanding. Another option would have been to allow the people to choose electors to write the constitution, as had been attempted with the Constituent Assembly elections of 1917. Finally, the executive and legislative branches themselves could have cooperated more effectively to arrive at a version they agreed on and which they could have then presented to the people.

Following the October Events, however, Yeltsin found none of these other options either necessary or appealing. Having gained the upper hand by disbanding the parliament, Yeltsin could now proffer the version he and his team had been drafting, with additional changes. By framing the vote on the constitution as either "yes" or "no," Yeltsin could possibly attract support from voters who preferred any new constitution to the old Soviet-era one, and who might not otherwise have supported him. The support shown for Yeltsin in the April referendum may have also given him confidence that such a move would work. After all, it was plausible that those who supported Yeltsin in April by voting "yes" on questions one and two of the referendum would now support him by approving the constitution (*see box, Lubricating Russian Voters*).

Lubricating Russian Voters

Of the many things Russia is known for, vodka is certainly among the most famous, and not only for the well-known custom of always finishing a bottle of vodka once it has been opened. This "national drink" also plays an influential role in electoral politics as well. In the 1991 presidential election, bottles of vodka were allegedly given out to voters who promised to vote for presidential candidate Nikolai Ryzhkov. In the same election, Vladimir Zhirinovskii's political platform included a promise to reduce the price of vodka. Perhaps no one, however, will surpass Moscow Mayor Yuri Luzhkov, who had bottles of vodka with his picture on it handed out during his December 1999 reelection campaign.

This may sound strange and abnormal to Americans, but this situation is not altogether different from practices which took place in America's past. Whether it was buying a round of beer for everyone in the bar, or distributing coupons for a free beer to voters, alcohol was also used to buy votes in the United States. That vodka is more appealing to Russian voters than beer is perhaps evidenced by the poor showing of the Beer Lovers' Party, a duly registered party that ran in the 1995 Duma elections but won less than 1 percent of the vote and quickly vanished from the scene.

Yeltsin thus felt confident in presenting the people with a constitution that created a strong presidency. The consitution provided that the president would be directly elected, for no more than two consecutive four-year terms. The president was to be commander-in-chief, would preside over the security council, and could declare martial law and states of emergency. There would be no office of vice president, and the president would hold important powers over the prime minister and the government in general. First, there was no provision that the prime minister would come from the parliament or even be a member of one of its parties. The government was subordinate to the president, who was to set the "basic direction of domestic and foreign policy." Moreover, the president could dismiss the prime minister and the government at will, and the government would be forced to resign on the election of a new president. Furthermore, the president could appoint and dismiss deputy prime ministers, and could appoint and dismiss other members of the government with the prime minister's consent. The president could also dissolve the parliament if it failed to confirm his appointment of a prime minister on three consecutive occasions. Finally, the president would have little reason to fear impeachment, since the procedures for such a move by parliament were difficult and severely restrained.

The new constitution also called for a new parliamentary structure, named the Federal Assembly, which was to be bicameral. The upper house, the Federation Council, would be composed of two representatives from each of Russia's eighty-nine subjects of the federation.[11] The lower house, the State Duma, would to be composed of 450 deputies, half of which were to be elected in single-member districts, with the remaining 225 seats to be filled by proportional representation based on party lists. Each voter would receive two ballots, one to cast for a candidate in his or her electoral district and one to cast for the party of one's choice (hence this system is known as a two-ballot system). The term of office for the Duma was to be four years, although the first Duma was scheduled to sit for only a two-year term because of the circumstances under which it was called.

The upper house of the Federal Assembly was designed to give equal representation by territory, much like the U.S. Senate, and representation in the lower house was based roughly on population, with each electoral district being of roughly equal size, approximately 500,000 registered voters. As Clem and Craumer point out, however, in practice the districts vary widely in size—the Astrakhan Oblast contains almost 724,000 voters, for example, and the Evenki A.O. contains only 13,863. The electoral districts had been carved out of the existing subjects of the federation, and each subject had been required to contain at least one district, which caused some malapportionment.[12]

The Constitutional Plebiscite

Once Yeltsin had succeeded in placing his constitution on the ballot, all that remained for him to do was to ensure its approval. One way Yeltsin pursued this objective was by playing on the fears of the people. In a televised address on the eve of the vote, Yeltsin told the country, "It is for you to decide whether or not there will be peace and calm in Russia . . . until the new constitution is adopted this threat will hang over the country and over each of us."[13] He also urged everyone involved in the 1993 elections, such as the various parties and candidates, to support the constitution or, failing that, to remain silent about objections that they may have.[14] This was backed up with the threat of a media blackout, which would mean almost certain defeat at the polls. Yeltsin's primary objective was approval of the constitution, for even if his supporters and other reform candidates lost in the concurrent parliamentary elections, he would still have won the powers of a strong presidency, which he would then be able to exercise constitutionally.

For the constitution to be ratified, there would have to be not only a majority of votes cast in its favor but a turnout of at least 50 percent of the electorate as well. This was a more lenient requirement than many opposition leaders had wanted. This opposition group had sought to have approval based on 50 percent of the electorate, meaning that half of all eligible voters (not just those who cast votes on that particular day) would have to support its approval. Given the likelihood of a low turnout, such a requirement would have spelled almost certain defeat for the constitution. Under the less stringent requirements, however, the constitution stood a very good chance of being approved.

When the ballots were counted, the new constitution was approved by 58.4 percent of those who participated in the plebiscite. It thus went into effect when the official results were announced on December 25, 1993. Had the constitution's approval required support of a majority of the electorate, however, the outcome would have been different. Since 45.2 percent of the electorate did not participate, the 58 percent of voters who approved of the constitution only amounted to 31 percent of the total electorate. Some have questioned, moreover, whether the reported participation rate of 54.8 percent is even accurate.[15] White, Rose, and McAllister report that observers at the polls estimated turnout at about 38–43 percent of the electorate—well short of the 50 percent required for the vote to be binding. Whether a majority of those who participated actually did support the constitution is not in question, but some do question whether the requirement that half the electorate must participate was indeed met.

The constitution was rejected, not only by nearly 42 percent of voters nationwide, but also by a majority in seventeen of the subjects of the federation, including Dagestan, where 79.1 percent voted against it. The level of support for the constitution varied dramatically, from the low of Dagestan's 20.9 percent approval to 81.8 percent approval in Khanty-Mansi. The geographical pattern of the vote was again similar to that of previous elections, with the north, northwest, and Moscow City and Moscow Oblast being the most supportive, along with much of Siberia and the Russian Far East. The red belt, including Kaluga, Orel, Smolensk, and Voronezh, was the least supportive region. Approval of the constitution was greater than 70 percent in twenty regions, including Arkhangelsk, St. Petersburg, Perm, and Sverdlovsk (Yeltsin's home region). In only four regions did approval drop below 40 percent— Penza, Adygeya, Dagestan, and Tyva.

Ethnic regions were found at both extremes. Three of the four least supportive regions were ethnic regions, and ethnic regions such as the Nenets A.O., Kareliya, Taimyr, the Koryak A.O., and Tatarstan were among the most supportive (all with more than 70 percent approval). The role ethnicity played in shaping the levels of support, however, is uncertain, given the fluctuating levels of turnout. For instance, Tatarstan, with 74.9 percent approval, was one of the regions most supportive of the constitution, but it had the lowest turnout in the country, with less than 14 percent, as those who were against the constitution simply stayed home on election day. Overall, seven of the thirty-one ethnic regions that participated in the plebiscite (Chechnya did not take part) rejected the constitution, and only ten of the sixty-seven nonethnic regions rejected it.

According to survey data and analysis, those opposed to the constitution tended to be younger than those who supported it, and tended to live in European Russia. Those who had suffered the greatest from the transition from communism were also more likely to vote against the constitution.[16] Likewise, those with improved standards of living were more likely to support it.[17] Urbanized areas and regions with better educated populations were more likely to support the constitution, and agricultural regions tended to vote against it.[18]

Surveys also reveal much about the electorate's attitudes and opinions regarding the constitution. One found that 51 percent of those who voted in the plebiscite had never even read the constitution.[19] This did not prevent them from holding opinions about it, however. The same survey found that 21 percent of the electorate supported a strong presidential system, and that 19 percent preferred a parliament with greater powers than the president. A larger group (41 percent) favored allowing the parliament and president roughly equal powers.[20] Having not read the constitution themselves, or perhaps not understanding the implications of its provisions, voters were strongly influenced by the media and recommendations of parties and candidates. In the end, many factors influenced the decisions of voters, but, as Colton accurately describes the situation, "public opinion about non-constitutional subjects mattered more than opinion about constitutional subjects."

Can we then say that Yeltsin's gamble, that those who supported him in the April referendum would do the same in the constitutional plebiscite, had paid off? Roughly the same percentage of voters that had supported him in April supported the constitution in December, which seemingly indicates that this was in fact the case. Clem and Craumer found support for this hypothesis based upon a strong correlation ($r = .748$) between "yes" responses to question one in the referendum and votes of approval for the constitution.[21] Yeltsin not only won approval of the constitution; he did so with a greater percentage of the electorate than had supported him in April. He accomplished this, furthermore, after having disbanded the parliament and presenting the people with a constitution that would make a strong presidency a fact of life for future generations.

Electing the State Duma

Winning approval of the constitution was only half the battle, however. Yeltsin would still need support from the legislature to enact broad legislation and effectively implement changes in Russia's society, economy, and polity. Although the constitution created a strong presidency, it did reserve powers for the parliament and judiciary, and the system allowed for some regional autonomy as well.

The December 1993 elections, it is important to recall, were held under tumultuous circumstances—the parliament had recently been bombed, political leaders were behind bars, and, until October 18, public rallies and demonstrations had been banned and a curfew had been enforced. Moreover, many opposition groups and political parties had been banned, including the Communist Party of the Russian Federation (Kommunisticheskaya Partiya

Rossiiskoi Federatsii, or KPRF). Although most of these groups were eventually allowed to participate in the electoral process, others remained suspended, and Rutskoi and Khasbulatov were kept safely behind bars until the new parliament had already sat for its first session.

In addition to these circumstances, there had been little time to prepare, especially considering that Russia's party system was still in its early stages of development, and that the elections were to be held under new electoral rules and procedures. The elections to the State Duma had first been announced on September 21, but the country had remained in gridlock until armed action was taken against the White House on October 4. The ban on demonstrations and rallies, along with a curfew, had then remained in effect for another two weeks. This was hardly an environment conducive to the participation of civil society in the democratic process. And with the deadline for parties and electoral blocs to register with the Central Electoral Commission (CEC) set for November 6—by which time they needed to collect 100,000 valid signatures from across several regions—there were really only six weeks to prepare, only three of which were after the ban on rallies had been lifted. This time might be sufficient in established parliamentary democracies, but Russia's party system was still in its infancy, and the institutions open for election had only just been created. Under these circumstances, this was certainly insufficient time for parties and blocs to form and decide on candidates and then collect the requisite number of signatures, not to mention run an effective campaign.

Parties and Candidates

There were more than one hundred parties that were formed or forming at the time immediately before the 1993 elections, and thirty-five parties and electoral blocs attempted to get on the ballot.[22] Twenty-one managed to collect the required number of signatures, but the CEC disallowed eight for irregularities in the signature lists and accompanying documentation. As Colton points out, there was very little margin for error, as the average number of signatures collected by a party was 107,000.[23] Those that were disqualified included four nationalist and anti-Yeltsin parties, two centrist parties, and two pro-reform parties. The latter two, once disqualified, urged their members and supporters to back the pro-Yeltsin Russia's Choice.

Thirteen parties and electoral associations were thus accepted and registered by the CEC. Colton's taxonomy of these parties, which places each party into one of five ideological groupings, explains the general positions of the parties and where they rest along the political spectrum (see Table 4.3). The first group, labeled as radical reformist, contains only one party, Russia's Choice—the pro-Yeltsin party that was led by former prime minister Yegor Gaidar, and that included such notables as privatization minister Anatoly Chubais and foreign minister Andrei Kozyrev. The moderate reformist group, which supported the post-1991 system but was not as directly supportive of

Table 4-3 Political Party Orientation and Leadership, 1993 State
Duma Elections

Party or bloc	Political orientation	Top candidate
Russia's Choice	Radical Reformist	Yegor Gaidar
Yabloko	Moderate Reformist	Grigory Yavlinskii
Party of Russian Unity and Accord (PRES)	Moderate Reformist	Sergei Shakrai
Russian Movement for Democratic Reform (RDDR)	Moderate Reformist	Anatoly Sobchak
Women of Russia	Centrist	Alevtina Fedulova
Democratic Party of Russia (DPR)	Centrist	Nikolai Travkin
Civic Union for Stability, Justice, and Progress	Centrist	Arkady Volskii
Future of Russia—New Names	Centrist	Vyacheslav Lashchevskii
Constructive Ecological Movement of Russia (KEDR)	Centrist	Lyubov Lymar
Dignity and Compassion	Centrist	Konstantin Frolov
LDPR	Nationalist	Vladimir Zhirinovskii
KPRF	Socialist	Gennady Zyuganov
Agrarian Party	Socialist	Mikhail Lapshin

Source: Adapted from Timothy Colton, "Introduction: The 1993 Election and the New Russian Politics," in Timothy Colton and Jerry Hough, eds., *Growing Pains: Russian Democracy and the Election of 1993* (Washington, D.C.: Brookings Institution Press, 1998), 18–19.

the Yeltsin administration, included the Yavlinskii-Boldyrev-Lukin bloc (commonly known by its Russian acronym, *Yabloko*, or apple), the Party of Russian Unity and Accord (PRES), and the Russian Movement for Democratic Reform (RDDR). Yabloko, under the leadership of reform economist Grigorii Yavlinskii, supported continued privatization and the establishment of a free-market economy, and PRES followed a more populist line and favored a "regional" approach to governance. Finally, RDDR, under the leadership of St. Petersburg mayor Anatoly Sobchak and former Moscow mayor Gavril Popov, emphasized social protection.

Nearly half of the parties on the ballot occupied the center of the political spectrum, including Civic Union for Stability, Justice, and Progress; the Constructive Ecological Movement of Russia (KEDR); the Democratic Party of Russia (DPR); Dignity and Compassion; Future of Russia—New Names; and Women of Russia. These parties distanced themselves from the radical reformers, although they still supported the post-Soviet regime and its basis. Each also had ties with at least one voluntary association, such as various women's associations (Women of Russia), the Russian environmental movement (KEDR, or "cedar"), industrial and entrepreneurial associations (Civic Union), and the successor to the Komsomol (Future of Russia—New Names).

Finally, three parties on the ballot questioned the legitimacy of the new system and attacked the Yeltsin regime, either from the left or the right. Vladimir Zhirinovskii's misnamed Liberal Democratic Party of Russia (LDPR) advocated extreme nationalism and aimed its message at the disaffected groups of society, including the military, the elderly, and the poor. The successors to the Communist Party of the Soviet Union—the Communist Party of the Russian Federation (KPRF) and the Agrarian Party of Russia—completed the lineup. Both openly opposed reform and advocated a return to state control of the economy and the maintenance of a social safety net. These two parties differed most in their support bases—the Agrarians relied upon rural areas and were led by collective and state farm directors, and the KPRF drew its support from the urban regions and elderly and displaced workers in the cities.

The electoral contests in the single-member districts were less structured than the proportional representation contests, and consequently they are more difficult to classify. The CEC originally registered 1,578 individual candidates, although this number dropped to 1,519 by the time of the elections. On average, approximately seven candidates ran for each of the 224 seats available in the country's single-member districts. Only about 40 percent of the candidates got on the ballot by party nomination. Many of these candidates were not actually party members, although they were willing to support the party in exchange for its nomination. In any case, party affiliation was not listed on the voting sheets, and candidates were not obligated in any way to the parties that nominated them. The remaining candidates, nearly 60 percent, were independents who got on the ballot by gathering nominating signatures from at least 1 percent of the district's registered voters—no easy task to accomplish in such a short time.

The Campaign

The time constraints not only limited the voters' choices but also affected the way in which the campaign was conducted. Only five weeks remained after the November 6 party registration deadline, and, possibly as a result of the severe time constraints, the campaign was not very intense in terms of public rallies and candidate canvassing. Instead, it was primarily conducted via the mass media. As Colton explains, in contrast to democracies in the West—where elections and campaigns had begun in an earlier era, relying upon oral and simple print communication—in Russia, "the media revolution preceded rather than followed the emergence of parties and of the other institutional tissue of an orderly mass politics."[24] It is only natural that Russia would jump directly to what seems the most effective means of getting across political messages and ideas—the mass media.

This raises the question of how fair and effective this media coverage was. Research on this subject indicates that the Russian press collectively provided uncensored, wide-ranging coverage of the campaign. Although coverage by particular newspapers was fragmented, the press as a group provided an abundance of information that the electorate could use to make informed choices on election day, including analysis of the major electoral blocs and their campaign platforms.[25]

Probably the most effective vehicle for the campaigns was television, especially for Russia's Choice and the LDPR. Some expected that television reporting on the election would be "one long 'infomercial' for the 'governing party,'" but analysis indicates that this was not the case.[26] Instead, as one scholar argues, the media coverage of the election was evenly balanced and fair. In television news, which the government could have influenced to favor Russia's Choice, the primary themes were the legitimization of the electoral process itself and the acceptance of democratic procedures. Moreover, television supplied the information needed for the people to make informed choices, including information on important issues, party platforms, and candidate positions.[27]

On the eve of the election, at which point campaigning was banned, Yeltsin gave his televised address urging the people to adopt the constitution, but he again failed to voice his support for the reform parties. Others did attack the opposition, however, as that same evening a highly negative documentary on Vladimir Zhirinovskii was aired on national television. The stage was set, and all that remained was for the election to begin.

The Results

As the votes began to be tallied, it quickly became apparent that the result would not be the liberal victory that Yeltsin and the government had hoped for and that the pollsters had predicted. The results available first were for the national proportional representation, or party-list, contest. The early returns showed that Zhirinovskii's LDPR led the field with more than 20 percent of the vote, outdistancing the pro-government Russia's Choice. Television commentators, who had been prepared to talk about the future of reform and the victory of liberal parties, were thrown into a frenzy and scrambled to fill airtime.

In the party-list contest the LDPR garnered more votes than any other single party, with a final tally of 22.9 percent (*see Table 4.4 and Table 4.5*). The LDPR achieved this feat despite receiving negative media coverage and being attacked from virtually all sides. One reason for the LDPR victory may have been the CEC's policy of not allowing the four other nationalist parties to compete. By removing the LDPR's main competition (i.e., like-minded parties), the CEC effectively coordinated this segment of the electorate and placed all of its votes in the hands of the LDPR.

The reformist parties, in contrast, had very little coordination and effectively competed against each other. Consider that the four reformist parties (the radical reformist and moderate reformist parties) together received more than 34 percent of the vote, but Russia's Choice individually received only 15.5 percent. The moderate reformist parties together received 18.8 percent,

Table 4-4   Distribution of Votes by Party, 1993 State Duma Elections

Party	Percentage of party-list vote	Deputies from party list	Percentage of district vote	Deputies elected in district races
LDPR	22.9%	59	3.6%	5
Russia's Choice	15.5	40	8.3	25
KPRF	12.4	32	4.1	9
Women of Russia	8.1	21	0.7	2
Agrarian Party	7.9	21	6.4	16
Yabloko	7.9	20	4.2	7
PRES	6.8	18	3.2	3
DPR	5.5	14	2.5	1
RDDR	4.1	0	2.5	5
Civic Union	1.9	0	3.6	6
Future of Russia	1.3	0	0.9	1
KEDR	0.8	0	0.7	0
Dignity and Compassion	0.7	0	1.0	3
Against all parties	4.3	n.a.	n.a.	n.a.

Source: Adapted from Timothy Colton, "Introduction: The 1993 Election and the New Russian Politics," in *Growing Pains: Russian Democracy and the Election of 1993,* eds. Timothy Colton and Jerry Hough (Washington, D.C.: Brookings Institution Press, 1998), 22.

but individually each received barely half the number of votes that Russia's Choice did. Yabloko received 7.9 percent, PRES 6.8, and the RDDR only 4.1, and thus failing to cross the 5 percent threshold.

The centrist parties were somewhat successful as a group, as they garnered more than 18 percent of the vote, but individually they did not do well. Only Women of Russia (8.1 percent) and the Democratic Party of Russia (5.5) managed to cross the 5 percent threshold, and the remaining parties received less than 2 percent of the vote.

Finally, Russia's two socialist parties, the Communist Party (the KPRF) and the Agrarian Party, were quite successful. Despite being banned as a political party on October 4 and prevented from organizing until the order banning it was revoked later that month, the Communist Party received 12.4 percent of the vote and placed a strong third, a tremendous accomplishment under the circumstances. The Agrarian Party also did well, placing just ahead of the reformist Yabloko with 7.9 percent of the vote.

A total of 13 percent of the votes were cast for parties that failed to pass the 5 percent threshold or were cast for the option of "against all parties," and the seats represented by these votes thus had to be redistributed to the other parties. When the seat allocations were calculated, no single party even received a quarter of the seats *(Table 4.4)*. The LDPR, which garnered more than 22 percent of the vote, received fifty-nine party-list seats, and Russia's Choice received forty seats. The Communist Party also did fairly well, with thirty-two seats. Women of Russia and the Agrarian Party each received twenty-one party-list seats, and Yabloko received twenty seats. The remaining seats went to PRES (eighteen) and RDDR (fourteen).

Table 4-5   Distribution of Votes by Party Grouping, 1993 State Duma Elections

Party grouping	Percentage of party-list vote	Deputies from party list	Percentage of district vote	Deputies elected in district races
Radical Reformist	15.5%	40	8.3%	25
Moderate Reformist	18.8	38	9.9	15
Centrist	18.3	35	9.4	13
Nationalist	22.9	59	3.6	5
Socialist	20.3	53	10.5	25
Independent candidates	n.a.	n.a.	58.3	136

Source: Adapted from Timothy Colton, "Introduction: The 1993 Election and the New Russian Politics," in *Growing Pains: Russian Democracy and the Election of 1993,* eds. Timothy Colton and Jerry Hough (Washington, D.C.: Brookings Institution Press, 1998), 22.

The Regional Dimension of the Party-List Vote

The four reformist parties did their best in the northwest, the north, and certain regions in the center, Siberia, and the Far East. In Moscow and St. Petersburg, more than 60 percent of the vote went to the reformist parties, who received their lowest levels of support in the red belt. As a group, the reformist parties received more than 40 percent of the vote in twenty-two regions and failed to attract 30 percent in thirty-two regions. In particular, Russia's Choice did best in the cities of Moscow and St. Petersburg; in the Chelyabinsk, Perm, and Sverdlovsk oblasts in the Urals; and in the north, including Arkhangelsk, Kareliya, Komi, and Murmansk. Whereas Russia's Choice led the reformist parties in seventy-three regions and led all parties in eleven regions, Yabloko failed to gain a plurality of the vote in any single region. Despite its poor national showing, PRES led the reformist vote in ten regions and led all parties in three regions. Finally, the RDDR, which failed to pass the minimum threshold, made a good showing in several regions, including Sverdlovsk Oblast and the cities of Moscow and St. Petersburg.

The socialist parties had victories as well, leading the vote in twelve regions. The KPRF had particularly strong showings in Dagestan, Karachaevo-Cherkessiya, and North Ossetiya, and the Agrarian Party won a plurality in three regions, including Bashkortostan. These parties found consistently high support throughout the red belt, from Tver and Smolensk through the black-earth region, down through the north Caucasus and eastward through the Volga area.

The support shown for the socialist parties provides a clear geographical pattern, but the pattern of support for the LDPR is complex. The LDPR won a plurality in sixty-four regions and did best on the environs of the reform parties' support bases, winning in the northwest (except for the city of St. Petersburg) and the center (except for Moscow City). It also had a strong showing in the blackearth regions and in the non-ethnic regions of the north Caucasus, including the Krasnodar and Stavropol krais. Finally, Zhirinovskii's party found pockets of support in Siberia and the Russian Far East.

Several of the remaining centrist parties also had distinctive regional support bases. The DPR did comparatively well in the ethnic republics, winning a large majority in Ingushetiya, and Women of Russia also did well in the ethnic republics, receiving more than 17 percent of the vote in the Yamalo-Nenets A.O. and the Evenki A.O. Future of Russia found a pocket of support in Sakha (3.5 percent), Civic Union did the same in Nenets A.O. (8.2 percent), while Dignity and Compassion and KEDR rarely topped 1 percent of the vote in any region.

The District Races

The LDPR gained a sizable lead over Russia's Choice in the party-list contest, but the tables were turned in the single-member district races. Although most of the seats in the district races were won by independent candidates (136 seats out of 229), party-nominated candidates still won 83 seats. Russia's Choice won more than any other single party, with 25 seats, which was matched only by the socialist grouping as a whole, as the Agrarian Party received 16 seats and the KRPF received 9 seats. The LDPR—the big winner in the party-list contest—won a mere 5 seats, roughly on par with the RDDR and Civic Union, parties that had failed to clear the 5 percent threshold. Yabloko won 7 seats in the district races, and the remaining parties won between 1 and 3 seats, with Dignity and Compassion failing to win a single seat. The real winner of the parliamentary elections, therefore, was Russia's Choice, which received 65 total seats, thus edging out the LDPR by a single seat.

Regional variation in the district races often mirrored that in the national party-list vote. The reformist party candidates did their best in Chelyabinsk, Moscow City, and Murmansk, and they also had strong showings in Ivanovo, Khabarovsk, Perm, St. Petersburg, and Sverdlovsk. Surprisingly, candidates backed by Russia's Choice won seats in Voronezh Oblast and a district in Saratov Oblast, regions in which the socialist parties and the LDPR had topped the party-list vote. Candidates supported by the KPRF and the Agrarian Party won seats in most areas in which these parties did well in the national party voting, including Bryansk, Kursk, Rostov, Smolensk, Tambov, Tver, and Vladimir. Finally, LDPR candidates, who received only 3.6 percent of district votes, won in the Shchelkovo district of Moscow Oblast (won by Zhirinovskii himself) and in Kirov, Krasnoyarsk, Pskov, and Saratov. There was no discernable geographic pattern for the remaining party-supported candidates, with no other party winning in more than three districts.

The Resurrection of the State Duma

The creation of the State Duma in December 1993 was touted not as the establishment of a new institution but rather as the "resurrection" of Russia's true legislature. As discussed in chapter 2, the Duma has deep roots in Russian history and had only came to an end with the Bolshevik seizure of power

in 1917. The continuity with the past was emphasized by the practice of refer-
ring to the Duma elected in 1993 as the "Fifth Duma," that is, the successor
of the Fourth Duma, dissolved in 1917. With a diverse group of deputies, the
new State Duma was unwieldy and without direction, and, on several occasions, it proved very aggressive toward Yeltsin and his administration, just as,
ironically, the Dumas of the early twentieth century had acted toward Tsar
Nicholas II. The strength of the presidency under the new constitution, however, ensured that "Tsar Boris" could continue to pursue his agenda.

Whether the actions of the president in 1993 were just, and whether the
constitutional plebiscite was legitimate, are still matters for debate. But most
accept that the system in place, rooted as it was in the Soviet era, was inherently
flawed and plagued with myriad problems. In addition to the uncertain distribution of power between the executive and legislative branches, the question
of regional power and autonomy was also in doubt. Of course, the process
whereby Russia crafted and put into force its new constitution could be cri-
tiqued from many angles. And, with the Communist Party banned during much
of the campaign, several leading politicians behind bars, and comparatively little time allowed for campaigning, so could the fairness of the December elections themselves. When the dust settled, however, Russia had a new electoral
system, based both on the experience of Western democracies and on Russia's
historical traditions. Over the next several years the Russian people would go
through two electoral cycles, for both the parliament and the presidency. These
later elections perhaps can tell us more about the development of Russian electoral politics, but the elections of 1993 are what laid the democratic foundation.

For Further Reading

Clem, Ralph, and Peter Craumer. "The Geography of the April 25 (1993) Russian
    Referendum." *Post-Soviet Geography* 34 (1993): 481–496.
_____. "The Politics of Russia's Regions: A Geographical Analysis of the Russian
    Election and Constitutional Plebiscite of December 1993." *Post-Soviet Geogra-
    phy* 36 (1995): 67–86.
Colton, Timothy. *Transitional Citizens: Voters and What Influences Them in the New
    Russia.* Cambridge: Harvard Univ. Press, 2000.
Colton, Timothy, and Jerry F. Hough, eds. *Growing Pains: Russian Democracy and
    the Election of 1993.* Washington, D.C.: Brookings Institution Press, 1998.
Okunov, Lev. "The Stages of Constitutional Reform in Russia." In *Democratization
    in Russia: The Development of Legislative Institutions,* ed. Jeffrey W. Hahn.
    Armonk, N.Y.: M.E. Sharpe, 1996, 265–71.
Sakwa, Richard. "The Russian Elections of December 1993." *Europe-Asia Studies* 47
    (1995): 195–227.
_____. "The Struggle for the Constitution in Russia and the Triumph of Ethical Indi-
    vidualism." *Studies in East European Thought* 48 (1996): 115–57.

Notes

1. This phenomenon is not unique to Russia, nor to the time period of 1991–1993.
   For an erudite exposition of the problems of executive-legislative relations in Russia in the period from 1993–1999, see Thomas F. Remington, "The Evolution of

Executive-Legislative Relations in Russia since 1993," *Slavic Review* 59 (2000): 499–520.

2. As reported in Ralph Clem and Peter Craumer, "The Geography of the April 25 (1993) Russian Referendum," *Post-Soviet Geography* 34 (1993): 482.

3. Stephen White, Richard Rose, and Ian McAllister, *How Russia Votes* (Chatham, N.J.: Chatham House, 1997), 83–84.

4. Ibid., 85.

5. Clem and Craumer, "The Geography of the April 25 (1993) Russian Referendum," 487.

6. Lev Okunov, "The Stages of Constitutional Reform in Russia," 265.

7. White, Rose, and McAllister, *How Russia Votes*, 89.

8. Timothy Colton, "The 1993 Election and the New Russian Politics," in *Growing Pains: Russian Democracy and the Election of 1993*, ed. Colton and Hough, 7.

9. White, Rose, and McAllister, *How Russia Votes*, 101.

10. This statement is based upon the very strong bi-variate correlation (r = .813) between the turnout rates for the April referendum and the December elections as reported in Ralph Clem and Peter Craumer, "The Politics of Russia's Regions," 80.

11. As originally conceived, the Federation Council was to be filled ex officio by the executive and legislative heads of the eighty-nine regions. After encountering resistance to his disbanding of the CPD from many of the regional leaders, however, Yeltsin decided on October 11, 1993, that there would be direct election to the upper house. This decision was later changed again in 1995 to allow the executive and legislative heads to sit ex officio in the Federation Council. The Council is currently in a transition toward a system in which the executive and legislative branches of the government will each appoint one offical to sit in this body.

12. Clem and Craumer, "The Politics of Russia's Regions," 69.

13. *Rossiiskie Vesti,* December 11, 1993, 1. Quoted in Timothy Colton, "Public Opinion and the Constitutional Referendum," in *Growing Pains,* ed. Colton and Hough, 292–93.

14. Clem and Craumer, "The Politics of Russia's Regions," 69.

15. White, Rose, and McAllister, *How Russia Votes,* 100.

16. Ibid., 101.

17. Colton, "Public Opinion and the Constitutional Referendum," in *Growing Pains,* ed. Colton and Hough, 296.

18. Clem and Craumer, "The Politics of Russia's Regions," 84.

19. Colton, "Public Opinion and the Constitutional Referendum," in *Growing Pains,* ed. Colton and Hough, 293.

20. Ibid., 294.

21. Clem and Craumer, "The Politics of Russia's Regions," 81.

22. Before 2001, parliamentary seats could be contested by both established parties and electoral blocs. The former included loose quasi-parties that would be more accurately described as electoral associations, and the latter were coalitions of small parties and other organizations that banded together to compete as one unit. Following the established usage in the field, in the discussion that follows all of these bodies will be referred to in the text as parties.

23. Colton, "The 1993 Election and the New Russian Politics," in *Growing Pains,* ed. Colton and Hough, 17.

24. Colton, "The Mass Media and the Electorate," in *Growing Pains,* ed. Colton and Hough, 268.

25. Joel M. Ostrow, "The Press and the Campaign: Comprehensive but Fragmented Coverage," in *Growing Pains,* ed. Colton and Hough, 237–65.

26. Laura Roselle Helvey, "Television and the Campaign," in *Growing Pains,* ed. Colton and Hough, 211.

27. Ibid., 211–35.

5

From Fragmentation to Consolidation: The Parliamentary Elections of 1995 and 1999

The elections and constitutional plebiscite of 1993 laid the institutional foundation for a new Russia. The new institutions would soon be put to the test, however, as the Russian people would go to the polls for national parliamentary and presidential elections and numerous elections in the regions as well. Before turning to the presidential and regional elections in subsequent chapters, in this chapter I discuss the second and third elections to the State Duma, which were held in 1995 and 1999. The Duma elections of 1993, as the first elections to the new parliament, were unique in several ways, but the two legislative elections since then have been held under more normal conditions. The later elections can thus tell us more about the development of Russian electoral politics in general—about the behavior and preferences of the electorate, about how institutional structures has translated the wishes of the people into a sitting parliament, and about how the people have learned to act within a democratic political system.

This chapter, after first discussing the Electoral Law of 1995, focuses on the parties, candidates, campaigns, and results of the 1995 and 1999 Duma elections. It analyzes factors such as regional voting patterns, electoral coordination, and emerging trends in party support for each election. To provide a more detailed view of how the electoral process works, I then look at the conduct and results of the 1999 Duma election for the two electoral districts of Smolensk Oblast. Next, I analyze trends in party development, with an emphasis on changes in the levels of support the various parties received in the 1993, 1995, and 1999 elections. Finally, I examine changes in the behavior of voters, as they seek to maximize their votes and to adapt to the incentives and constraints of the new electoral system.

Changing the Rules of the Game: The Electoral Law of 1995

The president and members of the Duma and Federation Council all learned certain lessons from their experience with the elections of 1993, and they became increasingly aware of the way in which the outcome of the 1993 elections was affected by the electoral rules under which they had been held. They understood that certain electoral rules, such as those that set the number of legislative seats that would be contested in single-member district races, the number of signatures required to be placed on the ballot, and the minimum vote percentage required to gain party-list seats, for example, had affected the final composition of the Duma. Those who understood the influence of these rules would soon realize that they could change them to better serve their own interests.

Institutions set the rules of the game in all competitive political systems, and electoral institutions are particularly important in determining the method by which votes are converted into seats.[1] It is a fact of political life that individual and institutional actors will seek to change the rules in their own favor when given the opportunity—hence the obstacles most countries put in the way of changing them. The electoral regulations used in the Duma elections of 1993 were temporary, having been established by presidential decree without any legislative input, so this perilous issue was raised again in Russia in 1994. The president and parliament had to reach an agreement, the 1993 constitution stipulated, on a new electoral law before the next round of national elections. With the 1995 elections approaching, Russia's fledgling democracy thus had to cope with an issue that is among the most contentious political issues a political system can face.

The debate over the new electoral law centered on four issues: the number of signatures required for a party to be placed on the ballot, the minimum vote percentage required for a party to gain party-list seats, the electoral turnout required for the vote to be valid, and the method of choosing delegates to the Duma—that is, how many seats would be assigned on the basis of proportional representation, and how many would be contested in single-member districts races. Various possibilities were considered during the debate, including retaining the existing procedures and even postponing the elections and allowing the Duma to sit for a full four-year term. This last possibility, however, found little support, even among members of the Duma themselves.

The issue of which method should be used to constitute the legislature had been a subject of debate before the 1993 elections as well. In September 1993 Yeltsin had called for the Duma to be composed of 400 deputies, with one-third elected in party-list races and two-thirds in single-member district races. It was only after consultations with his advisers, who urged him to increase the number of deputies to 450, with half elected in each manner, that Yeltsin issued the decree of October 1 creating the present structure. The Yeltsin camp believed that pro-reform parties, such as Russia's Choice, would do better in the proportional-representation voting, and that such an arrangement would thus return a Duma amenable to Yeltsin's reform program.

Contrary to expectations, however, Russia's Choice did best in the district races in 1993, winning twenty-five seats, by far the largest number of single-member district seats. The LDPR received the largest share of the party-list vote but did poorly in the district races, winning only five district seats.

The latter result is even fewer than the six seats won by Civic Union, which received only 1.9 percent of the vote nationally. Yeltsin and his advisers, in light of these results, then reasoned that a reduction in the number of seats allocated on the basis of proportional representation would favor reform candidates and result in a more conciliatory Duma. They pointed to Zhirinovskii and the LDPR, who had benefited the most from the present electoral arrangements, as evidence. Had fewer seats been distributed according to proportional representation, the LDPR would have had much less of a presence—and influence—in the legislature.

The parties and their members in the Duma, however, recognized that such a change would endanger their positions, and that it was in their best interest to retain a large number of seats based on proportional representation. In particular, the parties who had fared better in the party-list races in 1993, such as the LDPR, were staunchly opposed to altering the existing configuration. As Duma leaders pointed out, increasing the number of seats contested in district races would weaken Russia's fledgling party system. In order to promote party development, so important to Russia's development as a democracy, it would be critical to retain an important role for party lists. After all, ranking candidates on party lists promotes party discipline, which in turn helps the parties pass legislation.

Another point raised by the Duma was that the district races favored candidates who had local appeal. A legislature with many seats allocated in district races would thus be filled with divergent local interests. If the Duma was primarily an "aggregation of local interests," it was argued, democratization would be stalled.[2] Of course, when drafting the U.S. Constitution, James Madison had argued exactly the opposite, that it was only in a legislature filled with a large number of divergent factions that the majority would be safe from the tyranny of any one faction, as compromise would be necessary.[3] Moreover, the faction most strongly represented in the Duma at that time was the Muscovites, as more than half of the candidates listed on the party lists were from the country's capital. How representative could the "national" legislature be if such a large percentage of the deputies came from the capital city and oblast? In order to ensure greater representation of those outside Moscow, limits should be placed, it was suggested, on the number of candidates from Moscow that could be put on the party lists.

The other issues in the debate—the number of signatures required to qualify for the ballot, and the minimum percentage of the national vote required to receive party-list seats—were less contentious. Those involved all favored provisions that would favor large parties and hinder fringe parties as they attempted to gain a foothold. Raising the number of signatures required would prevent fringe parties and candidates from participating and would thus lead to party consolidation, as the would-be supporters of these parties would be compelled to give their votes to larger parties. Raising the minimum threshold above 5 percent would prevent smaller parties from gaining representation, even if they were able to muster the required number of signatures and votes. This would again benefit the larger parties, since the wasted votes would be redistributed to the larger parties. Since the Duma was led by factions that would benefit from such measures, and the president also favored placing greater barriers to entry, both sides were in agreement on setting the rules to force party consolidation.

In November 1994 Yeltsin issued a draft electoral law that called for 300 seats to be contested in district races and 150 to be allocated according to the party-list vote. Such a system would likely secure a working majority for reform candidates who were willing to back Yeltsin's policy initiatives. Other provisions in the draft law included an increase of the minimum percentage requirement to 7 percent and an increase of the signature requirement to 250,000. When the Duma voted on the draft law in late November, it approved it only after extensive revision, including an amendment that switched the seat allocations back to the 225–225 split that was currently in effect. The Federation Council, which had supported the president's draft, quickly rejected the version presented to it by the Duma, with Speaker Vladimir Shumeiko arguing that Russia's party system was not developed enough to justify basing half the legislature's seats on proportional representation.

The Duma leaders, although they understood that the weakness of Russia's party system was an important concern, argued that diminishing the number of seats based on proportional representation would retard further party development. They thus decided to attempt to override the Federation Council's veto. The Duma had little trouble in mustering the two-thirds majority necessary, and once this was accomplished they sent the draft law directly to President Yeltsin. Yeltsin still favored increasing the number of seats contested in district races, however, and citing his support of the Federation Council, he vetoed the bill. This time the Duma was not able to generate the votes necessary to override the president's veto. A conciliation committee composed of Duma, Federation Council, and executive branch representatives was then given the task of crafting an electoral law that would be supported by all sides.

The draft completed by the committee retained the Duma's preferred seat allocation of 225 district seats and 225 party-list seats (*see box, The 1995 Electoral Law*). It also retained the 5 percent minimum threshold and the required turnout of 25 percent. A compromise was reached on the signature requirement, with all parties agreeing to an increase to 200,000 signatures, no more than 7 percent of which could come from any one region (a stricter requirement than that of the 1993 regulations, which had stipulated that no more than 15 percent come from one region). In another important change, there was a limit placed on the percentage of candidates from Moscow that could be placed on the party lists, in order to increase representation from outside the capital. Additionally, candidates on the party list who were from Moscow were not allowed to run simultaneously in a district race, whereas those from outside Moscow would be allowed to do so. The draft law was easily approved by the Duma but only managed to squeeze through the Federation Council after an all-night session. Finally, the new rules of the game went into effect on June 21, 1995, when Yeltsin signed it into law.

The 1995 Electoral Law

- The State Duma is composed of 450 seats, with half elected in single-member district races and half elected in a national party-list race, assigned on the basis of proportional representation, with the entire country as the district.
- Candidates for single-member district seats must submit signatures in an amount equal to 1 percent of the registered voters in their district.
- Parties must collect 200,000 signatures, with no more than 7 percent coming from any one region, in order to be registered.
- Except for the top twelve candidates, party lists must contain representatives from specific subjects of the federation.
- Candidates on the party list who are from Moscow are not allowed to also run in a single-member district race, although those from outside Moscow are permitted to do so.
- The required turnout for the vote to be valid is 25 percent.
- A party must win at least 5 percent of the party-list vote in order to receive a share of the proportional representation seats.
- The proportional representation seats will be divided among those parties that surpass the minimum threshold in relative proportion to the percentage of the vote they received.

Source: Compiled by the author.

The 1995 Duma Elections

With the new electoral law in force, the stage was set for the first test of Russia's fledgling democratic institutions. The parliamentary elections were scheduled to be held on December 17, 1995. In contrast to 1993, these elections were scheduled long in advance, at the time of the 1993 elections themselves. Moreover, the Duma was no longer such an unknown entity. The people now had experience with the country's political institutions, knew about the Duma's work, and, perhaps most importantly, had experience with many of the parties and politicians in the legislature.

Parties and Candidates

Of the hundreds of parties and political movements that expressed interest in participating in the December elections, forty-three collected the required 200,000 signatures and were registered by the Central Electoral Commission (CEC). Several parties, including Yabloko, had initially been denied registration by the CEC for procedural violations. Following protests and several Supreme Court reviews, all parties with the required number of signatures were eventually placed on the ballot. Even though the signature requirement had been doubled, because of the extra amount of time allowed to gather signatures, more than three times as many parties were able to register than in 1993. The new electoral law also stipulated that candidates for district seats needed to gather signatures in an amount equal to 1 percent of the registered voters in their district. A total of 2,627 candidates were nominated to run in the 225 district races (almost 12 candidates per district), with 1,055 running as independents.

The process of gathering signatures was largely a farce, as most parties paid "professionals" to do the job for them, and it resulted in the outright buying of signatures. Professional signature gatherers often paid citizens for their signatures and then sold the lists to parties and candidates. Although this was not explicitly illegal, it was certainly unethical. Moreover, many of the signatures were gathered in a fraudulent manner, with collectors going door to door asking people to sign petitions that were allegedly for such things as keeping rents low, or just forging signatures from readily available databases. Sixteen of the forty-three registered electoral blocs even received fewer than 200,000 votes on election day, suggesting that their signatories were not actual supporters.[4] In fact, some have argued that if all signatures had been collected honestly, only twelve parties would have qualified for the ballot.[5] Having such a large number of parties on the ballot may seem innocuous, but it has a very harmful consequence in splitting the vote among so many parties, as I will discuss below.

Almost all of the parties that were on the ballot in 1993 were back in 1995, although often with different names and new leadership. The parties and electoral blocs that were placed on the ballot represented the entire political spectrum—many times over! There was a proliferation of parties with ambiguous platforms, and parties that had clearly defined platforms competed with others having very similar platforms—justifying such a move by the likelihood that they could all clear the 5 percent minimum threshold. As opposed to 1993, as shown in the typology used in Table 4.3, the parties that took part in the 1995 election can be broken down into only four groups, rather than five (*see Table 5.1*). No party represented a radical reformist policy, as Russia's Choice had in 1993, in large measure because of the drastic economic downturn the country suffered between 1993 and 1995.

The most influential electoral bloc in the reformist group was Russia's Democratic Choice–United Democrats, a bloc centered on Russia's Democratic Choice, led by Yegor Gaidar. Gaidar had renamed the party, formerly Russia's Choice, at its founding congress in 1994, after many members had left for the centrist Our Home Is Russia (*Nash Dom—Rossiya*, or NDR), led by Viktor Chernomyrdin. In addition to Russia's Democratic Choice, the bloc included the Peasant Party of Russia, the Social Democratic Party, led by Aleksandr Yakovlev, and three other small parties. Its platform promoted

Table 5-1   Orientation and Leadership of Selected Parties, 1995 State
Duma Elections

Party or bloc	Political orientation	Top candidate
Yabloko	Reformist	Grigory Yavlinskii
Russia's Democratic Choice	Reformist	Yegor Gaidar
Bloc of Ivan Rybkin	Centrist	Ivan Rybkin
Women of Russia	Centrist	Alevtina Fedulova
Our Home Is Russia (NDR)	Centrist	Viktor Chernomyrdin
Liberal Democratic Party of Russia (LDPR)	Nationalist	Vladimir Zhirinovskii
Congress of Russian Communities (KRO)	Nationalist	Yuri Skokov
Communist Party (KPRF)	Socialist	Gennady Zyuganov
Agrarian Party	Socialist	Mikhail Lapshin

Source: Compiled from data contained in Laura Belin and Robert Orttung, *The Russian Parliamentary Elections of 1995: The Battle for the Duma* (Armonk, N.Y.: M.E. Sharpe, 1997).

"freedom, property, and legality," and it favored such policies as a reduction in the state's role in the economy, support for small business, privatization of agriculture, and military cutbacks. Although the bloc generally supported the Yeltsin government, it was critical of the war in Chechnya.

The other main reformist party was Yabloko, led by Grigorii Yavlinskii, which was largely free from association with the Yeltsin regime and promoted itself as a viable democratic alternative. Although Yabloko shared with Russia's Democratic Choice a commitment to economic reform, it was critical of Gaidar's shock therapy policies and favored a more gradual approach to economic reform. And although Yabloko supported the free market, it held that social protection was necessary for certain groups in society and that market forces could not adequately sustain science, health, culture, and education. In short, Yabloko favored a more evolutionary approach to reform, one coupled with social justice, morality, and protection of the environment.

Another reformist party on the ballot was Forward, Russia!, headed by Boris Fedorov, who had split off from Russia's Choice after the 1993 election. Fedorov promoted his party as patriotic-democratic, favored market reform, and supported military intervention in Chechnya. The remainder of the reformist field ranged from the Pamfilova-Gurov-Lysenko Bloc, which favored social justice and public order, to the Beer Lovers' Party, the Social Democrats, and the Party of Workers' Self-Management.

The most powerful party in the political center was Our Home Is Russia (NDR), a party with the primary purpose of supporting the Chernomyrdin government and laying the foundation for Yeltsin's reelection campaign the following summer. NDR assumed the role of the pro-government party, or the "party of power," just as Russia's Choice had in 1993. That the party of power in 1995 was a centrist party and not a reformist party reflects an overall change in policy of the Yeltsin government, in reaction to the severe economic downturn associated, rightly or wrongly, with the policies of rapid economic reform pursued from 1992 to 1995. Labeling its position as "reasonable centrism grounded in common sense," its party program called for "stability and development, democracy and patriotism, confidence and order."[6] More concrete policy objectives included a stronger state, support for domestic manufacturers, maintaining the integrity of the country, and the development of a market economy with social protection. Although it had been criticized for its close ties with the energy and metallurgical complexes, NDR emphasized its "firm foundation of responsibility and experience."[7]

The other centrist parties ranged from the pro-government Party of Russian Unity and Accord to KEDR, an environmentalist movement. Of particular interest is Women of Russia, touted as the female half of the "party of power,"[8] and the Bloc of Ivan Rybkin, speaker of the Duma. Finally, the left-center was represented by the Trade Unions and Industrialists of Russia and Transformation of the Fatherland.

The strongest nationalist party was Zhirinovskii's LDPR, which had scored the big upset in 1993. Based mostly on the charisma and image of its outspoken leader, the LDPR favored an anti-Western foreign policy, a pro-market economic policy, and a protectionist trade policy, and it supported the restoration of federal control in Chechnya. Aside from its more mainstream policies, the LDPR's party program also called for expanding Russia's borders, dividing the world into spheres of influence, and reducing the price of vodka—along with guaranteeing vodka's ready availability.[9]

The Congress of Russian Communities (*Kongress Russkikh Obschin*, or KRO) joined the nationalists as a newcomer, with a platform distinct from that of the LDPR. Party leaders Yuri Skokov and Aleksandr Lebed, although less eccentric than Zhirinovskii, were perhaps more sincere in their nationalist message. Skokov, who had been chairman of the Security Council, maintained close ties with the military-industrial complex, and Lebed was a retired general who had previously commanded the Fourteenth Army in the Trans-Dniestr region of Moldova. Founded on the platform of protecting the interests of ethnic Russians living in the near abroad, KRO favored the gradual restoration of the Soviet Union "by peaceful means," the preservation of traditional Russian institutions such as the church and family, and the restoration of Russia's status as a great power. The KRO was not the only party to support the latter objective: former vice president Aleksandr Rutskoi had formed a party titled *Derzhava* (great power).

Completing the political spectrum were the socialist parties, primarily the Communist Party of the Russian Federation (KPFR) and the Agrarian Party, as in 1993. The KPRF could claim a membership of five hundred thousand or more, probably the best network of local activists throughout the country, and many loyal supporters. The KPRF held several unconventional positions. It pledged to annul the Belavezhe Accords, which had dissolved the Soviet Union, and held that the 1993 constitution was invalid, since turnout had been less than the 50 percent required by law for any constitutional matter. Its platform also included the re-nationalization of certain industries, including natural resources, the restoration of social guarantees, and an end to inter-ethnic conflicts within the federation. Party leader Gennady Zyuganov, however, attempted to project the image of a tolerant, moderate party that would attempt to restore the positive aspects of the Soviet system but not its evils. The KPRF was joined on the ballot by the Agrarian Party, the Communists' ally in rural areas.

Failed Coordination

The plethora of parties that qualified for the ballot in 1995 represented almost every conceivable political niche. There were so many parties, in fact, that the ballot resembled a newspaper and was almost impossible to open completely in the voting booths. Such a situation is a recipe for disaster in terms of electoral coordination. Electorates are composed of different groups with diverse political leanings, and it is the job of political parties to bring like-minded people together into groups that will act collectively at the polls. If there are more parties on the ballot than distinct political divisions in the electorate, this means that several parties are attempting to represent roughly the same political interests. Such was the case in Russia's 1995 Duma elections. Many parties with similar and often vague platforms split the votes of their target constituencies. In an efficient party system, parties have clear platforms and distinguish themselves from their competitors. In Russia in 1995, however, the parties fragmented as politicians competed for leadership, a process that was made easier by the relative ease of qualifying for the ballot, as noted above. The electorate was left with a difficult choice, as it had to decipher ambiguous party platforms and choose from among a vast array of parties that were very difficult to distinguish from each other on the basis of anything other than the personalities of their leaders.

The issue of electoral coordination is particularly critical in single-member districts where simple majorities determine seats, as is the case with half of the 450 seats in the Duma. The reformist and socialist camps competing against each other in the 1995 elections appear to have recognized this. Boris Fedorov, leader of Forward, Russia!, stated that his party had agreed with Russia's Democratic Choice and Yabloko to not compete against each other in 90 percent of the districts.[10] However, the evidence indicates that the parties did in fact compete against each other. Although the reformist parties only fielded one candidate in 87 of the 225 districts, two or more reformist candidates competed against each other in 56 districts (and some districts had no reform candidates).[11] Further, the smaller reform parties also fielded candidates in the districts in which candidates of the three larger reform parties were running. Reform candidates ran unopposed by other reform candidates in only 40 electoral districts, and in some districts, such as those in Moscow and St. Petersburg, known to be reformist strongholds, eight or more reform candidates competed against each other.

The socialist camp proved only slightly more efficient at coordination. The four major socialist parties—the KPRF, the Agrarian Party, Power to the People, and Communists–Workers' Russia–For the Soviet Union—agreed not to field candidates against each other in 92 districts. In 101 districts, however, two or more of these socialist-leaning parties competed against each other, and the Agrarian Party and the KPRF faced each other in 56 districts.

The Campaign

During the official campaign, access to radio and television airtime, as well as to the print media, was strictly regulated by the Central Electoral Commission. The national television and radio stations were required to provide one hour of free airtime every day, which was to be shared by the forty-three parties and blocs that were on the ballot. The stations retained the authority to determine who received which time slot, and they were thus able to give favorable airtime to parties they supported. Individual candidates running in single-member districts were entitled to up to twenty minutes of airtime on local stations during the course of the campaign. According to a Western monitoring agency, the free airtime was allocated "fairly and in accordance with regulations," a few minor complaints notwithstanding.[12] Nevertheless, most parties made poor use of the free airtime allotted to them.[13]

Parties and candidates were not limited to the free airtime allotted to them but were able to buy additional time. In contrast to the practically unrehearsed monologues delivered during the free airtime, the paid commercials reflected a variety of styles and strategies, ranging from Vladimir Zhirinovskii's singing with a popular rock band to testimonials delivered by cultural icons in support of a particular party. During the two months leading up to the election, there were 195 separate commercials shown a total of about 4,500 times. In the vast majority of these, candidates and party leaders delivered dry monologues and failed to market themselves effectively. They also steered away from roundtable discussions, which they saw as giving too much control to the moderator. Unlike in the United States, there were very few televised debates, as the candidates were apparently afraid to face each other and debate the issues. One Russian journalist castigated the candidates for this, telling them that they "do not know what an election campaign is" or how to run for office.[14]

Our Home Is Russia was the largest consumer of political advertising, spending about four million dollars, or nearly one-quarter of the total amount spent by all parties and candidates.[15] The Communist Party and the Agrarian Party, on the other hand, used airtime sparingly, less than even the Beer Lovers' Party. The socialist parties relied most heavily upon their local networks and mass membership to rally support, and their numerous party papers and the Moscow-based *Pravda* and *Sovetskaya Rossiya* widely publicized their views and messages. The national press, while also important, played a lesser role. There was a clear tendency in the press, however, to support the reformist parties and candidates and provide negative coverage of the LDPR.

Electoral Turnout

When the people finally went to the polls on December 17, they did so in greater numbers than previous Duma elections and constitutional plebiscite of 1993. The healthy turnout of 64.4 percent, which represented an almost 10 point increase from the 1993 Duma elections and equaled that for the April 1993 referendum, signaled a rebound to comparatively high participation rates. Turnout ranged from a high of 74.4 percent in Belgorod Oblast to a low of 51.9 percent in Yeltsin's home region of Sverdlovsk. Despite the range of more than 20 points, there was little variation from region to region, and there were no discernable regional patterns. The variation in turnout was relatively stable across the country, with neighboring regions varying among themselves as much as did regions of the country distant from one another. For instance, in the blackearth region, which includes Belgorod Oblast, the lowest turnout of any of the oblasts was 63 percent, or just less than the national average. And in the Urals region, which includes Sverdlovsk Oblast, the surrounding regions all had higher participation rates than Sverdlovsk, including the Republic of Udmurtiya, which had a turnout of 56 percent. Significantly, participation was more than 50 percent in every subject of the federation.

The Communist Resurgence

As the electoral returns came in, it became apparent that LDPR's surprise showing in 1993 would not be repeated. This would not work to the advantage of the reformist parties, however. In both the national party-list vote and the single-member district races, the Communist Party led the field. When the final tally was in, the KPRF had received 22.3 percent of the party-list vote, almost twice as much as the second place finisher, LDPR, which received 11.2 percent. Our Home Is Russia, the new "party of power," did not do as well as Russia's Choice had in 1993 but still received 10.1 percent of the vote and placed a strong third. Finishing out the field of top finishers was Yabloko, which received 6.9 percent of the vote. (See Table 5.2 and Table 5.3).

The remaining thirty-nine parties all failed to reach the 5 percent minimum and qualify for seats. In fact, only ten parties received more than 2 percent of the vote, and 2.8 percent of the votes cast were against all parties. The four parties that qualified for proportional representation seats together received only about 50 percent of the total party-list vote—meaning that almost half of the party-list votes were wasted, an astonishing total that would be hard for those new to democracy to swallow. The high percentage of wasted votes led some to challenge the legitimacy of the elections and of the Duma itself, and to call for new elections. Although some parties, such as the Beer Lovers' Party, had little chance of reaching the minimum, others

Table 5-2 Distribution of Votes by Party, 1995 State Duma Elections

Party	Percentage of party-list vote	Deputies from party list	Deputies elected in district races	Total deputies elected
KPRF	22.3%	99	58	157
LDPR	11.2	50	1	51
Our Home Is Russia	10.1	45	10	55
Yabloko	6.9	31	14	45
Women of Russia	4.6	0	3	3
Communists-Workers' Russia-For the Soviet Union	4.5	0	1	1
Congress of Russian Communities	4.3	0	5	5
Party of Workers' Self-Management	4.0	0	1	1
Russia's Democratic Choice	3.9	0	9	9
Agrarian Party	3.8	0	20	20
Forward, Russia!	1.9	0	3	3
Power to the People	1.6	0	9	9
Pamfilova-Gurov-Lysenko Bloc	1.6	0	2	2
Trade Union and Industrialists	1.6	0	1	1
Bloc of Ivan Rybkin	1.1	0	3	3
Stanislav Govorukhin Bloc	1.0	0	1	1
My Fatherland	0.7	0	1	1
Common Cause	0.7	0	1	1
Transformation of the Fatherland	0.7	0	1	1
Party of Russian Unity and Accord	0.4	0	1	1
Party of Economic Freedom	0.1	0	1	1
89 Regions of Russia	0.1	0	1	1
Bloc of Independents	0.1	0	1	1
Against all parties	2.8	n.a.	n.a.	n.a.

Note: Parties that received less than 1 percent of the party vote and that did not win any single-member district races are excluded (8.9 percent of the votes cast went to such parties).
Source: Data compiled from *Vestnik Tsentral'noi Izbiratel'noi Komissii Rossiiskoi Federatsii* (1996): 18–51.

missed by only a few tenths of a point, such as Women of Russia, which received 4.6 percent.

In contrast to the party-list vote, in the single-member district races many parties—a total of twenty-three—won seats. Of the 225 district seats, 148 were won by candidates affiliated with a party, whereas in 1993 only 93 winners were affiliated with a party. Unlike the 1993 election, in which the LDPR won the largest share of the party-list vote and the reformist Russia's Choice won the most seats in the district races, the Communist Party emerged as the clear winner in both the district and party-list races.

The Agrarian Party placed second in the district races, winning 20 such races. The reformist and centrist parties also did fairly well in the district races. Yabloko, which received less than 7 percent of the party-list vote, was able to gain 14 seats in the district races, again doing better than in the party-list vote. Our Home Is Russia won 10 seats, Power to the People and Russia's Democratic Choice each won 9 seats, and the Congress of Russian Communities won 5. The remaining 16 parties won between 1 and 3 seats each, with the LDPR winning only 1 seat—that won by its leader, Vladimir Zhirinovskii.

Table 5-3   Distribution of Votes by Party Grouping, 1995 State Duma Elections

Party grouping	Percentage of party-list vote	Deputies from party list	Deputies elected in district races	Total deputies elected
Reformist	6.9%	31	14	45
Centrist	10.1	45	10	55
Nationalist	11.2	50	1	51
Socialist	22.3	99	58	157
Independent candidates	n.a.	n.a.	77	77

Source: Data compiled from *Vestnik Tsentral'noi Izbiratel'noi Komissii Rossiiskoi Federatsii* (1996): 18–51.

The Regional Dimension

The regional patterns of the 1995 elections closely resembled those of the 1993 Duma elections. Regions such as Moscow City and Oblast, St. Petersburg, Rostov, Krasnodar Krai, Tatarstan, and Bashkortostan strongly supported reformist parties. The reform parties won a plurality of the national party-list vote in eleven regions, with NDR taking eight and Yabloko the remaining three. The most important development was an absolute decline in support for reform parties, measured as a percentage of the overall vote. Support for reform parties declined most in the Urals region, including Chelyabinsk, Perm, and Sverdlovsk, which had given crucial support to Yeltsin in the April 1993 referendum and the constitutional plebiscite later that same year. An important exception was the strong support given reformists in several of the ethnic regions, including the republics of Kalmykiya, Chuvashiya, Mordoviya, Karachaevo-Cherkessiya, Dagestan, and the Yamalo-Nenets Autonomous Okrug, where support increased from 1993.

The KPRF, the big winner in the 1995 Duma elections, won in sixty-three of the eighty-nine regions. The geographical pattern of support for the KPRF was fairly consistent with that of 1993, with levels of support increased evenly from 1993 throughout. The KPRF increased its support in its traditional stronghold, the blackearth region, and was also able to gain support in new regions, particularly Moscow City and Oblast. In absolute terms there were more KPRF supporters in Moscow (1.4 million) than in all the oblasts of the blackearth region combined (1.26 million).[16] Besides Moscow, the KPRF made its biggest gains in Kemerovo, Krasnodar, and Rostov. The Agrarians lost about 1.7 million voters nationwide, and it seems that many defected to the KPRF.

The nationalist parties lost support overall, as the LDPR led in only thirteen regions. The LDPR received its strongest support, in terms of vote totals, in the North Caucasus, West Siberia, and in the regions of Saratov, Samara, and Nizhnii Novgorod. Regions in the Russian Far East, including Primorskii Krai and Magadan, were very supportive of the LDPR in terms of vote percentages. Overall, support for nationalist parties was very uniform across the country, with the variation primarily in which specific nationalist party found support in which region. Unlike in 1993, when the LDPR had practically no competition for the nationalist vote, it faced competition from the KRO and Derzhava, meaning that more nationalist parties were competing for the same votes. These parties thus split the nationalist vote, as different voters supported different nationalist parties.

As in the party-list vote, candidates supported by socialist parties did well in district races in the blackearth region, the North Caucasus, and parts of Siberia. Victories for reformist candidates were almost exclusively confined to Moscow, St. Petersburg, and Nizhnii Novgorod and parts of the Urals.

The levels of support parties received in the two types of races—proportional representation and district races—was not very consistent, even within a region. In fact, many regions gave their support to parties of different political orientations in the two kinds of races.[17] This phenomenon is referred to by Georgy Bovt as "the two faces of the Russian voter."[18] It did not hurt the Communists, however, for they received 22 percent of the party-list vote and won a little more than 25 percent of the single-member district seats, thus showing great consistency in both contests.

The Significance of the 1995 Elections

One of the most significant aspects of the 1995 parliamentary elections was the renewed support for the Communists. As a Russian political scientist remarked following the elections,

> The first thing to strike an observer is that, despite four years of unbridled anticommunist propaganda, what once again took first place in Russia were the popular ideas of socialism and the restoration of the Union and of Soviet power, for which at least one-third of the electorate voted, casting their ballots for the Communists and for parties ideologically close to them. The voters were not frightened by the semi-official news media's demagogic fantasy about impending gulags and repressions: They voted for the candidates who can give them a better life.[19]

Despite the old Communist regime's mistakes and failures, and the new regime's anticommunist stance and propaganda, the people still held on to many of socialism's ideals and popular nostalgia for the past. In a period of such tumultuous change, it had proved tempting to look to the past and remember the times when, even if there was not much freedom, the Soviet state provided a modest standard of living for all. This is not the only explanation, of course, for the strong support expressed for the Communists in the 1995 parliamentary elections. As one commentator remarked, "people in Russia do not vote for anyone; they vote against those who are in power and are getting fat at the expense of the people."[20] The victory of the Communists in 1995, therefore, may have been more a sign of protest against the inadequacies of the new regime than a genuine desire to return to the past.

When attempting to discern the political attitudes and values that the results of the 1995 Duma elections indicate, it is important to recall that, although many Russians expressed their dissatisfaction with current conditions by voting for the Communist Party, many others supported parties and candidates who favored continued reform. The support of such voters, however, was fragmented among the numerous reformist and centrist parties that competed against each other. The most damaging consequence of this fragmentation was that almost 50 percent of the votes cast in the election went to parties that failed to clear the 5 percent threshold and thus were wasted. Many of these votes were for reformist and centrist parties, such as Russia's Democratic Choice, Forward, Russia!, the Party of Workers' Self-Management, Women of Russia, and the Pamfilova-Gurov-Lysenko Bloc. In fact, the total votes cast for all reformist and centrist parties, including wasted votes, perhaps amounted to as much as 30 percent of the total votes cast and certainly exceeded the total votes received by the KPRF. Thus, the Russian electorate did not get the legislature it collectively desired, due to coordination failure. Because the electorate was presented with such a wide selection of parties and candidates with ambiguous and vague political platforms, an unacceptably high number of votes was wasted, and the political segment that was split among itself the least thereby won the most seats. The real question is how long will it take for parties, candidates, and voters to learn this difficult and painful lesson.

The 1999 Duma Elections

The greatly fragmented Duma that was elected in 1995 managed to complete its full term, despite a move by Yeltsin apparently aimed at compelling the Duma to dismiss itself during the confirmation of a relatively unknown prime minister in March 1998.[21] As Russians went to the polls in December 1999 to elect deputies to the third session of the State Duma, the idea of continuity with the pre-Soviet dumas, which had been promoted in 1993, was now conveniently brushed aside in order to emphasize the political development of Russia's post-Soviet institutions. The significance of the fact that the elections of 1999 would be the third set of national legislative elections to be held in Russia in one decade should not be lost. When Yeltsin disbanded the parliament in October 1993, some feared that such actions might become a recurring feature of post-Communist Russian politics, and that such actions might even be tolerated by the people. Fortunately, this has not happened. With every transfer of power that occurs through the voting booths, Russia's current structure becomes institutionalized, and democratic elections increasingly are considered the only legitimate means of transferring power, both by the people and the elites.

Parties and Candidates

Before the 1999 elections a total of thirty parties and electoral blocs registered with the Central Electoral Commission to be placed on the ballot. As in 1995, this could be done by submitting 200,000 signatures, with no more than 7 percent coming from any one region. Additionally, a new option was available, that of paying a deposit of 25,000 times the minimum wage, approximately 80,000 in U.S. dollars. Seventeen parties took advantage of this new option, in addition to the thirteen parties that submitted the required signatures. Four parties were eventually disqualified because of registration irregularities, leaving twenty-six parties on the ballot. This was still a large number of parties, but it represented a considerable reduction from 1995, when forty-three parties had competed.

Among the parties that competed in the December 1999 elections were both newcomers and established parties, including all four parties that crossed the 5 percent threshold in 1995—the KPRF, Yabloko, Our Home Is Russia, and Zhirinovskii's Bloc (see Table 5.4). Zhirinovskii initially faced difficulties getting the LDPR on the ballot, as two of the top candidates on the party list were disqualified for incomplete declarations, which thus disqualified the party itself. Zhirinovskii was able to join with other parties that were already registered, however, and together they ran as Zhirinovskii's Bloc (*Blok Zhirinovskogo*).

The LDPR not only ran under a different name but also altered its position on several points. The once quasi-fascist party toned down its anti-Semitic and expansionist rhetoric and transformed itself into "primarily a commercial operation, selling its votes to the highest bidder."[22] Moreover, Zhirinovskii himself came to be seen not so much as someone to be feared as a clown performing for the entertainment of society. The LDPR was not the only party to undergo change. The Communist Party adopted a less radical policy stance, a move which alienated some of its more left-leaning members. The KPRF now no longer sought to overthrow the capitalist system but rather to provide social protection to supplement the market. Both the nationalist and socialist camps, therefore, moved considerably closer to the center.

In contrast to the LDPR and the KPRF, Yabloko and Our Home Is Russia retained their traditional positions, as reformists and centrists, respectively. Yabloko's most significant move was probably in taking an outwardly oppositionist stance against the war in Chechnya, which was a risk in light of public opinion polls indicating approval of the war stood at 70 percent.

Several new parties also proved to be serious contenders. Joining the reformist camp was the Union of Rightist Forces (*Soyuz Pravikh Sil*, or SPS). Formed in September 1999 and led by the young former prime minister Sergei Kirienko, SPS was an electoral bloc composed of several smaller parties and associations. The nucleus of the SPS was the association Right Cause, which itself was composed of some thirteen parties and movements, including Common Cause, Yegor Gaidar's Russia's Democratic Choice, Democratic Russia, and Young Russia. Although it seems awkward for a bloc to contain so many different elements, the coalition, as planned by its architect, Anatoly Chubais, was to be an umbrella organization that could unite all rightist parties and groups in order to compete effectively. SPS was touted as the party of the

Table 5-4   Orientation and Leadership of Selected Parties, 1999 State
Duma Elections

Party or bloc	Political orientation	Top candidate
Union of Rightist Forces (SPS)	Reformist	Sergei Kirienko
Yabloko	Reformist	Grigory Yavlinskii
Unity (*Medved*)	Centrist	Sergei Shoigu
Fatherland—All Russia (OVR)	Centrist	Yevgeny Primakov
Our Home Is Russia	Centrist	Viktor Chernomyrdin
Zhirinovskii's Bloc (LDPR)	Nationalist	Vladimir Zhirinovskii
KPRF	Socialist	Gennady Zyuganov

Source: Compiled from data contained in Michael McFaul, Nikolai Petrov, and Andrei Ryabov, eds., *Primer on Russia's 1999 Duma Elections* (Washington, D.C.: Carnegie Endowment for International Peace, 1999).

young, and it eagerly solicited votes from younger members of the electorate, for example by holding rock concerts as part of its campaign strategy. Its appeal to young voters was based primarily on the fact that it was led by many young politicians, several of whom had even held important governmental posts in the past, including Gaidar, Kirienko, and Boris Nemtsov. It thus also assumed the appearance of a self-proclaimed new party of power, and indeed one of its biggest challenges was in distinguishing itself from the old party of power, Our Home Is Russia.

The other two major newcomers attempted to squeeze into the ever-crowded political center. The Fatherland—All Russia movement (*Otechestvo–Vsya Rossiya,* or OVR) was another umbrella organization of sorts, composed of regional leaders and senior politicians, including Moscow mayor Yuri Luzhkov, St. Petersburg governor Vladimir Yakovlev, and former prime minister Yevgeny Primakov. In addition to attracting many regional leaders from the political center, OVR joined with the Agrarian Party, a move meant to attract left-leaning voters to this centrist party. In the process, OVR absorbed most of the Agrarian Party's leadership and members, including its leader, Mikhail Lapshin, thus further fragmenting the socialist camp while not noticeably changing its own platform. Despite its pro-government slant, OVR failed to gain explicit support from either Yeltsin or Putin, for although it was a pro-regime party, it represented something of an "alternative regime" stance, with similar objectives and policies on its agenda, only under a different slate of leaders.

The other newcomer to the center, and OVR's closest competitor, was the Interregional Movement Unity (*Mezhregionalnoye Dvizheniye Edinstvo*), sometimes referred to by its Russian acronym *Medved,* or "Bear." A last-minute creation of the Kremlin, Unity attempted to compete directly against OVR and its alternative regime message. It received explicit support from Putin and was also touted as the latest party of power. Instead of being headed by politicians who would be susceptible to negative attacks for their previous policies, Unity was headed by well-known figures who were politically "clean," including Emergency Situations Minister Sergei Shoigu and Olympic champion wrestler Aleksandr Karelin. Unity was based on regional support, and it counted more than thirty governors among its supporters and members. The regions that supported Unity were not primarily in the country's center, as with OVR, but across the entire country, from Kaliningrad to the Far North and stretching to the Russian Far East. Moreover, Shoigu himself is from Tyva, an ethnic republic situated next to Mongolia, and his leadership role in Chechnya was perhaps meant to show that Russia's "unity" was not just an issue of Russian nationalism but in the interests of all ethnic groups.

The Campaign

In contrast to 1995, the media did not provide the unbiased political coverage that it should have. Although this was true for both the print and broadcast media, the former's coverage was less biased, perhaps because its owners and sources of financing were more diverse. Each television channel seemed to support a specific party. Significantly, neither state nor private broadcasts were impartial. For the national media the parties of choice were Unity and SPS, and Moscow television favored OVR. In the regions, local stations often gave preference to the party or bloc that was in favor with the regional administration. Explicit bias was not the only flaw in the media's campaign coverage, however, as journalists were prevented by the CEC from making editorial comments. The media campaign, therefore, was mostly limited to political commercials and debates among politicians, with media commentators unable to voice their own views on the campaign and the issues.

A positive change from 1995 was the more frequent use of televised debates, with one-third of the free airtime being allocated for this purpose. In particular, Yabloko leader Yavlinskii appeared in several televised debates, which provided him with very favorable coverage. Few other prominent leaders of major parties, however, participated in the debates. Several were simultaneously running in district races, and the election rules thus prohibited them from participating, for fear that this would give them an unfair advantage in their district races. Although this seems fair on one level, it is unfortunate that party leaders were limited in this way, for who is better qualified to speak on behalf of a party than its leader?

The Communist Party made greater use of the media in this campaign than in the past, using some of its free airtime to broadcast short political commercials. Other parties on the left that had effectively broken with the KPRF over its more mainstream policy positions, such as the Stalinist Bloc–For the Soviet Union and Communists–Workers' Russia–For the Soviet Union, made even greater use of television and billboard advertising. They used their free airtime to broadcast short monologues and to promote traditional communist values, as they sought to appeal to the more radical electorate that the

KPRF had abandoned. Perhaps the most terrifying political commercial from the left was one for the Congress of Russian Communities. The commercial began with a red map, against a white background, outlining the territory of medieval Russia, and it continued by showing the growth of Russia's territory over the centuries. After a brief pause at the borders of the Soviet Union, it then receded to those of the present Russian Federation, leaving an outline of the borders of the Soviet Union. Finally, as a voice said "vote for the Congress of Russian Communities," the borders of the Russian Federation then "bled" over to fill in the outline that once marked the borders of the Soviet Union. Whether the color red was meant to symbolize Communism or bloodshed was left to the viewer's imagination.

The centrist and liberal camps ran some of the most successful campaigns. One of Unity's commercials featured Karelin hurling his wrestling opponent to the mat, then led into a political message. Overall, Unity and SPS, which both had huge campaign budgets, made strategic use of the national media and received favorable coverage on the state-run channels ORT and RTR. Whereas OVR received favorable coverage on Moscow's TV-Center, it suffered a tremendous blow when Yuri Luzhkov, an OVR party leader who was also running for reelection as mayor of Moscow, was attacked on the *Dorenko Show*. In a show that was ostensibly a political exposé, numerous charges were leveled against Luzhkov, as it showed aerial photos of his lavish home outside Moscow and made allegations of financial improprieties.[23] Luzhkov later successfully sued *Dorenko*, but he never had the opportunity to respond to the charges on the show, and the damage to his credibility and campaign had already been done.

In addition to the official media coverage of the campaign, several politicians took advantage of the positions they already held to gain favorable exposure. For example, Unity leader Sergei Shoigu, as Minister of Emergency Situations, was on television almost constantly, ostensibly in relation to the events in Chechnya that he was managing. On the eve of the elections, SPS leader Sergei Kirienko was shown meeting with Prime Minister Putin, indicating that the SPS had close connections to the Putin government, although it never received an official endorsement. The importance of these plugs should not be overemphasized, but Western analyses of the campaign in general have considered such incidents news coverage and, therefore their analyses did not consider them.

Electoral Turnout

The electorate's turnout of 61.7 percent on December 19, 1999, was roughly equal to the turnout for the 1995 Duma elections. The turnout did decline almost 3 points, but it was still high compared to many other countries. Turnout ranged from a high of 78.1 percent in Kabardino-Balkariya to a low of 49.8 percent in Leningrad Oblast. The high of 78.1 percent represents an increase from the high of 1995, and Leningrad set a new low. Leningrad took the distinction of having the lowest turnout rate away from

Sverdlovsk, but this was because of the former's decline rather than any increase in the latter, as Sverdlovsk's turnout only increased from 51.9 percent in 1995 to 52 percent in 1999. The range in turnout was slightly greater than in 1995, but there was again very little regional variation. One discernable trend is the correlation between levels of turnout and support for the Communist Party. In many regions in European Russia, higher levels of turnout seem to be correlated with greater support for the KPRF. This is in line with the trend of high turnout among Communist Party supporters. Turnout declined slightly but remained above or near 50 percent in every region, although in several individual districts turnout was lower than this level. In fact, the vote was invalid in nine districts because either turnout was below 25 percent or the total votes cast "against all candidates" exceeded the total for the leading candidate. In such districts, elections were to be held again in conjunction with the presidential election in March 2000.

Party Emergence and Consolidation

As the early electoral returns came in, it seemed that Unity was about to score a tremendous upset. Since Russia is spread across eleven time zones, the polls are already closed in several regions in the Russian Far East before they have even opened in some places in European Russia. The early returns, therefore, reflected the strong support for Unity in the Far East and Siberia, where Unity's support was as high as 73 percent in Shoigu's home republic of Tyva. When the returns from the blackearth region began to be counted, however, it became clear that this was going to be a very close race. The early returns from the Far East showing Unity in the lead may have even mobilized Communist Party supporters in European Russia and prompted some who were not planning on making the trip to the polling stations to venture out on this cold December day.

Once the final tallies were in, the Communist Party of the Russian Federation had again received the largest share of the party-list vote, with 24.29 percent (*see Table 5.5 and Table 5.6*). Unity also did well, receiving 23.32 percent, the second largest vote share. This was the first post-Soviet legislative election in which two parties were so close in the polls. Unity was the leading party in forty-eight regions, compared to the KPRF, which was the leading party in only thirty-two regions. But the Communist Party was able to attract more supporters in the more populous regions and thus win a larger share of the overall vote. The Fatherland–All Russia bloc also faired well, receiving 13.32 percent, the third largest share, although it led in only eight regions.

Of the remaining twenty-three parties, only three managed to clear the 5 percent threshold, meaning that almost 19 percent of the votes cast were wasted. The Union of Rightist Forces (SPS), a recent creation, received 8.52 percent, edging out Zhirinovskii's Bloc and Yabloko, which each received just less than 6 percent. It displaced Our Home Is Russia (NDR), its main competitor in the center, which seemed to have been successfully attacked by both

Table 5-5   Distribution of Votes by Party, 1999 State Duma Elections

Party	Percentage of party-list vote	Deputies from party list	Deputies elected in district races	Total deputies elected
KPRF	24.29%	67	56	123
Unity (*Medved*)	23.32	64	8	72
Fatherland—All Russia (OVR)	13.32	37	30	67
Union of Rightist Forces (SPS)	8.52	24	5	29
Zhirinovskii's Bloc (LDPR)	5.98	17	1	18
Yabloko	5.93	16	4	20
Our Home Is Russia	1.19	0	9	9
Movement to Support the Army	0.58	0	2	2
Party of Pensioners	1.95	0	1	1
Congress of Russian Communities	0.61	0	1	1
Bloc of General Nikolaev and Academician Fedorov	0.56	0	2	2
Russian National Union	0.37	0	2	2
Russian Socialist Party	0.24	0	1	1
Spiritual Heritage	0.10	0	1	1
Against all parties	3.3	n.a.	n.a.	n.a.

Source: Troy McGrath, "Political Shifts in Russia's Duma: A December to Remember," *Analysis of Current Events* 11 (December 1999): 5.

SPS and Unity. Another explanation for the success of the SPS is the strong support given it by Putin and the favorable coverage it received in the mass media. Although Yabloko's performance represented a decline of only a few percentage points, half of Zhirinovskii's support had eroded since its 1995 levels, which had represented a decline of 50 percent from 1993. Whether Zhirinovskii and his party will be able to hold on to this segment of the electorate or if this trend will continue remains to be seen.

The Regional Dimension

The most discernable regional pattern was that discussed above: the strength of Unity's support in the Russian Far East and Siberia and the Communist Party's continued strong support in the blackearth region. The Communist Party's support was relatively stable from region to region, as it received up to 40 percent and at least 12 percent of the vote in every region except three, a further sign that the party's electorate is stable and consolidated and faces no real competition from the left. Another pattern was the propensity of a given region's centrist supporters to vote for either OVR or Unity. In fact, there was a clear trend whereby the higher the vote was for one party, the less it was for the other. This indicates that both parties were appealing to the same segment of the electorate, and that their relative success varied from region to region.

In the district races, 2,320 candidates competed in 224 districts (again, no elections were held in Chechnya). Of the approximately 10 candidates that

Table 5-6   Distribution of Votes by Party Grouping, 1999 State Duma Elections

Party	Percentage of party-list vote	Deputies from party list	Deputies elected in district races	Total deputies elected
Reformist	14.45%	40	9	49
Centrist	36.65	101	38	139
Nationalist	5.98	17	1	18
Socialist	24.29	67	56	123
Independent candidates	n.a.	n.a.	93	93

Source: Troy McGrath, "Political Shifts in Russia's Duma: A December to Remember," *Analysis of Current Events* 11 (December 1999): 5.

ran in each district, almost 50 percent were nominated by parties. Although independents won in 93 districts, party-supported candidates did exceptionally well, winning 123 of the 224 seats, with 113 of the winners representing one of Russia's seven top parties (as ranked in Table 5.5). The Communist Party was again the clear winner in the district races, with 56 deputies elected. Unity did poorly in the district races and only managed to win 8 seats. The same is true for SPS and Yabloko, which won 5 and 4 seats, respectively. Finally, Zhirinovskii's Bloc only won a single seat. In contrast, OVR-supported candidates were elected in 30 districts. The relative success of these candidates is mostly attributable to the strong support of regional leaders in OVR-friendly regions. Perhaps an opposite reason can explain the defeat of candidates supported by the Unity and SPS parties—these new parties did well nationally in the party-list vote, but their organizations were unable to provide adequate support for their candidates throughout the country.

As the preceding paragraphs illustrate, much of what explains electoral behavior takes place at the district level. As the saying goes, "all politics is local." This is particularly true for electoral politics, as the district level is the most informative when gauging the effects of institutional constraints and incentives on political outcomes. To provide a closer view of the electoral process itself, we will next take a closer look at the two electoral districts of Smolensk Oblast, a region located in the red belt and traditionally considered a Communist stronghold.[24]

The View from Smolensk

Smolensk is an average-sized oblast located in Russia's central region along the border of Belarus, approximately 400 kilometers southwest of Moscow. It has a population of nearly 1.2 million, 94 percent of whom are ethnically Russian, with an additional 4 percent being of Belarusian and Ukrainian ethnicity. The region has a strong industrial base and is relatively urbanized. More than one-quarter of the region's population lives in the capital city of Smolensk, and another 10 percent resides in one of the region's other large cities (Roslavl and Vyazma). Economically, Smolensk is in a depressed economic state, as are most of the regions of central Russia. The population is relatively well educated, and public information is easily accessible. Based on several of the above attributes, Smolensk can be considered an average region in Russia's red belt.

As with many regions in Russia, the level of competition for elected offices is high. For example, in the 1998 gubernatorial election, more than five serious candidates ran for the office. In the December 1999 Duma elections, nine and twelve candidates ran in Smolensk Oblast's two single-member districts, respectively. The candidates in these elections represented virtually the entire political spectrum, from Zhirinovskii's Bloc and the Union of Rightist Forces to the Communist Party and the Pensioners' Party. Many others chose not to affiliate with any party, thus widening the field further. Some candidates justified such a position by claiming that they represented the interests of constituents, not party interests.[25]

The district-level results for Smolensk differ from the national level results in two important ways. First, support for the first- and second-place parties was substantially higher, with the KPRF and Unity together receiving approximately 58 percent of the vote, compared to the 47 percent the two parties received nationally. This is an important development, for if Russia is to develop an effective party system the number of parties in the legislature must be reduced to a manageable number. Smolensk, in giving the majority of its support to only two parties, thus contributed to this process.

Second, whereas only five parties passed the 5 percent threshold, these five parties represented 78 percent of the total ballots cast. In comparison to the country as a whole, 3 percent more of the votes were wasted, but a larger percentage of ballots were cast for fewer parties. This trend also works in favor of the development of a manageable party system, both directly, by eliminating fringe parties, and indirectly, by providing an incentive for such parties to unite and coordinate their actions. Unfortunately, it will take time for the parties to react to these incentives. In the case of Smolensk, the liberal opposition failed to coordinate, and parties such as the SPS, Unity, and OVR, which are all ideologically close, split the reformist vote by running against each other, and thereby reduced their influence. The net result was that the Communist Party won a plurality with less than 25 percent of the vote, although together the three liberal parties secured 45 percent.

That these parties failed to coordinate, and thus competed directly against each other, is readily apparent when one considers the electoral results in the region's two single-member districts, Smolensk district 169 and Vyazma district 168. The Communist Party incumbents won in both districts despite running very meager campaigns, whereas their competitors had been very active and had used the media extensively. The Communist Party also won a plurality in the party-list vote. One factor which contributed to its success may be that the rural electorate was the most active segment of the electorate in both districts, and the rural population has continually proven itself to be the most supportive of the Communist Party across Russia.[26]

In both of Smolensk's single-member districts, support for the Communist Party candidates was approximately equal to the support given to the Communist Party in the party-list vote. In the Smolensk district, for instance, the KPRF received 31.37 percent, and Anatoly Lukyanov, running on the Communist Party ticket, received 31.88 percent (*see Table 5.7*). The Vyazma district showed a slightly different pattern, however. The KPRF received 31.69 percent of the party-list vote, but KPRF candidate Dmitrii Abramenkov received only 24.2 percent. In fact, he barely edged out local entrepreneur Viktor Derenkovskii, who received 21.57 percent. The Communist Party won in both districts, but it did not account for more than 32 percent of the votes cast.

A liberal opposition exists in both districts that seemingly has support exceeding the support for the Communist Party. In both the Smolensk and Vyazma districts, the second- and third-place finishers were liberal, reform-oriented candidates. Together, their support exceeded that of the Communist victor in each district. For instance, the second- and third-place finishers in Smolensk district together received more than 41 percent of the vote, whereas in Vyazma the second- and third-place finishers together received approximately 34 percent. Moreover, the race in Vyazma was particularly very close, with the fourth- and fifth-place candidates each receiving slightly more than 7 and 6 percent, respectively. This race is an egregious case of failed coordination, as the reformist segment of the electorate split its support among four candidates. It also seems to be symptomatic of Russia's fledgling electoral system, in which candidates often do not sufficiently distinguish themselves from one another, voters have extreme difficulty deciding whom to support, and the net result is failed coordination and minority victories at the polls.

Although 30 percent of Smolensk's electorate may favor the Communist Party, a majority of its voters favors reform candidates. In each district, the candidates who finished in second, third, and fourth place were each liberal reformers, including entrepreneurs and businessmen. As the electorate had to choose among so many candidates, however, the votes of those who wished to support more liberal, reform-oriented candidates were split. As we have seen, this occurred not only in the district races but in the party-list races as well. By failing to coordinate strategically, the reform candidates thus handed the election to the KPRF. This is a pattern, furthermore, that is evident across the country.

Factors Contributing to Coordination and Consolidation

The 1999 Duma elections were held on schedule, were conducted in a reasonably free and fair manner, and were participated in by a majority of the electorate—all of which portends well for the development of the Russian electoral system. But perhaps most important was the further consolidation of Russian political parties. First, there were significantly fewer parties on the ballot in 1999 than in 1995—twenty-six, a decline from forty-three. Second, the valid vote was high, as more than 80 percent of the votes cast went to par-

Table 5-7   Results of the 1999 Duma Elections in Smolensk's Electoral Districts

Candidate	Party affiliation	Electoral district	Percentage of vote received
Anatoly Lukyanov	KPRF	Smolensk	31.88%
Yevgeny Kamanin	Yabloko	Smolensk	22.21
Sergei Kolesnikov	Independent (liberal)	Smolensk	18.88
Dmitry Abramenkov	KPRF	Vyazma	24.20
Viktor Derenkovskii	Fatherland—All Russia[a]	Vyazma	21.57
Vladimir Kishenin	Independent (liberal)	Vyazma	12.39

Source: Compiled from data obtained from the local press and from the Smolensk branch of the Central Electoral Commission.
[a]Although Derenkovskii is the head of the local branch of OVR, he ran as an independent in the district race. I use his party affiliation here simply to label his political orientation.

ties that passed the minimum threshold. Considering that in 1995 fully 50 percent of the votes were wasted, this is a significant improvement.

These accomplishments are attributable to the actions of both the parties themselves and the electorate. The parties made great strides in coordinating with each other and consolidating the party structure. Under the guidance of Anatoly Chubais, the Union of Rightist Forces consolidated numerous rightist parties into an effective electoral bloc. For the district races, SPS also coordinated with its closest competitor, Yabloko, as the two agreed not to compete against each other in several districts. For example, in Moscow they ran against each other in only five of the fifteen districts, and they did not field candidates in the districts in which the other's party higher-ups were running.[27]

The socialist camp also consolidated, although under quite different circumstances. With the fragmentation of the Agrarian Party and the incorporation of most of its members into Fatherland–All Russia, the Communist Party's ally and sometimes competitor was eliminated, and the KPRF's hold on the left was thus consolidated. This development, coupled with the Communist Party's status as Russia's most firmly established and well-organized political party, has left the KPRF as *the* leftist party. With its position consolidated, it now faces only a disorganized liberal opposition.

The left and right consolidated, but the center, as it grew, fractured further with the formation of two new centrist parties—OVR and Unity. As Figure 5.1 illustrates, the center is now the largest segment of the Russian electorate, accounting for 36 percent of the votes cast. Its strength was diluted, however, as the centrist vote was split between two alternatives, or three including SPS. The two parties were able to garner enough support to come in second and third, but they have little incentive to cooperate in the future, since they are competitors for the same votes. A coalition of the two, however, would be a real force.

The process that probably contributed the most to party consolidation was strategic voting among the electorate. Public opinion polls taken before

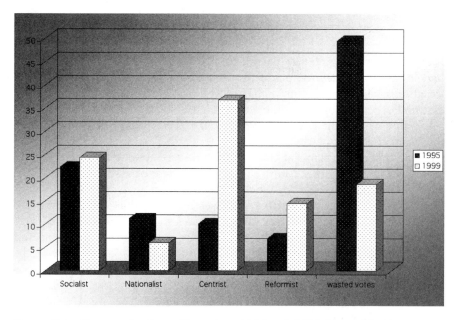

Figure 5-1 Support by Party Grouping, 1995 and 1999 Duma Elections

the election illustrate that voters, to avoid wasting their votes as they had in 1995, were using information about which parties were likely to receive at least 5 percent of the vote to make their decisions. One need only compare the percentage of wasted votes in 1995 with that of 1999 to see that this indeed occurred. Although twenty of the thirty parties on the ballot failed to pass the 5 percent threshold in 1999, 81.37 percent of the votes cast went to parties that did meet the minimum requirement. In the elections of 1995 only four out of forty-three parties passed the threshold, with the consequence that the legislature was elected by only slightly more than 50 percent of the voting population. Voters still need to make better choices about which parties to support, however, since they did continue to split their votes among parties with similar policy positions. Although the parties are partly to blame for this problem, voters should shift their support to the party that both represents their interests and has the best chance of gaining representation in the legislature.

A factor that will contribute to party consolidation is a punitive provision in the electoral law, whereby losers have to pay for their electoral failures. For starters, the seventeen blocs that paid a deposit of $80,000 to register and then gained less than 3 percent of the vote will not get their deposits back. In addition, the eighteen blocs that gained less than 2 percent of the vote will have to repay the CEC for funds allocated during the campaign, and they will have to compensate the print and broadcast media for their free airtime. These charges, if they do not bankrupt these small parties, may deter them from running in the future.

Conclusion

The development of Russian electoral politics from 1995 to 1999 has been largely positive. Fewer parties competed, the parties that did compete had more clearly defined platforms, and fewer votes went to parties that failed to reach the minimum threshold. Problems in party consolidation and electoral coordination remain, but the situation has vastly improved.[28]

More significant than the elections of December 1999, however, were the events that took place immediately afterwards. Within days following the elections it became clear that Unity and OVR were not going to form a coalition government together. Many had expected them to do so, as both are centrist parties and together they would have held more seats than the Communists. They are direct competitors, however, and their political platforms are significantly different in at least one regard—Unity is a pro-Kremlin party while OVR supports allowing the regions more autonomy and authority and is an alternative regime party. Instead, Unity formed a coalition with the KPRF, creating perhaps the strongest coalition in Russia's history. Whereas the coalition is still several votes shy of an absolute majority, it will likely prove more effective at passing legislation than its predecessors.

Even this event seemed trivial in comparison with Yeltsin's surprise resignation on New Year's Eve, a mere two weeks after the Duma elections. The exact reasons for his resignation are unknown. Russia's political system had survived another electoral competition, the regime had performed rather well, and things seemed to be secure in the hands of Prime Minister Vladimir Putin. Perhaps it thus seemed an opportune moment to pass the torch to Putin. Despite the advantages he possessed, Putin would still have to face the electorate and secure for himself by democratic means the post vacated by Yeltsin.

For Further Reading

Belin, Laura, and Robert Orttung, with Ralph S. Clem and Peter R. Craumer. *The Russian Parliamentary Elections of 1995: The Battle for the Duma.* Armonk, N.Y.: M.E. Sharpe, 1997.

Berezkin, Andrei, Mikhail Myagkov, and Peter Ordeshook. "The Urban-Rural Divide in the Russian Electorate and the Effect of Distance from Urban Centers." *Post-Soviet Geography and Economics* 40 (1999): 395–406.

Clark, William. "The Russian State Duma: 1993, 1995, and 1999." *Problems of Post-Communism* 46 (November/December 1999): 3–11.

Clem, Ralph, and Peter Craumer. "Regional Patterns of Political Preferences in Russia: The December 1999 Duma Elections." *Post-Soviet Geography and Economics* 41 (2000): 1–29.

Colton, Timothy, and Michael McFaul. "Reinventing Russia's Party of Power: 'Unity' and the 1999 Duma Election." *Post-Soviet Affairs* 16 (2000): 201–24.

Fish, M. Steven, "The Predicament of Russian Liberalism: Evidence from the December 1995 Parliamentary Elections." *Europe-Asia Studies* 49 (1997): 191–220.

Marsh, Christopher. "Civic Community, Communist Support, and Democratization in Russia: The View from Smolensk," *Demokratizatsiya* 8 (fall 2000): 447–60.

McFaul, Michael. "Russia's 1999 Parliamentary Elections: Party Consolidation and Fragmentation." *Demokratizatsiya* 8 (spring 2000): 5–23.

McFaul, Michael, Nikolai Petrov, and Andrei Ryabov, eds. *Rossiya v Izbiratel'nom Tsikle 1999–2000 godov.* Moscow: Moscow Carnegie Center, 2000.

McFaul, Michael, Nikolai Petrov, and Andrei Ryabov, with Elizabeth Reisch, eds. *Primer on Russia's 1999 Duma Elections.* Washington, D.C.: Carnegie Endowment for International Peace, 1999.

McGrath, Troy, "Political Shifts in Russia's Duma: A December to Remember," *Analysis of Current Events* 11 (1999): 1–5.

Oates, Sarah, "The Dirty Road to the Duma: The 1999 Russian Duma Elections." *Problems of Post-Communism* 47 (May/June 2000): 3–14.

Ovchinnikov, B.V., "Elektoral'naya Evoliutsiya: Prostranstvo Regionov i Prostranstvo Partii v 1995 i 1999 godakh." *Polis: Politicheskie Issledovaniya* 55 (2000): 68–79.

White, Stephen, Matthew Wyman, and Sarah Oates. "Parties and Voters in the 1995 Russian Duma Election," *Europe-Asia Studies* 49 (1997): 767–98.

Notes

1. Rein Taagepera and Mathew Soberg Shugart, *Seats and Votes: The Effects and Determinants of Electoral Systems* (New Haven: Yale Univ. Press, 1989).
2. *Nezavisimaya Gazeta,* April 12, 1995, 2.
3. James Madison, "Federalist No. 51," in Alexander Hamilton, John Jay, and James Madison, *The Federalist Papers* (New York: Modern Library, 1937).
4. Laura Belin and Robert Orttung, *The Russian Parliamentary Elections of 1995: The Battle for the Duma* (Armonk, N.Y.: M.E. Sharpe, 1997), 59.
5. Quoted in ibid., 59.
6. Ibid., 34.
7. Stephen White, Matthew Wyman, and Sarah Oates, "Parties and Voters in the 1995 Russian Duma Election," *Europe-Asia Studies* 49 (1997): 770.
8. Ibid., 772.
9. Belin and Orttung, *The Russian Parliamentary Elections of 1995,* 49–50.
10. Ibid., 57.
11. Ibid. The figures used in this section come from Belin and Orttung's excellent analysis of the subject in the section of chapter 4 titled "Failure to Cooperate in Single-Member Districts," 57–58.
12. White, Wyman, and Oates, "Parties and Voters in the 1995 Russian Duma Election," 776–77.
13. Laura Belin, "Television Plays a Limited Role in Duma Elections," *Transition,* February 23, 1996, 20–23.
14. Ibid., 22.
15. White, Wyman, and Oates, "Parties and Voters in the 1995 Russian Duma Election," 777.
16. Ralph Clem and Peter Craumer, "The Regional Dimension," in Belin and Orttung, *The Russian Parliamentary Elections of 1995,* 156–57.
17. Ibid., 150–53.
18. Georgy Bovt, "The Two Faces of the Russian Voter: Charisma vs. Ideas," *Kommersant-Daily,* December 20, 1995, 1–3.
19. Boris Slavin, "The Ideas that the People Went For," *Pravda,* December 23, 1995, 1.
20. Aleksandr Tsipko, "Why Gennady Zyuganov's Party Could Win the December Elections," *Nezavisimaya Gazeta,* November 9, 1995, 5.
21. Research for this section was supported by a grant from the International Research and Exchanges Board, with funds provided by the U.S. Department of State (under the Title VIII program) and the National Endowment for the Humanities. None of these organizations is responsible for the views expressed below.
22. Michael McFaul, "Russia's 1999 Parliamentary Elections: Party Consolidation and Fragmentation," *Demokratizatsiya* 8 (spring 2000): 9.

23. Sarah Oates, "The Dirty Road to the Duma: The 1999 Russian Duma Elections," *Problems of Post-Communism* 47 (May–June 2000): 7.

24. A fuller examination of democratic development in Smolensk is provided in Christopher Marsh, "Civic Community, Communist Support, and Democratization in Russia: The View from Smolensk," *Demokratizatsiya* 8 (fall 2000): 447–60.

25. One candidate who explicitly took this position was Sergei Kolesnikov, an unsuccessful Duma candidate from the Smolensk district. See Sergei Kolesnikov, "Khochu Gordit'sya Svoei Stranoi," *Robochii Put'*, December 17, 1999, 2.

26. For the most detailed analysis of this phenomenon to date, see Andrei Berezkin, Mikhail Myagkov, and Peter Ordeshook, "The Urban-Rural Divide in the Russian Electorate and the Effect of Distance from Urban Centers," *Post-Soviet Geography and Economics* 40 (1999): 395–406. For a less quantitatively rigorous discussion of this issue, see Jerry Hough, Evelyn Davidheiser, and Susan Goodrich Lehmann, *The 1996 Russian Presidential Election* (Washington, D.C.: Brookings Institution Press, 1996), and Robert Orttung and Anna Paretskaya, "Presidential Election Demonstrates Rural-Urban Divide," *Transition* 2 (1996): 33–38.

27. Aleksei Kuzmin and Boris Ovchinnikov, "Yabloko," in *Primer on Russia's 1999 Duma Elections,* ed. Michael McFaul, Nikolai Petrov, and Andrei Ryabov (Moscow: Moscow Carnegie Center, 1999), 89.

28. An anonymous reviewer pointed out that the trend of party consolidation and coordination is not as clear when the 1993 results are considered in addition to the results of 1995 and 1999. But the apparent success in coordination and party consolidation in 1993 was actually a consequence of the spur-of-the-moment nature of the elections and the restrictions placed on party activity and registration. The 1995 and 1999 elections, therefore, are the only ones that are truly comparable.

6

The Presidential Elections of 1996 and 2000

The March 26, 2000, presidential election in Russia not only marked the true beginning of the post-Yeltsin era; it also served as the culmination of a full decade with a president residing in the Kremlin. On March 16, 1990, Mikhail Gorbachev was chosen to serve as the first president of the Soviet Union, and before the end of the year many of the republics were preparing to introduce their own presidencies. In June 1991, little more than one year after the post was first introduced into the Soviet political system, Russia elected Boris Yeltsin as its first president—a post he would hold until his resignation just hours before the clock struck midnight on the eve of 2000.

Yeltsin's authoritarian tendencies led many to speculate that he was actually prepared to cancel the presidential elections that were originally scheduled for June 2000. Yet Yeltsin's wish to "go down into history as the president who ensured the first legitimate changing of power" in Russia was realized.[1] The manner in which he handed over the reigns of power, however, would cause speculation about his motives. Many believed that Yeltsin resigned in favor of then–prime minister Vladimir Putin in order to give Putin an edge in the coming elections, and that this transfer of power was part of a negotiated settlement whereby Yeltsin would receive immunity from prosecution for crimes and irregularities committed during his tenure in office. Although no one knows for certain whether not such an explicit plan existed, within several months legislation was enacted that did just that.

This chapter focuses on the 1996 and 2000 elections to Russia's highest political office—the office of president. From early speculation that Yeltsin would cancel the 1996 election because he feared that he may lose, to the early election in 2000 that was made necessary by Yeltsin's resignation, presidential elections in Russia have been the most telling events on the Russian political scene. This chapter discusses presidential elections in post-Soviet Russia, including the candidates and campaigns, voting patterns, regional variation, and the implications of the elections for Russian political development and democratization. It concludes with a discussion of continuity and change in Russian presidential elections, from the standpoint of the candidates and the preferences of the electorate, and the implications for the further democratic development of Russia.

The 1996 Presidential Election

After engineering the creation of the Russian presidency, Yeltsin became the country's first democratically elected president in 1991, winning a five-year term. The Soviet Union would not even survive the year, but Yeltsin was able to hold on to his post, although not without incident. After relations between the parliament and Yeltsin became increasingly bitter, Yeltsin first went to the people for a popular mandate with the referendum of April 1993. Although a solid majority indicated that they supported his policies, only a slim majority voted against having him stand for early reelection. Once it became apparent later in the year that the referendum had not resolved the power struggle in his favor, Yeltsin disbanded the parliament and resorted to force.

Although Yeltsin succeeded in using this historic opportunity to introduce a new constitution and political system, his popularity dropped precipitously from this point on. A short two years later his popularity was so low that he trailed Communist Party leader Gennady Zyuganov in the polls. In a survey conducted in January 1996, 21 percent of those polled said that they intended to vote for Zyuganov, and only 8 percent intended to vote for Yeltsin.[2] Yeltsin, however, did not at this time understand the seriousness of the situation. At a February meeting of his close advisers held to discuss his campaign strategy, Yeltsin stated flatly, to the astonishment of those in the room, that his rating must surely be the highest of any politician's. As one of his advisers recalled later, "We all sat there in silence. We were shocked, wondering, where did he get this idea? A few tried to suggest, very gently, that maybe the numbers were not so high—but only gently."[3]

The Election That Almost Wasn't

Once Yeltsin realized just how poorly he was doing, he and his advisers seriously considered canceling the election. One of Yeltsin's closest aides, Aleksandr Korzhakov, was even given the responsibility of preparing a contingency plan on how this could be done. In early 1996, as campaign preparations got under way, there were really two campaign teams. The first was led by close Yeltsin aides Korzhakov and Oleg Soskovets. According to some accounts, this team had as its main objective discrediting the elections themselves and thus convincing Yeltsin to cancel them. The second team was composed of a group representing business interests, including Vladimir Gusinskii and Boris Berezovskii, and led by Anatoly Chubais. This team included a group of American campaign consultants, one of whom Yeltsin assigned the task of predicting whether he would win or lose, so that he could call off the election if need be. The two teams worked against each other, with Korzhakov's team trying to convince Yeltsin that he should cancel the election and the other team trying to help Yeltsin win, albeit to protect their own interests.[4]

In early March Korzhakov presented Yeltsin with his plan to cancel the elections. The Duma had recently passed a resolution denouncing—and perhaps voiding, depending on your reading of it—the dissolution of the Soviet Union in December 1991 by Yeltsin and the leaders of Belarus and Ukraine. Korzhakov warned Yeltsin that this could lead to his arrest and prosecution if the Communists were to win the election in June. Yeltsin thus gave the plan serious consideration, and he even had drafts of presidential decrees drawn up dissolving the parliament, banning the Communist Party, and canceling the election.[5] Once Yeltsin learned that his minister of internal affairs, Anatoly Kulikov, could not guarantee the loyalty of his troops if he took such actions, Yeltsin seems to have changed his mind. Instead of signing the decrees, Yeltsin put all of his efforts into winning reelection.

One of the most important moves Yeltsin then made was to establish an election council consisting of members of both teams. At the urging of his more progressive advisers and the international community, Yeltsin decided to go through with the elections. After all, if he did not win reelection, he could always void the results. A top Kremlin official was quoted as saying in private that even if 80 percent of the people voted against him, Yeltsin would not leave office.[6] What was the advantage in canceling the elections before they were held rather than voiding them afterward? In fact, if Yeltsin had lost to a radical nationalist or anti-reformist candidate and then voided the results, the West would probably not even have balked at such a move.

Yeltsin's Electoral Strategy

Once Yeltsin decided to pursue reelection, he planned to go after Communist Party leader Gennady Zyuganov—the frontrunner in the polls—by framing the election as a choice between two systems, the old and the new. Although many people had suffered under the new system, many more had suffered under the Soviet regime. The rationale behind this strategy was that, if the election was framed as a choice between the two regimes, the people would choose the Yeltsin regime and the "continuity, stability, and progress" that it represented.

In distinguishing himself from Zyuganov, Yeltsin could not shift too far toward the liberal, reformist end of the political spectrum, however, as support for this position was waning in the midst of the economic and social dislocations associated with the early years of the Yeltsin regime. The waning support for politicians of a liberal and reformist persuasion was made apparent by the poor performance of reform-oriented parties in the December 1995 Duma elections. Yeltsin's team logically concluded that in order to win they would have to distance themselves from more reformist political positions.[7]

The Campaign

Some commentators have emphasized the critical role played by Yeltsin's Western advisers, but the most important advantage Yeltsin had was his position of power and the access to resources that it provided.[8] Yeltsin proved himself quite effective at politicking. In addition to staging rock concerts to attract young voters, he traveled extensively throughout the country, promising everything from the payment of wage arrears to special privileges for regional authorities. Yeltsin didn't stop there, however—he actually handed out cash during political rallies![9] His seemingly incessant traveling had another purpose as well, to dispel the rumors that his health was failing.

In contrast to previous elections, when the television media had focused on legitimizing the elections and democratic procedures, during the 1996 presidential campaign the pro-Yeltsin media presented a Yeltsin victory as crucial to the continuation of free and fair elections.[10] Rather than highlighting the achievements of his administration, Yeltsin's major campaign strategy was to vilify the Communists. Yeltsin and his supporters sought to evoke fear of a Communist return to power through such methods as broadcasting films and documentaries that reminded the people of the evils of the Soviet system. Perhaps the most effective was the award-winning film *Burnt by the Sun*, which powerfully illustrates the deep pain felt by victims and malefactors alike during the Stalin period. This tactic was used in campaign commercials as well. One frequently aired commercial, shown against a backdrop of executions, famines, and other Soviet-era atrocities, announced that "Russia's Communists have not even changed the name of their party; they will not change their tactics either."[11] Finally, Yeltsin's campaign equated the old CPSU with the new KPRF, an analogy that, although tempting on a simplistic level, is actually far from accurate.[12]

Zyuganov welcomed Yeltsin's move of equating the KPRF with the Communist Party of the Soviet Union. He pointed out that there had always been two factions in the CPSU—the radical faction, led by such men as Trotsky, Khrushchev, Gorbachev, and Yeltsin, and the liberal faction, with which Zyuganov was more closely associated, led by such men as Andropov, Gagarin, and Stakhanov.[13] Moreover, Zyuganov did not seek to distance himself too much from Stalin, whose crimes, he claimed, "were not as bad as some portrayed."

In the early stages it seemed likely that Zyuganov would win. All that he had to do was present himself as *the* opposition candidate and unite all anti-Yeltsin elements behind him. If he could successfully accomplish this, he seemed assured of victory. Zyuganov was well situated to do so. After all, he had the best-organized party apparatus working for him, with a strong infrastructure down to the grassroots level—although he seems to have relied on the party infrastructure too heavily, at the expense of television and radio campaigning.

Zyuganov also attempted—although he would not be very successful—to unite other leftist and nationalist parties behind him, except for Zhirinovskii, from whom he tried quite wisely to distance himself. Zyuganov even presented himself as the leader of a nationalist bloc—not in the sense of ethnic Russian superiority, but rather based on support for national self-determination and opposition to more exclusionary forms of Russian nationalism, such as that proposed by Zhirinovskii. As Clover states, Zyuganov modeled "himself a Bashkir nationalist, a Tatar nationalist, and a fierce defender of Kalmykian Buddhism," in seeking the support of Russia's many nationalities.[14]

He also portrayed himself as being a moderate, instead of the radical Communist ideologue that Yeltsin and the liberal opposition tried to make him out to be. He expressed his willingness to work within Russia's new democratic political structure and sought to distance himself from extremist elements on both the right (nationalists) and the left (neo-Marxists and even some of his own party members). Unfortunately for him, the Yeltsin-biased media focused on his more radical and nationalist statements and did not air his more moderate proclamations.

Finally, Zyuganov's campaign tried to ensure that Yeltsin would not succeed in distancing himself from the difficulties of his period in office. Zyuganov sought to make the election a referendum on Yeltsin's performance and the conditions in contemporary Russian society, focusing on the rampant corruption, agricultural and industrial decline, and skyrocketing crime.

Although it was obvious early on that this would be a two-candidate election, between Yeltsin and Zyuganov, the Central Electoral Commission initially certified eleven candidates, including former Soviet president Mikhail Gorbachev. The rest of the field included Lebed, Yavlinskii, and Zhirinovskii. Together, they could have put together a potential "third force," but neither Yavlinskii nor Lebed wanted to unite with the radical Zhirinovskii. Although Yavlinskii and Lebed talked about working together, it appears that Yeltsin approached Lebed with a better deal—to stay in the race for the first round, in order to detract voters from Zhirinovskii and maybe even Zyuganov.[15]

Round One

Turnout in the first round of the election was very high, 69.7 percent, up from the previous winter's legislative elections. Although the regional variation in turnout ranged 20 percentage points, with a low of 59 percent in Murmansk and a high of 79 percent in Bashkortostan, participation was high across the country. Yeltsin received 35 percent of the vote, barely edging out Zyuganov, who received 32 percent. Aleksandr Lebed came in a distant third with 14.5 percent of the vote, and Yavlinskii and Zhirinovskii received 7.3 and 5.7 percent of the vote, respectively (see Table 6.1). The other candidates all received less than 1 percent of the vote, including Gorbachev, who received only 386,000 votes, or about half of 1 percent.

Yeltsin could claim his first place finish, but Zyuganov had actually placed first in forty-three of the eighty-nine regions and received more than 50 percent of the vote in eleven regions. His strongest pockets of support were in the central and blackearth regions, although he also found support in regions in the Volga area and the North Caucasus. Yeltsin was the leading candidate in forty-five regions, and he tied with Lebed in the region of Ivanovo. Yeltsin found the most support in regions in the north, northwest,

Table 6-1   Results of the 1996 Presidential Election, First Round

Candidate	Number of votes	Percentage of the vote
Boris Yeltsin	26,665,495	35.3%
Gennady Zyuganov	24,211,686	32.0
Aleksandr Lebed	10,974,736	14.5
Grigory Yavlinskii	5,550,752	7.3
Vladimir Zhirinovskii	4,311,479	5.7
Svyatoslav Fyodorov	699,158	0.9
Mikhail Gorbachev	386,069	0.5
Martin Shakkum	277,068	0.4
Yuri Vlasov	151,282	0.2
Vladimir Bryntsalov	123,065	0.2
Against all	1,163,921	1.5

Source: Tsentral'naya Izbiratel'naya Komissiya Rossiiskoi Federatsii, *Vybory Prezidenta Rossiiskoi Federatsii 1996: Elektoral'naya Statistika* (Moscow: Ves' Mir, 1996).

and the Russian Far East, in addition to cities and more urban areas. Yeltsin's support was also strong in the ethnic regions, as he lost to Zyuganov in only four of Russia's thirty-one ethnic republics and autonomous okrugs. It appears, therefore, that Zyuganov's attempt to present himself a "Bashkir, Tatar, and Kalmykian nationalist" to Russia's ethnic minorities was less than successful.

Although Yeltsin had defeated Zyuganov in the first round, Russian electoral law stipulates that the president must be elected by a majority of those who take part in the election. Since no candidate received a majority, there would be a runoff election between the two top vote-getters. Yeltsin's 3 percent margin of victory was certainly not enough to allay the fears of his supporters regarding the second round. The victory would hinge on how those who had voted for candidates other than Yeltsin and Zyuganov in the first round—33 percent of the electorate—would realign in the runoff election on July 3.

Events between the Rounds

The weak support shown for Zhirinovskii may have brought a sigh of relief to many in Russia and abroad, but the strong support Zyuganov had received made clear—particularly to Western leaders and Yeltsin himself—that the threat of a Communist victory was very real. At the precise moment that he needed to surge ahead with his campaign, however, Yeltsin suffered a heart attack. Fearing that it might reduce the people's confidence in him and his health, Yeltsin kept his illness a secret. Although he would quickly recover, his heart attack prevented him from taking several trips to the regions as planned. In fact, Yeltsin effectively stopped campaigning after his attack.

Zyuganov attempted to seize the advantage that Yeltsin's poor health offered. First, he portrayed Yeltsin as medically unfit to hold office. He challenged Yeltsin to a televised debate and, after he did not receive a response, implied that Yeltsin was either afraid or medically unfit, with the latter of course being the case. As evidence of his own health and vigor, Zyuganov made sure he was seen on television playing volleyball and dancing at a night club.

His heart attack should have given Zyuganov an advantage, but Yeltsin still had a few tricks up his sleeve. He approached Lebed in order to gain his support, and thus his first-round supporters. Although Lebed never outwardly backed Yeltsin, he did publicly take a stand against Zyuganov. In exchange for his "services" in the campaign, Yeltsin would later bring Lebed on as national security adviser.

Another significant between-round move that Yeltsin made was to have the date of the runoff election switched from a Sunday to a Wednesday, so that his supporters would be more likely to turn out. Yeltsin understood that his target voters were the well-to-do and the young, groups that were both likely to take advantage of a nice summer weekend by vacationing or traveling to their *dachas* (cottages). If the election was held on a weekday, Yeltsin hoped, they would be more likely to vote. Finally, the Central Electoral Commission did its part by running a "get out the vote" campaign, and private interests broadcast commercials warning against a return to power of the Communist Party.

Following the first round of the elections, Yeltsin had stated, "I think that you did not so much vote for our past life as you voted against the hardships of life today."[16] Yeltsin recognized the temptation for people to look to the past in difficult times and to remember the positive aspects of the Soviet system. In order to work against this tendency, he delivered a public address in the days leading up to the second round in which he appealed to the people to remember the true past: "It is said that it is characteristic of the human memory to remember only the good things. When life became difficult and unsettled, our past began to seem to many people to have been better not only than the present but even than the future. But did the common people really live that well under the old regime? Can even elderly Russian citizens remember a time when there was plenty of everything in our country? Such a thing never happened in 70 years. Only the Party bosses lived well."[17]

Round Two

To many observers, the second round between Yeltsin and Zyuganov seemed to be a choice between continued democratization and liberalization, on the one hand, and a potential retreat to Russia's authoritarian past, on the other. As a Russian journalist observed at the time, "Whatever we say of Yeltsin . . . he is still the only guarantor of democracy and the irreversibility of economic reform."[18] When given this choice, the people responded with a resounding call for continued reform. With a nearly 69 percent turnout, 53.8 percent of the electorate voted in favor of Yeltsin, only 40.3 percent supported Zyuganov, and slightly more than 4.8 percent voted against both candidates (*see Table 6.2*). That electoral turnout remained high certainly con-

Table 6-2   Results of the 1996 Presidential Election Runoff

Candidate	Percentage of valid vote	Percentage of the vote
Boris Yeltsin	40,203,948	53.8%
Gennady Zyuganov	30,102,288	40.3
Against all	3,604,462	4.8

Source: Tsentral'naya Izbiratel'naya Komissiya Rossiiskoi Federatsii, *Vybory Prezidenta Rossiiskoi Federatsii 1996: Elektoral'-naya Statistika* (Moscow: Ves' Mir, 1996).

tributed to Yeltsin's victory, as did Lebed's silent nod of approval for the Yeltsin regime. What probably contributed the most to Yeltsin's victory, however, was his campaigning. Before his heart attack following the first round, he had lost weight, quit drinking, and wooed the Russian electorate. Yeltsin effectively turned the election into a referendum on the new system—not specifically on its performance but rather on its freedoms and the progress that had been made. And as it turns out, a majority of Russians were still willing to give the new system a chance.

Yeltsin was the candidate of choice in fifty-six of the regions, and he tied with Zyuganov in Khakassiya. There was tremendous variation in voting patterns across the country. Yeltsin's support was as high as 79.8 in Ingushetiya (which was attributed by some to vote fraud) but reached a low of 32 percent in Orel. Zyuganov's support was also high in some regions, as high as 63 percent in Orel. But Zyuganov received extremely low support in certain regions, such as the Yamalo-Nenets Autonomous Okrug, where he received only 15 percent of the vote.

The ethnic regions again mostly supported Yeltsin, giving him a majority of the vote in all but six regions. Interestingly, Tatarstan swung squarely behind Yeltsin in the second round, increasing its support of him from 38 percent in the first round to 61.5 percent in the second. The increase was mostly among voters who had supported other candidates in the first round, as Zyuganov's support only dropped from 38.1 to 32.3 percent. As it turns out, the ethnic regions were slightly more likely than the rest of the country to support Yeltsin, with the average level of support for Yeltsin in the ethnic regions being 58 percent, whereas it was only 50 percent in the Russian regions.[19]

The division between Russia's rural and urban areas was also marked, as Yeltsin again did best in urban centers, and Zyuganov had an advantage in more rural areas. In addition to winning in the urban regions of Moscow, St. Petersburg, and Nizhnii Novgorod, Yeltsin also won in 86 of Russia's 100 largest cities. Support for Yeltsin was also strongest among the better-educated, the young, and those with higher income levels.[20] Zyuganov found his greatest support in the countryside and more rural regions, particularly in the blackearth regions of the Russian southwest. The elderly and pensioners were among his strongest supporters, perhaps in part because of nostalgia among this group. The relationship between education and electoral support is complicated—those with very little education tended to vote for Zyuganov, those with average educational levels voted for Yeltsin, and those with very high levels of education (including advanced degrees) voted for Zyuganov.[21] Since it can take quite a long time to earn an advanced degree, support for Zyuganov among the latter category might also be a function of age.

Several early analyses argued that vote falsification was very high, but it now seems that, although electoral fraud certainly took place, it did so on a much smaller scale than previously estimated, and had only a minimal impact. The Communist Party alleged early on that 600,000 votes had been illegally added in Tatarstan in favor of Yeltsin, and they later won their case in a court of law. Probably the most egregious improprieties that took place during the 1996 elections, however, involved Yeltsin throwing money around and making illegal promises, while the elites in control of the media used all of their resources to support Yeltsin and discredit the Communist Party.

The 1996 Election in Retrospect

Although Yeltsin did stand for reelection in 1996, these elections were not truly democratic, for several reasons. First, there was the evidence of voting fraud, a fact about which even the Constitutional Court agreed. Second, Yeltsin had several advantages, including preferential media access and a team of American campaign advisers. Finally, Yeltsin probably would not have respected the results if he had lost—and may even have been supported by the West had he voided the election, considering the alternative. Thanks to Yeltsin's several advantages and the unified opposition to Zyuganov in the second round, Yeltsin did win reelection, and this possibility can now be conveniently overlooked.

Yeltsin's manipulation of the system did not end once he won reelection. In fact, one of the most characteristic traits of Yeltsin's second term as president was his constant shuffling of prime ministers in an attempt to retain ultimate control and to leverage the Duma.[22] In most established democracies in which a prime minister serves as head of government, this office is usually given to the head of the largest political party in the parliament or the head of a ruling coalition. Russia, however, has yet to evolve along these lines. Yeltsin, who as president had the authority to appoint the prime minister (subject to confirmation by the Duma), instead chose to use this power to manipulate the Duma. Yeltsin suddenly dismissed Viktor Chernomyrdin, prime minister since 1992, in March 1998 under the pretext that Chernomyrdin needed time to prepare for the 2000 presidential race. Other explanations for this action seem more plausible. For example, the Russian constitution stipulates that the Duma be dismissed if it fails to approve the president's choice for prime minister on three consecutive occasions, and Yeltsin may have sought to force such a move in order to change the composition of the Duma. Regardless of his intentions, Yeltsin's dismissal of Chernomyrdin began a long process of constantly shuffling prime ministers, from Chernomyrdin's immediate replacement, Sergei Kirienko, to the appointment of Yevgeny Primakov, following the Duma's refusal to bring back Chernomyrdin, to the appointment of Sergei Stepashin in May 1999. This process only ended with the appointment of Vladimir Putin as prime minister in August 1999. In his last manipulative move, Yeltsin resigned his own post soon after the 1999 Duma elections, leaving Putin in the position of acting president, a very advantageous position from which to launch his own presidential bid the next spring.

The 2000 Presidential Election

As with any presidential system, the Russian system allows incumbents several advantages, and being able to serve as acting president gave Putin a major advantage in his electoral campaign. Yeltsin of course intended as much, for he had hand-picked Putin to be his successor. Putin's popularity had reached record heights, the electorate had just voiced its support for various centrist parties (including the Putin-backed Unity) in the 1999 Duma elections, and the war in Chechnya was not too unpopular. It thus seemed to be the most opportune moment for Putin to stand for election. All indications are that Yeltsin resigned specifically to give an advantage to Putin. His resignation forced the election, which had been scheduled for June, to be moved forward to March.[23] Putin could then exploit these advantages to their fullest.

Putin's Flight to Victory

To the casual observer, the March presidential election was nowhere near as big an event as the December 1999 Duma elections. In fact, on the day of the elections Russian television stations even discussed, by way of contrast to the present elections, how elections in the Soviet period used to be real public events, with festivities, celebrations, and parties. Overlooked in this discussion was the significant difference that multiple candidates now compete against each other for their posts, as compared to the sham elections of the Soviet period, which had served little more than a system legitimizing function. It is ironic that now, when elections actually do determine who will hold power, many are nostalgic for the old days, when elections were big events even if only a rubber stamp.

The election coincided with a switch to daylight savings time, and the switch may have received equal billing with the election. In fact, changing the clocks was inextricably tied to the elections themselves. As Laura Belin points out, the term "new time" (*novoe vremia*) was used to refer to what is typically called "summer time" (*letnee vremia*) in Russian, a play on the whole idea of a new epoch in Russia, as Yeltsin left power. Putin even mentioned in a televised address that the "transition to the new time" was symbolic of an old era ending and a new one beginning.[24]

Although it was widely reported in the West that Putin did not participate in traditional campaigning, it would be a grave error to think that he did not run a campaign. In fact, Putin's campaign was brilliant. Putin avoided facing his opponents tête-à-tête in televised debates, during which he might have to answer questions about his amorphous platform and policy ideas, and he even turned this refusal to his advantage by explaining to the press, "You're supposed to look millions of people in the eye and make promises that you know you can't keep. I haven't learned to do that."[25] Putin also did not plaster campaign literature all over the country. In fact, one would have been hard pressed to find Putin campaign paraphernalia in the country's capital. This stands in sharp contrast to the Duma elections in December 1999, for instance, when Moscow mayor Yuri Luzhkov had handed out bottles of vodka with his picture on them.

Instead of running the sort of campaign that has become typical in the new Russia, Putin's primary strategy was to look busy running the affairs of state, much as Yeltsin had done in his 1991 campaign. In order to take full advantage of the incumbency advantage, Putin traversed the country and met with leaders, troops, and crowds. This tactic was very effective in giving people the impression that he would be an active president. Among his more noteworthy appearances was his flight into Grozny as copilot of a SU-27 fighter jet, immediately following which he gave a short interview in his flight uniform, calling the aircraft "very responsive."[26] Then on a trip to Nizhnii Novgorod, he took the new Volga 3111 for a test drive. He revved up the engine and sped around for a while, "showing pretty good driving skills," according to one reporter.[27] Finally, the publication of Putin's book *Ot Pervogo Litsa (In the First Person)* was timed perfectly to coincide with the electoral campaign, with bookstores receiving advance copies the week prior to the election.[28] The Central Electoral Commission recognized this move for what it was—a sly campaign tactic—and it prohibited the book's publication until after the election. The book, which contained stories of a fire at Putin's dacha and depicted him as an honorable man, was nevertheless available online before the election, and the stories became favorite topics of discussion among Russians. Overall, Putin successfully identified himself with the people and showed that he understood their problems, and he distinguished himself quite effectively from the other candidates and from Yeltsin.

As had been done in 1996, the movie *Burnt by the Sun* was re-aired, along with documentaries highlighting the evils of the Stalin era, including *A World Revolution for Comrade Stalin,* which effectively put the blame for the Soviet Union's disastrous policy during World War II on Stalin's shoulders. This is reminiscent of the Twentieth Party Congress speech of 1956, during which Khrushchev had blamed Stalin for the Soviet Union's past failures.

The Putin "Bargain"

On March 26 slightly less than 69 percent of Russia's eligible voters turned out to elect their new president. The early returns from the Russian Far East showed Putin only receiving approximately 48 percent of the vote, but as more ballots were counted Putin's support rose steadily. When the final tallies were in, the people had given Putin 52.94 percent of their votes, thus awarding him a first-round victory (*see Table 6.3*). In so doing, the Russian people saved a billion rubles that would have had to be spent on a second round. As he had pointed out during his electoral campaign, the cost of a second round "is almost as much as all the pensioners in Moscow Oblast get."[29]

The electoral turnout of almost 69 percent represents an increase from the turnout of 61 percent in the 1999 Duma elections. This is a significant increase, but presidential elections almost always draw a higher turnout than legislative elections. In fact, the turnout in March 2000 was equivalent to that for the 1996 presidential race. There was little regional variation in voter turnout, with all but four regions having a turnout of between 60 and 80 percent. The Evenk Autonomous Okrug had the lowest turnout, with 57 percent (a figure still enough to make many Western democracies envious), and Ingushetiya (92.8) and Kabardino-Balkariya (88.5) had turnout rates that greatly exceeded the national average. These two regions were also among the most supportive of Putin, giving him 75 and 86 percent of their votes, respectively.

High voter turnout seems to have contributed to Putin's first-round victory. Communist Party members are the most mobilized segment of the electorate, and members of the electorate who favored the status quo—and who thus tended to support Putin—were among the groups usually less likely to turn out. Putin accordingly made a televised appeal to the Russian people to turn out to vote, which was shown repeatedly in the days up to the election. The Central Electoral Commission ran an extensive campaign to get out the vote (telling voters that they had a "decisive voice," or *reshaiushchii golos*), which also contributed to Putin's victory.

Communist Party leader Gennady Zyuganov received slightly less than 30 percent of the vote, which, although approximately 3 percent less than he had received in the first round of the 1996 election, evidenced his relatively stable support among more than a quarter of the electorate. Grigorii Yavlinskii, head of the Yabloko faction in the Duma, received slightly less than 6 percent, down from 7 percent in 1996. Putin, Zyuganov, and Yavlinskii were the only candidates to receive more than 5 percent of the vote. In fact, Putin and Zyuganov together won a plurality in every region of Russia except Kemerovo, where presidential candidate (and regional governor) Aman Tuleev received 51.57 percent of the vote, compared to his 3 percent showing nationwide.

Other noteworthy candidates included Vladimir Zhirinovskii, who has run in every presidential election since the post was created in 1991. Zhirinovskii received his lowest level of support yet, 2.7 percent, compared to almost 6 percent in 1996. This low total, coupled with the low level of support Zhirinovskii's Bloc received in the December 1999 Duma elections, is further evidence that support for the ultra-nationalist is on the wane. Finally, more people (1.9 percent) cast their ballot "against all" than for any of the remaining candidates, including Ella Pamfilova, former procurator general Yuri Skuratov, and Konstantin Titov.

Table 6-3   Results of the 2000 Presidential Election

Candidate	Percentage of valid vote	Percentage of the vote
Vladimir Putin	39,740,434	52.94%
Gennadii Zyuganov	21,928,471	29.17
Grigory Yavlinskii	4,351,452	5.79
Aman Tuleev	2,217,361	2.95
Vladimir Zhirinovskii	2,026,513	2.70
Konstantin Titov	1,107,269	1.47
Ella Pamfilova	758,966	1.01
Stanislav Govorukhin	328,723	0.44
Yuri Skuratov	319,263	0.42
Aleksei Podberezkin	98,175	0.13
Umar Dzhabrailov	78,498	0.10
Against all	1,414,648	1.88

Source: Tsentral'naya Izbiratel'naya Komissiya Rossiiskoi Federatsii, *Vybory Prezidenta RF 26 Marta 2000 goda.* Available at http://www.fci.ru.

Analysis of the correlates of the election reveals patterns similar to those in previous elections. Younger and better-off voters leaned toward reformist and centrist candidates, and pensioners and economically disadvantaged voters continued to lean toward the left. In particular, Zyuganov received much of his support from the less-educated and lower-income segments of the electorate and from agricultural areas.[30]

The Regional Dimension

At first glance it may seem that there was little regional variation in the March 2000 election, as Putin's support was almost uniform across Russia's vast territory, but deeper analysis uncovers several significant patterns. The voting patterns exhibited the kind of regional differences in political choice that have characterized all Russian elections, and the spatial pattern of support for Putin resembles that for Yeltsin in 1996.[31] Putin won every region that Yeltsin won in the second round of the 1996 election, and he picked up thirty-one other regions as well. Putin received an absolute majority in fifty-six of Russia's eighty-nine regions and a plurality in all but five (losing to Zyuganov in the Altai Republic, Bryansk, Lipetsk, and Omsk and to Tuleev in Kemerovo). Putin's support was strong in his home region, Leningrad Oblast and St. Petersburg, where he received 67.1 and 62.7 percent of the vote, respectively, and his support was lower in the city of Moscow and Moscow Oblast, where he received 46.6 and 48.3 percent.

Much of the regional variation in voting patterns involves Putin's opponents. Just as Tuleev did his best in his home region of Kemerovo, Konstantin Titov did his best in Samara Oblast, where he is governor, receiving slightly more than 20 percent of the vote. It seems that most of this support was taken from Putin, who received only 41.3 percent there, whereas Zyuganov was able to hold on to 30.2 percent. Vladimir Zhirinovskii did his best in the Russian Far East, where he was able to get more than 5 percent of the vote in six regions, including Khabarovsk, Magadan, and Primorskii Krai. Support for Zyuganov showed the most clearly defined geographical pattern. As in 1996, support for the Communist Party leader was strongest in the red belt and along Russia's southern border, from Krasnodar Krai (37.7 percent) to Primorskii Krai (36.2 percent). In contrast to the 1996 elections, however, his strong support in these areas did not secure him an absolute majority in even one region, although twenty-six regions gave him more than 35 percent of the vote and eleven gave him more than 40 percent. He was able to muster a victory in four regions, however, two of which (Bryansk and Lipetsk) were in the red belt. In other regions considered Communist strongholds, such as Smolensk, Zyuganov retained his 30 percent of support, but the remainder of the electorate swung firmly behind Putin. According to the local press in Smolensk, Putin carried the region because of the people's faith in his ability to lead the country into the future.[32]

Russia's ethnic republics and autonomous areas were among the most supportive of Putin's presidential bid.[33] Overall, Putin won a plurality in every ethnic region except the Altai Republic, where he received his lowest level of support (38.4 percent). His support was highest in places such as Dagestan (81.6 percent) and Ingushetiya (86.1 percent), though he also received considerable support from the republics of Tatarstan (69.9 percent) and Bashkortostan (61.1 percent). Putin's support did dip rather low in some areas, however, as he received only 45 percent in Adygeya, Chuvashiya, and Mari El and slightly less than 43 percent in Buryatiya and Khakassiya. In each region Putin still edged out Zyuganov, whose support ranged from 44.9 percent in Adygeya (Putin won there by only 0.23 percent of the vote) to over 36.8 percent in Khakassiya. In each of these regions the outcome between Putin and Zyuganov was decided by less than 6 percent of the vote.

In the 1996 presidential elections Yeltsin received his highest levels of support in the ethnic regions, and the bounce Putin received from the ethnic regions was even more pronounced in 2000. Putin won in every ethnic region except the Altai Republic, where Zyuganov surpassed him by 5 percentage points (and where Yeltsin also lost in 1996). When comparing the average levels of support for Putin among the ethnic and Russian regions, the difference is even greater than that for Yeltsin in 1996. Whereas Putin received an average of 52.3 percent of the vote in the Russian regions, he received an exceptionally high 60 percent in the ethnic regions.

Perhaps the reason Putin found such strong support in the ethnic regions was the widespread perception that a Putin regime would be friendly to the ethnic minorities. This perception may have been encouraged by the fact that his beloved Unity movement was headed by Sergei Shoigu, who himself is ethnically Tyvan. Voters would have also assumed, however, that the "party of power" would try to hold the federation together at any cost. Indeed, numerous television ads were aired during the 1999 Duma campaign that showed Shoigu in Chechnya on "official business" as Minister of Emergency Situations. The message of these ads was clear—all of Russia's multinational people are supportive of ending the "terrorist activity" in the territory of Chechnya.

Putin's stance on nationalities, which became apparent during his campaign, was apparently based upon the principle that no special privileges should be granted to the ethnic republics. In the week prior to the election, Putin met individually with President Shaimiev of Tatarstan and President Rakhimov of Bashkortostan and told each of them that the constitution must be followed and that their days of being "more equal than the others" were over.[34] Putin even got Rakhimov to sign an agreement under which Bashkortostan began to transfer taxes to the federal budget instead of retaining all of the money that it collects.[35] Although Shaimiev stated that "the freedom we've gained isn't going to be given up that easily," he did not withdraw his support for Putin and even pledged to help him get elected.[36]

Electoral Miracles and the March of the Dead Souls

A discussion of the 2000 presidential election would not be complete without considering vote fraud. Even before the official results were in, one local commentator flatly accused the Putin administration of widescale election fraud, citing as evidence the high vote totals Putin received in regions such as Bashkortostan, Chechnya, Ingushetiya, and Tatarstan. According to this individual, it just did not make sense that these ethnic regions would support Putin in such large numbers: "The only plausible explanation for these electoral miracles is purported massive vote-rigging."[37] As we saw with the 1996 presidential elections, however, the ethnic regions *are* more likely than the Russian-populated areas to vote for a pro-regime candidate and against the Communist Party. Another explanation for Putin's support in such regions could be that local leaders who endorsed Putin were able to give him favorable coverage in the media, thus increasing his support.

Although we may never know the exact scale of the vote fraud that took place, we can speculate as to what its impact may have been. The commentator mentioned above cited as evidence statements made by "tens of thousands" of Communist Party observers who were at the polling stations during the election, and who maintained that Putin only received 45 percent of the vote. This estimate, which was made by the opposition and should be taken as an extreme, would have meant a difference of approximately 8 percentage points, or almost 6 million ballots. To stuff the ballot boxes with so many illegitimate votes would have been a huge undertaking, and it is difficult to believe that something on that scale could have taken place without Western observers, who themselves numbered in the thousands, taking notice. As a matter of fact, the Organization for Security and Cooperation in Europe, which monitored the election, found the elections on the whole "democratic and a step forward for Russia," although it did cite witnessing "abuses."

Just how pervasive these abuses actually were only began to come to light in September 2000. In its weekend edition of September 9, the *Moscow Times* released a special report on election fraud, in which it proclaimed that ballot papers had been burned, voters bullied, and entire blocks of voters invented in favor of Putin. One Russian voter reported being very confused: "the form listed 209 apartments in the building, while he knew in reality there were only 180 there. Twenty-nine apartments, filled no doubt with at least 60 or 70 fictional voters," had miraculously appeared on the voting ballot.[38] Other accounts spoke of additional floors, and even entire buildings, being created.

Perhaps the biggest question was the so-called "baby boom" that caused an increase in the number of registered voters between the December 1999 Duma election and the March presidential race, during which time 1.3 million new voters were placed on the election rolls. The Central Electoral Commission explained that elections had not been held in Chechnya the previous December, which accounted for almost half a million voters, and that another half-million Russians turned eighteen between the elections and were thus automatically added to the voting rolls. Demographic experts, however, dismissed such claims, maintaining that there was no birth spike eighteen years ago and that the Russian population had actually shrunk by 836,000 between the elections.

If, for argument's sake, we proceed from the Communist Party's estimate that Putin actually received only 45 percent of the vote, what impact did electoral fraud actually have? This total would still have been more than that of any other candidate, but it would have been insufficient to award Putin a first-round victory. Considering that Zyuganov would have been unlikely to pick up a great number of voters in a runoff, it seems clear that Putin would have won a second-round race with little difficulty. In the final analysis, Putin could have been elected president without fraud. But with his victory based on fraud and manipulation, his reputation and that of his administration surely must be tarnished.

Putin and the Path to Democracy

The March election was only one step along the long path to democracy, but it has immediate significance for several reasons. For one, it was a truly "Russian" election. Western campaign advisers, who in 1996 had done their best to keep Yeltsin in power, were largely absent. Moreover, the people continued not only to take part in the electoral process but also to show that they believe contested elections to be the only legitimate means for the transfer of governmental power. The most significant aspect of the 2000 election was probably that, in contradistinction to the "forced-choice" election of 1996, the winner was genuinely supported by the Russian people (*see box, Vladimir Putin: Is He Russia's Jefferson?*). Although it is widely agreed that the people did not so much vote "for" Yeltsin in 1996 as they voted "against" Zyuganov, Putin's supporters genuinely wished to have him as their president. A poll conducted just

Vladimir Putin: Is He Russia's Jefferson?

When Thomas Jefferson was inaugurated as America's third president in 1801, he noted that the American experiment in democracy had passed a crucial test with the transfer of power peacefully from one president to the next after a bitter electoral campaign. Two centuries later, another newly elected president, Vladimir Putin, echoing Jefferson, paid homage to the democratic process: the "transfer of power is always a test of the constitutional system, a test of its strength." In the presence of Mikhail Gorbachev and Boris Yeltsin, the new leader promised to "safeguard what has been achieved" and to "ensure that the authorities elected by the people work in their interests."

Despite the apparent similarity between the eighteenth-century Virginia farmer and the twentieth-century former KGB operative, Putin is not likely to draw on the sage of Monticello for inspiration. Jefferson called for a "wise and frugal government" that would "restrain men from injuring one another" but "leave them otherwise free to regulate their own pursuits of industry and improvement." Putin is more spiritually akin to Peter Stolypin, prime minister under Nicholas II (1906–12), whose battle cry against revolutionaries was, "You want great upheavals, but we want a Great Russia!" An echo of Stolypin's words can be heard in Putin's declaration that he seeks to restore "the guiding and regulating role of the state to a degree which is necessary, proceeding from the traditions and present state of the country. . . . Russia needs strong state power and must have it."

Perhaps Stolypin's model is attractive to Putin because, in the short run, it was successful. The economy grew at a rapid pace, the Russian military was modernized, and plans were drafted for a dramatic expansion of social services. Stolypin's policies led Lenin to conclude that his generation might not even see the "approaching battles of the revolution." Unfortunately, time was not on Stolypin's side; his assassination and Russia's entry into World War I wrecked his work, and the Russian Revolution followed. As if haunted by Stolypin's ghost, Putin pointed out in his inaugural address that the reform process is "still far from completion." To see this process through, Putin is likely to adopt some very un-Jeffersonian policies and procedures.

Source: Nikolas Gvosdev, "Vladimir Putin—Not the Jefferson of Russia: Progress at the Expense of Democratic Process," at TomPaine.Com, online at www.tompaine.com/history/2000/05/19/1.html, May 19, 2001.

before the election found that most people supported Putin because "he is young and energetic" (27 percent), "he is capable of establishing order in the country" (23 percent), or "he understands the interests and problems of ordinary people" (12.5 percent). Of those who stated that they were likely to vote for Putin, only 9 percent said that they would support him because they thought that he was the only candidate with a real chance of winning.[39] For the first time in quite a while, therefore, Russia has a leader who is genuinely supported by the people. The only question is, How long will he be able to retain that support?

Russia's First Presidential Turnover

When Vladimir Putin was inaugurated as Russia's second president on May 7, 2000, the country underwent its first turnover of presidential power, and it did do so in accordance with its constitution. Significantly, as Russia continues to operate within democratic institutions and according to constitutionally prescribed procedures, democracy as a system of government in Russia continues to develop. How long it will take, however, until we can be sure that a democratic system has taken root in Russia, nobody knows. Samuel Huntington's "two-turnover test" can help us understand how far this process still has to go. According to Huntington, a democracy can be considered consolidated "if the party or group that takes power in the initial election at the time of transition loses a subsequent election and turns over power to those election winners, and if those election winners then peacefully turn over power to the winners of a later election."[40] Based on these criteria, the Putin presidency at best is only the first step toward consolidation. Additionally, the fact that Yeltsin hand-picked Putin may mean that Russia has yet to experience even its first genuine turnover.

Although the holding of frequent, contested elections to governmental offices is a necessary condition for the establishment of a democratic polity, it is by no means a sufficient condition. A flourishing democracy must be based upon an efficacious civil society, in which informed voters freely participate in the electoral process and place demands on their leaders. Many of the practices that have taken place during Russia's two post-Communist presidential elections, such as ballot stuffing and media bias, have certainly blemished Russia's transition to democracy. There is still cause for optimism, however. After all, Russians themselves have been the ones to point out these flaws, indicating that they are not as complacent as some suspect. This is, of course, how democracy works, since Russia's citizens have to hold their own leaders accountable. One thing we can be certain of is that it will still take quite some time before either we can say that democracy has failed to take root in Russia, or we can feel confident that democracy has become firmly established and is the only game in town.

For Further Reading

Clem, Ralph, and Peter Craumer. "Spatial Patterns of Political Choice in the Post-Yeltsin Era: The Electoral Geography of Russia's 2000 Presidential Election." *Post-Soviet Geography and Economics* 41 (2000): 1–18.

_____. "Roadmap to Victory: Boris Yeltsin and the Russian Presidential Elections of 1996." *Post-Soviet Geography and Economics* 37 (1996): 335–54.

Hough, Jerry, Evelyn Davidheiser, and Susan Goodrich Lehmann. *The 1996 Russian Presidential Election.* Washington, D.C.: Brookings Institution, 1996.

Huskey, Eugene, *Presidential Power in Russia.* Armonk, N.Y.: M.E. Sharpe, 1999.

Marsh, Christopher. "One Down, One to Go: The 2000 Election and Russia's First Presidential Turnover." *Analysis of Current Events* 12 (May 2000): 1–5.

Marsh, Christopher, and James Warhola. "Ethnicity, Modernization, and Regime Support in Russia's Regions under Yeltsin." *Nationalism and Ethnic Politics* 6 (fall 2000): 32–47.

Mason, David S., and Svetlana Siderenko-Stephenson. "Public Opinion and the 1996 Elections in Russia: Nostalgic and Statist, yet Pro-Market and Pro-Yeltsin." *Slavic Review* 56 (winter 1997): 698–717.

McFaul, Michael. *Russia's 1996 Presidential Election: The End of Polarized Politics.* Stanford, Calif.: Hoover Institution, 1997.

_____. "Russia under Putin: One Step Forward, Two Steps Back." *Journal of Democracy* 11 (2000): 19–33.

Nichols, Thomas. *The Russian Presidency: Society and Politics in the Second Russian Republic.* New York: St. Martin's, 1999.

Rose, Richard, Neil Munro, and Stephen White. "How Strong Is Vladimir Putin's Support?" *Post-Soviet Affairs* 16 (2000): 287–312.

Rutland, Peter. "Putin's Path to Power." *Post-Soviet Affairs* 16 (2000): 313–54.

Treisman, Daniel. "After Yelstin Comes . . . Yeltsin." *Foreign Policy* 117 (winter 1999–2000): 74–86.

Notes

1. *ITAR-TASS,* June 8, 1999.
2. VTsIOM survey, as published in *Izvestiya,* June 11, 1996, from Stephen White, Richard Rose, and Ian McAllister, *How Russia Votes* (Chatham, N.J.: Chatham House, 1997), 258.
3. Remarks of Emil Payin, from David Remnick, *Resurrection: The Struggle for a New Russia* (New York: Random House, 1997), 329.
4. Ibid., 329–35.
5. Ibid., 331–32.
6. Kevin Fedarko, "Yeltsin's Secret Report on How to Call off the Vote," *Time,* April 8, 1996.
7. Michael McFaul, *Russia's 1996 Presidential Election: the End of Polarized Politics* (Stanford, Calif.: Hoover Institution, 1977), ch. 5.
8. Michael Kramer, "Rescuing Boris," *Time,* July 15, 1996, 28–37.
9. Remnick, *The Struggle for a New Russia,* 335.
10. Sarah Oates and Laura Roselle Helvey, "Russian Television's Mixed Messages: Parties, Candidates and Control on 'Vremya,' 1995–1996" (paper presented at the 1997 annual meeting of the American Political Science Association, Washington, D.C., August 28–31, 1997).
11. McFaul, *Russia's 1996 Presidential Election,* 31.
12. To equate the two would be a mistake on several accounts, not the least of which is that the KPRF is not the only successor party to the CPSU and is only one of many remaining splinter organizations. For more on the Communist Party of the Russian Federation, see Joan Barth Urban and Valerii Solovei, *Russia's Communists at the Crossroads* (Boulder: Westview, 1997).
13. McFaul, *Russia's 1996 Presidential Election,* 43.
14. Charles Clover, "Dreams of the Eurasian Heartland," *Foreign Affairs* 78 (1999): 12.
15. Although it is difficult to find evidence to support this claim, White, Rose, and McAllister point out that the Lebed campaign received an influx of money after

meeting with Yeltsin's campaign team, and that Lebed was the only other candidate besides Yeltsin to receive mostly favorable coverage on television (*How Russia Votes,* 253).

16. "The New Life is More to be Cherished than Grievances," *Rossisskaya Gazeta,* June 28, 1996, 3.

17. Ibid.

18. Oleg Moroz, *Literaturnaya Gazeta* 46 (1995): 10, quoted in Sakwa, *Russian Politics and Society* (London: Routledge, 1996), 171.

19. For a more detailed account of this and related phenomena, see Christopher Marsh and James W. Warhola, "Ethnicity, Modernization, and Regime Support in Russia's Regions under Yeltsin," *Nationalism and Ethnic Politics* 6 (fall 2000): 32–47.

20. For more on the effect such factors had on support for Yeltsin and democratization, see Marsh, *Making Russian Democracy Work: Social Capital, Economic Development, and Democratization* (Lewiston, N.Y.,: Edwin Mellen Press, 2000), ch. 4 and 6.

21. Ralph Clem and Peter Craumer, "Roadmap to Victory: Boris Yeltsin and the Russian Presidential Elections of 1996," *Post-Soviet Geography and Economics* 37 (1996): 351–53.

22. For more on this issue, see Eugene Huskey, *Presidential Power in Russia* (Armonk, N.Y.: M.E. Sharpe, 1999).

23. The elections were required to be rescheduled by a provision in the 1993 constitution stating that elections must be held within ninety days of the president's resignation, impeachment, death, or inability to carry out the functions of the presidency because of health problems.

24. *RFE/FL Russian Election Report,* April 7, 2000, 8.

25. *Segodnya,* March 20, 2000, 1.

26. *Kommersant,* March 21, 2000, 1.

27. *Nezavisimaya Gazeta,* March 22, 2000, 1.

28. *Kommersant-Vlast',* March 21, 2000, 2.

29. *Segodnya,* March 20, 2000, 1.

30. Clem and Craumer, "Spatial Patterns of Political Choice in the Post-Yeltsin Era: The Electoral Geography of Russia's 2000 Presidential Election," *Post-Soviet Geography and Economics* 41 (2000):15.

31. Ibid., 2.

32. *Rabochii Put',* March 28, 2000, 1.

33. For more on the ethnic dimension of Putin's electoral support, see Christopher Marsh and James W. Warhola, "Ethnicity, Ethnoregionalism, and the Political Geography of Putin's Electoral Support," *Post-Soviet Geography and Economics,* 42 (2001).

34. *Izvestiya,* March 23, 2000, 1.

35. *Izvestiya,* March 24, 2000, 3.

36. "Shaimiev Will Get People of Tatarstan to Back Putin," *Kommersant,* February 3, 2000.

37. Pavel Felgenhauer, "Miracles, or Election Fraud?" *Moscow Times,* March 30, 2000.

38. Yevgenia Borisova, "Baby Boom or Dead Souls," *Moscow Times,* September 9, 2000.

39. *Nezavisimaya Gazeta,* March 21, 2000, 8.

40. Samuel Huntington, *The Third Wave: Democratization in the Late Twentieth Century* (Norman, Okla.: University of Oklahoma Press, 1991), 266–67.

7

Elections at the Grassroots:
Governors, Mayors, and Regional Assemblies

While Russia has had a series of presidential and legislative elections on the national level, there have been literally thousands of elections at the local and regional level, for offices such as republic presidents, regional governors, and mayors, and for various legislative bodies including regional assemblies and city soviets. In such elections citizens vote for local politicians who will be more directly responsible for and closely associated with local conditions. Local and regional elections in contemporary Russia, therefore, are an important dimension of Russian electoral politics more generally.

This chapter serves as an overview of the numerous elections being held on the regional and local level. Since we cannot review them all, nor do we need to, this chapter surveys the various types of elections and their characteristics, with examples from some of the more interesting. The chapter begins with the introduction of electoral competition at the sub-national level of government. It then continues with an examination of the various elections to executive positions in local and regional government, including republic president, regional governor, and mayor. We then consider elections to regional and city legislative institutions, with an in-depth look at one of the most controversial elections in post-Soviet Russia, the 1998 elections to the St. Petersburg Legislative Assembly. Finally, the chapter concludes with an assessment of the problems with local elections in Russia and their implications for the country's further political development.

Elections at the Grassroots

During the last decade Russia's republics, regions, cities, and towns have all undergone political reforms alongside those taking place on the national level. The latter have been intricately connected with the former, as those seeking to change the system quickly understood that no real reform of the Soviet system was going to be possible unless accompanied by similar reforms at the grassroots level. One significant component of these reforms has been the introduction of electoral competition for the many positions of political leadership in the republics, regions, and cities. Unfortunately, the relative success of reform on the national level has not been matched in regional and local politics.

When Soviet citizens went to the polls in March 1989 and again in March 1990 to elect the Soviet and Russian legislatures, many also had the opportunity to vote for their regional and city legislatures. Although the liberal opposition emerged victorious in Leningrad, Moscow, and Sverdlovsk (now renamed Yekaterinburg), the old elite held onto power in more cases than it lost it. In fact, in no case did a reformist group unambiguously capture a regional legislature.[1] To withstand the electoral challenge, local elites used their positions of influence to eliminate candidates at various stages of the electoral process and to manipulate the local media. These tactics proved quite effective, and by and large the radical transformation that took place on the national level in 1989–1990 was not accompanied by similar changes in the regions. In fact, one of the biggest problems Russia faces even today is completing the reforms being carried out unevenly in the regions.

The liberal opposition continued to make progress in certain regions, and in the summer of 1991 it won important victories in Moscow and Leningrad. While Yeltsin was running for the Russian presidency, elections were also being held for head of the city administrations in Moscow and Leningrad, with Gavril Popov winning election in Moscow and Anatoly Sobchak doing the same in Leningrad. Along with their staffs—Yuri Luzhkov was Popov's deputy, and Vladimir Putin a protégé of Sobchak—these two reformers ensured that progress was made in regional administration as well. Although they succeeded in implementing significant reforms, however, their impact largely remained limited to Russia's two historic capitals.

Following the coup attempt in August 1991, the Russian parliament established the post of "head of administration" at the regional level, including for the krais, oblasts, and autonomous regions. Yeltsin was able to appoint officials directly to the post as a means of ensuring effective government at the local level, and to manipulate local affairs in the process. It had been expected, however, that these officials would eventually be elected, and elections had been initially scheduled for December 1991. Because of problems associated with rapid economic reform and the even more rapid collapse of the Soviet Union, however, these elections were postponed until December 1992.

In April 1993 Yeltsin authorized seven regions to conduct elections, and in five of these regions the incumbent, that is, Yeltsin's appointee, lost his reelection bid. Fearing that this might indicate a trend, Yeltsin then postponed further gubernatorial elections. As he was battling the Supreme Soviet during the fall of 1993 and attempting to put a new political system into place, Yeltsin also prepared to initiate reforms in the regions. In October he called for local and regional elections to be held between December 1993 (coinciding with the numerous national votes scheduled to take place) and the following spring. He gave great discretion to local authorities—particularly the governors and republic presidents—over how these elections would be conducted.

In one of the first local elections, held in Penza in January 1994, former Communist Party functionaries won forty of the forty-five seats in the regional assembly. Recognizing that this was the beginning of a dangerous trend, Yeltsin again suspended the process and passed a decree postponing gubernatorial elections until December 1996 (following the presidential election scheduled for that June), with legislative elections also postponed. Several exceptions were made, but between October 1993 and August 1995 only one gubernatorial election had been permitted. In late summer 1995, a short round of gubernatorial elections were held. Only a dozen elections were conducted before they were postponed yet again, this time so as not to interfere with the summer 1996 presidential election that was quickly approaching. In all about a dozen regions held elections in December 1995 (coinciding with the State Duma elections), and Moscow's second mayoral election was held in June 1996 (coinciding with the presidential election itself).

Electing Russia's Governors

Seventy regions held elections between late summer 1995 and spring 1997, but the first real round of gubernatorial elections took place between June 1996 and March 1997, during which time elections were conducted in fifty-five regions. The average number of candidates on the ballot was slightly less than five, although in a few regions many more candidates took to the field—for example, in Chelyabinsk ten candidates competed. In most regions there were no more than three candidates on the ballot, a number that indicates a well-structured race, one that provides a real choice but does not offer such a wide selection that no real consensus can emerge. Another positive characteristic was the strong presence of entrepreneurs and economic figures on the ballot, alongside local officials such as legislative heads, mayors, and public administrators. This indicates that regional politics in Russia is becoming professionalized.

As usual, incumbency proved useful, as almost half of the incumbents won reelection. Moreover, the incumbents in these elections had not always previously been elected, since approximately 90 percent of the incumbent governors had been appointed by Yeltsin and had yet to face the electorate.[2] The 50 percent turnover rate, however, indicates considerable voter dissatisfaction with the situation in the regions, and with the performance of the regional authorities in particular. The December 1995 Duma elections and the summer 1996 presidential elections showed that the Russian electorate was split between those who supported the regime and those who favored various opposition candidates, and the gubernatorial elections showed a similar split. In fact, whether a region supported Yelstin was perhaps the greatest determinant of the results, as regions that favored Yeltsin in his reelection bid tended to reelect his appointees, and those that supported opposition parties in the Duma elections chose to oust their appointed governors.[3]

An interesting case in point is Pskov, a region that is traditionally supportive of the Communist Party and that supported Communist Party candidate Zyuganov in the 1996 presidential election. Although incumbent governor Vladislav Tumanov, who had been appointed by Yeltsin in 1992 and had the support of Our Home Is Russia, placed first with 31 percent of the vote in the first round of the region's gubernatorial race, LDPR candidate Evgenii Mikhailov defeated him in the runoff, as he increased his first-round showing of 23 percent to more than 57 percent, thus becoming Russia's first LDPR governor. Mikhailov's victory is also interesting in that it was based on a strange but pragmatic alliance between the LDPR and the KPRF.[4]

The 1995–1997 gubernatorial elections indicate that Russian voters behave quite differently in regional elections than they do in national elections. Although Russia's citizenry made its decisions in the 1995–1996 legislative and presidential elections based on their beliefs on fundamental issues such as property ownership and political reform, in regional elections they showed more interest in local conditions and short-term benefits.[5] They thus tended to vote for candidates they perceived as able to improve local conditions. Such candidates, however, usually have the closest ties to Moscow and would thus have the best chance of extracting special dispensations from the capital, so the two types of elections were not entirely divorced. A nod of support from the Kremlin goes a long way toward facilitating the election of a governor.

Since many of Russia's governors were elected between 1995 and 1997, their terms began to expire in 1999, and another round of gubernatorial races began. In 2000 alone, forty-four republics and regions held executive elections, and some interesting trends emerged (*see Table 7.1*). For one, incumbents did well and were able to hold onto power more often than not. Since many incumbent governors were Communists, this meant that the Communists retained their strength in local politics. The Communist governors who won reelection include Nikolai Vinogradov of Vladimir, Viktor Shershunov of Kostroma, and Yuri Lodkin of Bryansk. In Bryansk the opposition fielded a candidate with the same name as Lodkin in order to confuse voters and diminish his support. The governor's team then did the same for the primary opposition candidates, so that two Demochkins, two Denins, and two Lodkins were on the ballot.[6] In the end, the voters were smart enough to see through the ploy and selected the same Lodkin as they had four years earlier.

Incumbents from other parties tended to win reelection as well. In Khabarovsk Krai, Governor Viktor Ishaev's only competition was Svetlana Zhukova, the director of a local personnel agency. Ishaev walked away with 88 percent of the vote, but Zhukova was not disappointed since she had been able to use the free airtime she was given to promote her business.[7] The races were much closer for Governor Oleg Bogomolov of Kurgan, who barely received 50 percent of the vote in a runoff election, and for Governor Vladimir Platov of Tver, an outspoken supporter of Unity, who edged out Communist Party candidate Vladimir Bayunov by only about three thousand votes.

There was turnover as well. In a widely publicized election, retired general Boris Gromov beat Gennady Seleznev for the post of Moscow Oblast governor in a runoff election in January 2000. After defeating the incumbent in the first round election, which had coincided with the December 1999 Duma elections, Gromov and Seleznev faced each other in a runoff election that

Table 7.1   Elections for Selected Regional Executive Heads, 2000

Region or republic	Winner	Status of winner
Astrakhan	Anatoly Guzhvin	incumbent
Bryansk	Yuri Lodkin	incumbent
Kaliningrad	Vladimir Yegorov	challenger
Khabarovsk Krai	Viktor Ishaev	incumbent
Koryak A.O.	Vladimir Loginov	challenger
Kostroma	Viktor Shershunov	incumbent
Kurgan	Oleg Bogomolov	incumbent
Kursk	Aleksandr Mikhailov	challenger
Mari El	Leonid Markelov	challenger
Moscow City	Yuri Luzhkov	incumbent
Moscow Oblast	Boris Gromov	challenger
Orenburg	Aleksei Chernyshev	challenger
Perm	Yuri Trutnev	challenger
St. Petersburg	Vladimir Yakovlev	incumbent
Tambov	Oleg Betin	challenger
Tver	Vladimir Platov	incumbent
Ulyanovsk	Vladimir Shamanov	challenger
Vladimir	Nikolai Vinogradov	incumbent
Voronezh	Vladimir Kulakov	challenger

Sources: Compiled from data contained in various issues of the *EWI Russian Regional Report,* online at www.ewi.org, and Russian newspapers.

reflected the competition for power between the Kremlin and the "alternative regime," as discussed in chapter 5, that was currently under way in the nation as a whole. Seleznev, a leading figure in the Communist Party and the former speaker of the State Duma, had the explicit support of Putin, and Gromov, who is a member of the Fatherland–All Russia movement (OVR), had Moscow mayor Yuri Luzhkov behind him. Unlike the 1999 Duma elections, the Kremlin and its Communist allies lost this contest.

The Communist Party is by no means disappearing from the scene; nor is its alliance with the Kremlin complete. In a contest that illustrates the competition between the two camps, Governor Vladimir Yelagin of Orenburg, a member of Unity, lost his reelection bid to Communist Party candidate Aleksei Chernyshev. Communist Party candidate and incumbent governor Aleksandr Ryabov of Tambov also lost reelection, to a long-time enemy, former governor Oleg Betin. Betin, a Yeltsin appointee, had been defeated by Ryabov in 1995. This was a highly unusual race, since Betin had the support of both OVR and Unity. In fact, although Luzhkov had been outspoken in his support of Betin, Unity leader Sergei Shoigu made a visit to the region in a show of support.

The most publicized gubernatorial race in 2000 was probably the battle in Kursk, where incumbent governor Aleksandr Rutskoi was disqualified from running for reelection based on charges that he had made false tax declarations and violated electoral rules during his campaign.[8] These charges had been filed against Rutskoi by Chief Federal Inspector Viktor Suzhikov and

Kursk mayor Sergei Maltsev, both of whom were also running for the post. After he failed to convince the Supreme Court to overturn his disqualification, Rutskoi was out of the running. The Yeltsin and Putin administrations had both wanted Rutskoi out for a while. Yeltsin's animosity toward Rutskoi dates from the standoff between the two that ended in the bombing of the White House in October 1993. Putin's distaste for Rutskoi is much more recent, however, and is based on Putin's desire to rein in regional bosses.

Suzhikov and Maltsev perhaps hoped that they had removed their most serious competitor, but Communist Party regional secretary and State Duma deputy Aleksandr Mikhailov gave them a run for their money. In fact, Mikhailov edged out Suzhikov in the first round, thus forcing a runoff election between the two. While Suzhikov sought to win over those who had supported the other candidates in the first round, Mikhailov ran a quiet and confident campaign. This was the best tactic in a region like Kursk, where 65 percent of the electorate is fifty-five years old or older and there is a solid Communist majority.[9] Taking full advantage of his Communist affiliation, Mikhailov easily won the runoff on November 5 with 55 percent of the vote, compared to Suzhikov's 38 percent, with a turnout of almost 50 percent.

The situation was just the opposite down the road in Voronezh, where Communist incumbent Ivan Shabanov lost his reelection bid in December 2000 to former regional Federal Security Bureau (FSB) director Vladimir Kulakov. Shabanov, who had been the Communist Party regional committee head and led Voronezh through a rather slow transition in the early 1990s, was first elected governor in 1995. His administration was plagued with corruption, however, and on the eve of the elections his support in the polls was hovering around 5–6 percent. Although Shabanov was able to garner 15 percent of the vote on election day, Kulakov won a landslide victory with slightly less than 60 percent. One factor that contributed to Kulakov's win was his energetic and professional campaign. In addition to televised advertising, his campaign made informational literature widely available, and his campaign representatives (mostly members of Unity) were on hand in various locations throughout the city weeks prior to the election.[10] Overall, it was a competitive and professionally run election, with six candidates on the ballot representing diverse platforms.

Emerging Trends in Gubernatorial Politics

The election of former regional FSB director Vladimir Kulakov's election as governor of Voronezh is part of an emerging trend in Russian regional politics (see box, A Commanding Presence in Russia's Regions). Many other representatives of the security and military establishment have hung up their uniforms to run for political office. Putin himself made the jump from FSB head to prime minister and then president, and this trend is perhaps partially attributable to his successful career change and the popularity of his leadership style. With such an example having been set, it was

---

A Commanding Presence in Russia's Regions

Although Aleksandr Lebed is perhaps the best known general-turned-governor in Russia, he is neither the first nor the last to make such a change of career. Aleksandr Rutskoi, who was governor of Kursk from 1996 to 2000, also had a long and illustrious career as a general, as did Dzokhar Dudaev, former leader of the Chechen independence movement.

More recently, it seems that the lack of qualified personnel in the regions has led the Kremlin to "suggest" to military figures that they consider running for gubernatorial posts. In December 2000, Baltic Fleet Commander Vladimir Yegorov won election as governor of Kaliningrad, and Vladimir Shamanov, former commander-in-chief of Russia's ground forces, became governor of Ulyanovsk. They join Vladimir Semyonov, president of Karachaevo-Cherkessiya, and Boris Gromov, who was elected governor of Moscow Oblast in January 2000. Given that former military leaders have the respect and admiration of such a large segment of the Russian electorate, this is a trend that will probably continue.

---

only a matter of time before regional politicians followed suit. In this sense, Kulakov and others like him are sort of local versions of Putin, or perhaps "Lilli-Putins."

There are broader reasons for this trend as well. Although explicit support from Putin himself is certainly helpful, as the elections in Orenburg, Kursk, and Moscow Oblast illustrate, often it is not enough. In the new Russia, to gain a position of leadership in the regions one cannot simply depend on an appointment by the Kremlin—would-be "provincial tsars" must win at the polls. Of course, the Kremlin can assist considerably, not only by providing an endorsement and the possibility of future benefits but by offering party support as well. This proved particularly useful in Kulakov's case. Although he is not a member of Unity, the party of power threw its full weight and resources behind him, mostly running his successful campaign, although without taking credit for it. This was certainly useful for Kulakov's election bid. But why didn't Kulakov run on the party ticket, and why did Unity downplay its role in his campaign?

The answer may be in order to appeal to the Communist Party's support base, which is traditionally strong in Voronezh and the other blackearth regions, particularly among the elderly.[11] Although joining Unity would probably have contributed little or nothing to Kulakov's support among his target electorate—that is, the young and emerging middle class—running as an independent was a strategic move to keep from alienating the KPRF's traditional electorate. Instead, he sought to present himself as a more appealing alternative to the Communists. This last task was not very difficult in Voronezh, where the people were fed up with the corruption surrounding Shabanov and his administration.[12] The extent of the corruption was certainly not on par with that in some other regions, such as Primorskii Krai, but the citizens of Voronezh are perhaps not as tolerant of it, and they were ready for change. The question was, what kind of change?

In contemporary Russia, where corruption sometimes seems ubiquitous and can be a terrible problem, the reorganized KGB seems like the place to turn for honest and accountable leadership. During the Soviet period, two organizations had represented Soviet power most concretely—the Communist Party and the KGB. Although the corruption and special favors of the Communist Party were perhaps always known, the KGB was considered the "cleanest" and most honest organization in Soviet society. (Of course, the institution's role as the main arm of Soviet totalitarianism is now conveniently forgotten.) What better way to appeal to an electorate with a history of KPRF support, therefore, than to present them with a restyled officer from the security services?

Such was Kulakov's strategy in Voronezh. Kulakov avoided identifying himself with a reform party such as Unity while running a campaign that sought to appeal to all citizens.[13] In addition to his calls for "accountable power" (*otvetstvennaya vlast'*) and his wish for "people to live honestly," which were of course indirect attacks against the Shabanov regime's record of corruption, Kulakov also emphasized his own work in "the defense of the security and national interests" of Russia. This latter position is increasingly popular among a strong segment of society, which wants to restore Russian greatness and to find uniquely Russian answers to the country's problems, rather than simply adopt ready-made Western models. Because they can appeal to such a broad range of the electorate, representatives of the security and military establishment—Lilli-Putins—have a distinct electoral advantage and are likely to have an increasing presence in Russian regional politics in the future.

Russia's Twenty-One Presidents

Although the Federal Treaty of March 1992 sought to make all the subjects of the Russian Federation equal, the ethnic republics had been able not only to retain their special status as republics, but also to add to their trappings of statehood and economic autonomy. The concessions they won were later confirmed with the Constitution of 1993. Among them are the right of republics to adopt constitutions, whereas ordinary regions may only have charters, and the right of republics to elect presidents, as opposed to simply an executive head. This is actually only the beginning of the tremendous diversity among the regions, however, since these powers gave the republics great autonomy in determining the qualifications and powers of the executive heads.

There is great diversity among the executives that sit atop Russia's eighty-nine constituent units—who are collectively referred to as executive heads (*glavy ispolnitel' noi vlasti*). Although the republics retain the right to name their leaders as presidents, the heads of the other regions are often referred to as governor (*gubernator*), and many are officially known as the head of administration (*glava administratsii*). In all but one region (Dagestan) these officials are directly elected, with the term of office four years in most, although it is set at five years in several regions and even seven years in Kalmykiya, where Kirsan Iliumzhunov was elected in 1995. The required qualifications for these positions also vary, with residency requirements ranging from seven years in Kareliya and Khakassiya to fifteen years in Sakha to none at all in some. Minimum age requirements vary from thirty-five to forty years, but there is no minimum age in some regions, such as in Pskov, where thirty-three-year-old Evgenii Mikhailov was elected the youngest governor in Russia in 1996. Where established, the maximum age is ordinarily set at sixty to sixty-five years. Some regions require a minimum electoral turnout of 25 percent for a vote to be considered valid. Many regions have dropped this provision, however, due to difficulties reaching it even after conducting multiple rounds. Since low turnout has proven to be a particular problem, many regions try to schedule their elections to coincide with national elections. Liberal leaders in particular try to do so, since those who fail to turn out for off-year elections tend to be younger, more liberal members of the electorate.

Since Russia's republics have the right to elect presidents instead of ordinary executive heads, the leaders of the twenty-one ethnic republics have somewhat more prestige attached to their position, although their prestige is often hollow. For instance, while the president of Udmurtiya wields little influence, Moscow's mayor is one of the most powerful figures in Russian politics. Unlike the leaders of Russia's other subjects of the federation, the leaders of the republics were not initially appointed by Yeltsin, instead being chosen by their electorates from the start. Of the twenty-one executive heads of the republics, fourteen hold the title of president, and the rest are titled either head (*glava*) or chairman (*predsedatel'*). The one exception is the Republic of Dagestan, which is headed by a parliamentary-style government, with the executive chosen by the legislature.

Sixteen of these twenty-one ethnic republics were formerly Autonomous Soviet Socialist Republics within the Soviet Union, and Adygeya, Gorno-Altai, Karachaevo-Cherkessiya, and Khakassiya were autonomous oblasts. Additionally, the Chechen-Ingush Republic split into two republics. Following the collapse of the Soviet Union in December 1991, therefore, Russia was left with twenty-one ethnic republics.[14] Managing the nationalist aspirations of the ethnic republics was not easy, however, and between 1991 and 1993 many republics sought increased autonomy and in some cases even outright independence.[15] As the Yeltsin administration consolidated its power, these calls for independence diminished, as the republics instead sought to obtain privileges and concessions through negotiations with Moscow. Chechnya, however, remains an example of the failure of this process to be settled in such a way.

Many of the republic presidents had been elected to their first terms by 1993, and their terms thus began to expire in late 1997 and early 1998. In several instances incumbents won reelection with virtually no competition, as was the case with Leonid Potapov in Buryatiya, Nikolai Merkushkin in Mordoviya, and Murtaza Rakhimov in Bashkortostan. Many citizens chose to vote "against all" as a sign of protest rather than voting for the incumbent.[16] No candidate won by a greater landslide than did Valerii Kokov, who won reelection in Kabardino-Balkariya with 99.35 percent of the vote. This total even surpassed Mintimer Shaimiev's total when he won reelection in Tatarstan in 1996, with 97.14 percent of the vote.

In republics such as North Ossetiya and Ingushetiya, although the incumbents had a sizable advantage, there was still a genuine battle. President Ruslan Aushev in Ingushetiya faced serious competition from a local legal figure and State Duma deputy, but he was still able to muster 66 percent of the vote to win. Of all the republics to hold presidential elections in 1998, only in Kareliya did an incumbent lose, as Viktor Stepanov lost his post to Petrozavodsk city administrator Sergei Katanandov in a very close race.

An interesting race for a republic presidency took place in December 2000 in Mari El, where incumbent president Vyacheslav Kislitsyn was defeated by LDPR candidate Leonid Markelov. Markelov led the field with 29 percent of the vote in the first round held earlier in the month, and Kislitsyn followed at a close second with 25 percent. This was a virtual repeat of the 1996 election, in which Kislitsyn had edged out Markelov by a similar margin. The surprise this time around was Ivan Teterin, head of the Emergency Ministry's North Caucasus Regional Center. A virtual unknown just weeks earlier, Teterin emerged on the scene with strong financial backing (the dubious origins of which led police to question his campaign funders) and practically swept the ethnic Mari vote, which constitutes slightly more than 40 percent of the population.[17] This was only enough, however, to secure him a third-place finish, with slightly less than 19 percent of the vote. In the runoff, Markelov picked up almost all of the remaining votes, increasing his percentage to 58 percent, while Kislitsyn was only able to increase his to 33 percent. Markelov thus became the only LDPR member to win election to a republic presidency and only the second to win election as a regional executive head. Pskov governor Evgenii Mikhailov changed his party affiliation during his successful reelection bid in October 2000, so the LDPR can still only claim one Russian region.

Russia's Fourteen Thousand Mayors

Russia's republic presidents and governors are not the only "provincial tsars." Mayors are also important executives who wield considerable influence throughout Russia. Usually referred to as the head of the local administration (*glava mestnogo samoupravleniya*), municipal executives can be found in approximately fourteen thousand cities, districts, villages, urban settlements, and just about every territorial division in Russia. Only about ten thousand are directly elected—the rest are chosen by local assemblies of various sorts. The biggest difference among these officials is not their title or method of selection, however, but rather the territory they govern. Just as in the United States, mayors of large cities are quite powerful, whereas others are of limited importance. For instance, New York mayor Rudolph Giuliani is one of the most powerful mayors in the world. In Russia, too, some mayors are extremely powerful, none more so than the mayors of Moscow, and, secondly, St. Petersburg.

As mentioned above, Gavril Popov and Anatoly Sobchak were elected head of the Moscow and Leningrad city administrations, respectively, in June 1991. Popov resigned in 1992, leaving his deputy Yuri Luzhkov as mayor of Moscow, as the post was later officially renamed, on an acting basis. Luzhkov, who became one of Russia's most popular politicians and is credited with the extensive development and construction that took place in the capital throughout the 1990s, easily won reelection in June 1996, in a race that coincided with the first round of the presidential election. Luzhkov continued to play an ever more influential role in Russian politics, eventually emerging at the forefront of the Fatherland–All Russia (OVR) movement.

As OVR was attempting to make its mark on the Duma in the December 1999 legislative elections, Luzhkov, although his term was not set to expire until June 2000, ran for early reelection, probably for two reasons (*see box, Movin' on Up*). First, he would be able to take advantage of the publicity that was then surrounding OVR, and to jointly campaign for the party and his own reelection. There may have been another reason as well. Although he never made an official announcement, Luzhkov was certainly considering making a bid for the national presidency in June 2000.[18] Of course, he would not have been able to run for both posts simultaneously, so by securing reelection as mayor in December, Luzhkov would be prepared to make his bid for the presidency the following summer. Yeltsin's resignation and Putin's sky-high popularity, however, forced him to change his plan. Although Luzhkov is very popular in Moscow and easily won reelection as mayor with almost 70 percent of the vote, his appeal outside of the capital remains limited, as evidenced by the meager showing of OVR in the 1999 Duma elections. Perhaps this explains why he chose not to face Putin at the polls in March 2000.

Putin's political career, which culminated with his election as president in March, began with his service as deputy to Anatoly Sobchak, when Sobchak served as head of Leningrad. Putin's close relationship with Sobchak predates either's political career, as Putin was Sobchak's student at the Leningrad State University Institute of Law. Once Sobchak was elected head of the Leningrad city administration in 1991, Putin joined his mentor and embarked on a career in politics.

Movin' on Up

Luzhkov's plan to jump from mayor to president is indicative of a larger trend emerging in Russia, which already exists in other countries. Just as Ronald Reagan and George W. Bush used their positions as governor to launch their successful bids for the U.S. presidency, Russian governors are attempting the same thing. Thus far, however, they have found little success.

Although mayors have successfully moved up to governor in several regions, including in Kareliya, Novosibirsk, Penza, and Smolensk, no Russian mayor or governor has been able to capture the presidency. But this does not mean that none have tried. Aman Tuleev, governor of Kemerovo, has run in every Russian presidential election, and Konstantin Titov, governor of Samara, ran for the presidency in 2000. Both have found little support outside their home region, however. Aleksandr Lebed took a slightly different path—after placing third in 1996 he took the job of governor of Krasnoyarsk Krai in 1998, with an eye on running for election in 2000, although he eventually gave up the idea. Both Yeltsin and Putin have had careers in city politics (Yeltsin in Sverdlovsk and Putin in St. Petersburg), but their successful bids for the presidency were not tied to these jobs but to the position of speaker of the Russian parliament, for Yeltsin, and the office of prime minister, for Putin. So although the position of mayor may be a good position from which to launch a bid for a governorship, governors are probably still too limited in their national appeal to successfully win the presidency.

Sobchak's relationship with another deputy of his, Vladimir Yakovlev, was not as cordial. Yakovlev ran against his boss in the June 1996 gubernatorial election in St. Petersburg (n.b. that, although often referred to as mayor, the executive head of St. Petersburg is officially the governor). Yakovlev, who gained the endorsement of such parties as Yabloko, Common Cause, and Forward, Russia!, narrowly defeated Sobchak in the first round of voting. Putin then moved to Moscow and began his career in national politics. Sobchak missed seeing his protégé elected president by only a matter of weeks, as he died in February 2000—a terrible loss for Putin.

Vladimir Yakovlev stood for reelection in May 2000, and although Sobchak was out of the picture, Yakovlev had others to contend with. In addition to Yuri Boldyrev, a founding member of Yabloko who has since left the party (the "b" in the acronym *Yabloko* reflects Boldyrev's name), Yakovlev also faced Igor Artemev, the local Yabloko leader. Artemev had withdrawn in 1996 in order to support Yakovlev's bid against Sobchak, but he choose to run against him this time around. Artemev earned 15 percent of the vote and placed second, but Yakovlev won a landslide victory, with 72 percent of the vote.

Elections to Russia's Regional Assemblies

In addition to the various executive positions in Russia's regions, each oblast, krai, and republic also has a popularly elected legislative body, as do thousands of cities and towns. The city soviets and town councils are mostly of only local significance, but the importance of Russia's regional assemblies increased dramatically in 1995, when the law on the formation of the Federation Council provided that the chairmen of the regional assemblies hold half the seats in the upper house. Although this is changing under Putin, the regional assemblies are still significant representative institutions and an important dimension of grassroots political participation in Russia.

In 1989 and 1990 elections were held for legislative assemblies at all levels of government, including for regional and city legislatures. These elections were relatively free and competitive, which was a significant step toward democracy, but reformers and democrats competing for legislative posts faired poorly. Competitive elections had thus been introduced, but otherwise the city and regional soviets remained essentially as they had been throughout the Soviet period—large unwieldy organs dominated by Communist Party members, who were now busy obstructing reforms. In July 1991 these institutions were remodeled, so that they would be similar to the national legislature. Each regional soviet was required to form a "small" soviet one-fifth the size of the full soviet, with the small soviet functioning in a manner similar to the national Supreme Soviet, with its primary role being the management of the legislature's daily affairs. The full soviet then functioned as did the Congress of People's Deputies, mostly performing supervisory functions.

Following the October Events of 1993, during which many town and village soviets had supported Khasbulatov and the Supreme Soviet, Yeltsin issued a decree dissolving most local assemblies, except for those on the republic and regional level. Yeltsin planned to shift power toward regional and city executives, and away from the legislative bodies, much as he was doing with the national government. His attack on local legislatures soon abated, however, and although the assemblies were made largely subordinate to local executive authorities, these legislatures retained the right to pass laws. In particular, the new legislatures were charged with adopting regional statutes, drafting and overseeing regional budgets, and approving economic development programs.[19] Their membership was also professionalized, as deputies were now to be full-time legislators serving two-year terms. Additionally, most assemblies elected a chairman (*predsedatel'*) to function as the legislative head.

The new assemblies were much smaller than the old soviets, which had ranged in size from 200 to 400 members. There were between 15 and 50 deputies in the new regional assemblies and between 100 and 150 in the republic assemblies. Although Moscow did not specify what these new bodies were to be called, many local authorities chose to give up the name soviet in favor of older Russian terms, such as duma or *sobranie* (assembly), sometimes adding the term *zakonodatel'noe* (legislative), as in the *zakonodatel'naya duma* in Khabarovsk. The ethnic republics also looked back to their cultural traditions, coming up with some interesting designations: *Narodnyi Khural* in Buryatiya, *El Kurultaya* in Altai, and *Verkhovnyi Khural* in Kalmykiya and Tyva.

The initial elections to the new assemblies were scheduled to begin on December 12, 1993, coinciding with the constitutional plebiscite and elections to the Duma and Federation Council. Although it was also intended that they would be complete by March 1994, by that time only Moscow, St. Petersburg, and sixty-six other regions had held elections. Other regions procrastinated, and although most had held elections by 1995, a few waited even longer.

Moscow's declarations in other areas also went unheeded, as local officials attempted to alter the system to their own advantage.[20] Although Moscow had mandated that the elections be held in single-member districts, some regions adopted multimember district systems similar to the old zemstvos. This was the case in Bashkortostan, Sverdlovsk, and Tatarstan, as well as in a few other regions. Moscow also intended there to be a minimum turnout requirement of 25 percent, but this, too, would be changed, since it proved very difficult to meet. Because of the turnout requirement many elections were concluded only after several rounds of voting, and in many regions unoccupied seats were not filled until repeat elections were held coinciding with the December 1995 Duma elections.[21]

The most significant trend in the elections to Russia's regional assemblies between December 1993 and December 1995 was the frequent election of regional administrative and economic elites.[22] Local administrators and businessmen have many advantages, of course, such as comparatively high profiles and financial resources. In addition to managers of local enterprises and farm directors, however, many administrative officials were also elected. In Bashkortostan, heads of administration ran and won in every single district. The large-scale election of these executive officials is problematic, since often they had been appointed to their posts by the regional governor and could be removed by him. Their presense in the legislature thus limited the ability of the legislative branch to serve as an effective check on executive authority. Moreover, such officials were often reluctant to resign their lucrative and relatively powerful posts in the regional administration in order to become full-time lawmakers. In late December 1993 Yeltsin accordingly amended an earlier decree and allowed some to work as deputies on an unpaid, part-time basis. This did not resolve all of the problems, however, since these executive officials/part-time lawmakers were likely to resolve any confrontation between executive and legislative power in favor of the legislators' primary occupation. This fact, coupled with the already dominant position of regional executive authorities, ensured that local elites remained in power and that the regional assemblies remained weak.

Another important aspect was the critical role played by the Communist Party and its affiliated organizations. As mentioned above, in one of the first local elections held in Penza in January 1994, former Communist Party functionaries won forty of the forty-five seats in the regional assembly, which led Yeltsin to postpone gubernatorial elections until December 1996 and legislative elections until December 1997. Yeltsin changed his mind in 1996, however, and gave the local assemblies authority to schedule their own elections. As Yeltsin feared, the Communist Party was a major player in the regional legislative elections. Between 1995 and 1998, Communists ran in sixty-nine regions and won seats in fifty-five regional assemblies.[23] Other parties played a much smaller role, including Our Home Is Russia, which, although it managed to put candidates on the ballot in twenty-five regions, only won in twelve regions.[24]

Although the initial elections for all of Russia's regional assemblies were not concluded until 1998, many regions had already held their second set of elections by this time. One region that held its second legislative elections in 1998 was St. Petersburg, elections which proved to be among the most dirty, scandalous, and criminal held in Russia yet.[25] These elections would establish some trends that have since been replicated in other parts of the country.

The Elections to the St. Petersburg Legislative Assembly

There were several widely publicized events during the campaign for the 1998 St. Petersburg Legislative Assembly, including the murder of the leader of an electoral bloc and political party, the arrest of a candidate, and shots fired at the apartment window of yet another candidate. Why so much intrigue? A seat in the St. Petersburg legislature is a very lucrative position, much more valuable than a seat in any other regional assembly. In addition to an official car, an office in a palace, and a salary that is roughly seventeen times the minimum monthly wage (plus additional funds to cover "staff" expenses), the deputies each have at their disposal a reserve fund of about six to nine million rubles, which they can allocate practically as they see fit.[26]

A total of 587 candidates registered for the 1998 elections to the St. Petersburg Legislative Assembly (*Zakonodatel'noe Sobranie*), which has fifty seats and at the time had forty-eight sitting deputies (the other two having since moved on to positions as deputy governors). By election day that number had only been reduced to 577, which left an average of almost 12 candidates competing for each seat in the city's fifty single-member districts. Only 111 of the candidates had been officially nominated by approximately fourteen parties and electoral blocs. St. Petersburg is known as a Yabloko stronghold, sometimes being referred to as the "Apple" (*yabloko*) capital of Russia. Accordingly, Yabloko put forward 30 party candidates, more than any other party. A coalition of various Communist organizations, united under the banner Communists of Leningrad, put forward 29, and a democratic bloc named *Soglasie* (accord) put forward 20. Other parties and blocs, including the Congress of Russian Communities and the LDPR, also put forward candidates, though no more than 10 each. The real number of party candidates was actually significantly higher than 111, since many candidates who ran as independents also represented parties and movements.

The campaign included what one observer called "some of the dirtiest campaign tactics yet seen in Russia."[27] One of the more innocuous "dirty tricks" was that of running a candidate with the same name as a popular politician, in order to draw away support.[28] This has since become a common tactic, but the 1998 elections in St. Petersburg perhaps set the example. Threat tactics were also common. Candidates were arrested on questionable charges, and some even had their homes shot at. The most violent tactic may have been the assassination of popular democratic leader Galina Starovoitova, although her murder has never been officially related to her political career.

Turnout was slightly more than 40 percent in the first round of voting, which, although it seems low, is actually above average for a local election (bear in mind that many regions have had difficulty attaining a 25 percent turnout). This rate was higher than the turnout for the Moscow City Duma election the year before and the legislative elections held almost simultaneously in Krasnodar Krai and Volgograd Oblast. Voters may have had other motivations for turning out than their civic mindedness, however. Candidates and criminal elements engaged in large-scale vote buying, with prices as high as 300 rubles per vote, roughly the equivalent of one month's pension. There were numerous documented cases of hundreds of people being driven by bus to the polls. In one case, passengers were given Christmas cards with 25 rubles and "encouraged" to vote for Yuri Molchanov as they were exiting the bus. The Central Electoral Commission refused to do anything about the alleged vote buying, stating that it could not prevent people from voting simply because they arrived by bus.[29] There were other voting irregularities as well, including people casting multiple ballots, people casting votes in the place of others, and voting officials promoting candidates.

Only six candidates won in the first round of voting, all of whom were current deputies seeking reelection. Eventually twenty deputies won reelection. Competition in most districts was intense, and in many the margin between first and second place was very slight—a fraction of a percentage in some.[30] Yuri Boldyrev's bloc won the most seats of any party with fifteen, and Yabloko won eight. The Communist coalition won five, and four other parties and blocs won one seat each, with the remaining eighteen seats going to independents.

Yabloko's meager showing was surprising given that it supposedly had strong support in St. Petersburg and was labeled the favorite going into the election. Since there had only been three Yabloko deputies in the previous assembly, an increase to eight can be considered an improvement, but party leader Grigory Yavlinskii was hoping for sixteen seats. One reason why

Yabloko did not perform as well as expected may have been the strong opposition of candidates and local politicians. For instance, Governor Vladimir Yakovlev vehemently opposed Yabloko and used his government resources to run a propaganda campaign against the party. Yuri Boldyrev, who had been a founding member of Yabloko, also actively campaigned against the party, seeking to draw its supporters to his own bloc. Although he was successful in that endeavor, he was not able to effectively compete against Yakovlev in May 2000, when he lost his bid for governor of St. Petersburg, as discussed above.

Dirty Tricks and Democrats in Russia's Regions

Voters behave quite differently in Russia's regional elections than they do in national ones. Russian voters have made several very progressive choices in national elections on fundamental issues, such as the role of the state in economic and political affairs. When it comes to regional elections, however, voters seem to be more interested in local conditions and short-term benefits, thus tending to vote for candidates they think can improve their lives. Quite often, this means voting for candidates with real or imagined connections to the Kremlin, in the hope that such candidates will be able to deliver special concessions. Support from the Kremlin, therefore, whether it be an endorsement or assistance by pro-Kremlin parties during the campaign, goes a long way in facilitating the election of a regional leader. Since their decisions are so closely tied to economic perks and the performance of the economy, however, voters are also likely to vote out incumbents who fail to deliver on their promises, as illustrated by the roughly 50 percent turnover rate for incumbents seeking reelection. Moscow's strong role in regional politics indicates a less than effective separation of powers between the national and subnational levels of government—another troubling trend.

Local and regional elections have other problems as well, some of which are more easily remedied than others. For instance, turnout for regional elections is drastically less than that for national elections, meaning that local authorities are elected by only a small percentage of the electorate. Low turnout proved to be such a problem that the minimum requirement of 25 percent had to be eliminated in many regions—but this of course does not address the underlying problem. A possible solution, which has been used in several cases, would be to coordinate regional and local elections with national elections. Elections are held on strange schedules in the regions, leaving citizens confused about when they will be held. Moreover, the flexibility in the electoral schedule allows those in power to manipulate the outcome by choosing when elections will be held. Regional leaders may schedule an election to coincide with a particular event or national election in order to increase the likelihood of a certain segment of the electorate turning out—or staying home, as the case may be. For instance, an anti-reformist government would find it beneficial to schedule an election during the warm summer months, to ensure that the middle-class electorate would be away at their dachas or traveling abroad. Likewise, holding elections in the middle of winter in a Siberian region would also ensure a low turnout. With the almost complete lack of standardized electoral schedules, elected officials are allowed the very tempting opportunity to manipulate the schedules to their advantage.

Another problem in local and regional elections, particularly for executive positions, is the frequently low level of competition. In some regional elections no serious candidates run against the incumbents, which is slightly reminiscent of Soviet-era elections. In these cases the elections are merely pro forma, as the outcome is known before they are held. Regional leaders in these cases win landslide victories with more than 90 percent of the vote. Whether this is a sign of consensus or local authoritarianism is difficult to discern, but for Russia's diverse electorate to be so united behind a single candidate—when such unity is almost never found on the national level—is cause for suspicion.

The last disturbing trend in regional elections is the prevalence of dirty tricks, voter intimidation, and even political assassinations. The practice of running a candidate with the same name as a popular politician in order to cut into his or her support, for example, has caught on in regional elections. Other facets of regional politics are more disturbing. Local authorities have used their political and personal connections to deprive opponents of airtime and permits to hold rallies, candidates have been intimidated and arrested, and candidates and party leaders have even been murdered. These are the issues that should be of greatest concern. Such practices not only affect life in the regions but may also retard the further development of democracy in Russia as a whole.

For Further Reading

Golosov, Grigorii. "From Adygeya to Yaroslavl: Factors of Party Development in the Regions of Russia, 1995–1998." *Europe-Asia Studies* 51 (1999): 1333–65.

Hahn, Jeffrey. *Soviet Grassroots: Citizen Participation in Soviet Local Government.* Princeton: Princeton Univ. Press, 1988.

Kolosov, V. A., and R. F. Turovskii. "Fall and Winter Elections of Regional Executive Heads: Scenarios for Change." *Russian Politics and Law* 36 (March–April 1998): 67–85.

Lazareva, Natalia. *Elections and Professional Campaigning in Russia.* Gainesville, Fla.: Blue Unicorn, 1999.

Mote, Max. *Soviet Local and Republic Elections.* Stanford: Hoover Institution Press, 1965.

Orttung, Robert, ed. *The Republics and Regions of the Russian Federation.* Armonk, N.Y.: M. E. Sharpe, 2000.

Radio Free Europe/Radio Liberty, *RFE/RL Russian Federation Report,* online at www.rferl.org/russianreport.

Slider, Darrell. "Elections to Russia's Regional Assemblies." *Post-Soviet Affairs* 12 (1996): 243–64.

————. "Pskov under the LDPR: Elections and Dysfunctional Federalism in One Region." *Europe-Asia Studies* 51 (1999): 755–67.

Solnick, Steven, "Gubernatorial Elections in Russia, 1996–1997." *Post-Soviet Affairs* 14 (January–March 1998): 48–80.

Tsentral'naya Izbiratel'naya Komissiya Rossiiskoi Federatsii. *Vybory Glav Ispolnitel'noi Vlasti Sub'ektov Rossiiskoi Federatsii, 1995–1997.* Moscow: Ves' Mir, 1997.

Notes

1. Gavin Helf and Jeffrey Hahn, "Old Dogs and New Tricks: Party Elites in the Russian Regional Elections of 1990," *Slavic Review* 51 (fall 1992): 511–30.
2. Steven Solnick, "Gubernatorial Elections in Russia, 1996–1997," *Post-Soviet Affairs* 14 (January–March 1998): 48.
3. V. A. Kolosov and R. F. Turovskii, "Fall and Winter Elections of Regional Executive Heads: Scenarios for Change," *Russian Politics and Law* 36 (March–April 1998): 67. Although he is less explicit on this position, see also Solnick, "Gubernatorial Elections in Russia, 1996–1997," 48–80.
4. For more on this subject, see Darrell Slider, "Pskov under the LDPR: Elections and Dysfunctional Federalism in One Region," *Europe-Asia Studies* 57(1999): 755–67.
5. Leonid Smirnyagin, "V Gubernatorskikh Vyborakh, Rossiiskii Izbiratel'—Pobeditel'," *Rossiiskie Novosti,* December 3, 1996, 1–2.
6. "Bryansk: Lodkin Wins with 31 Percent," *EWI Russian Regional Report* 5 (18 December 2000), online at www.ewi.org.
7. "Khabarovsk: Ishaev Wins Decisive Victory," *EWI Russian Regional Report* 5 (18 December 2000), online at www.ewi.org.
8. "Communist Wins Controversial Russian Regional Election," *Russia Today* (6 November 2000), online at www.russiatoday.com.
9. Sergei Sarychev, "Communist Mikhailov Defeats Kremlin's FSB Man in Kursk," *EWI Russian Regional Report* 5 (8 November 2000), online at www.ewi.org.
10. Observed by the author during field research in Voronezh, November–December 2000.
11. This account was given to the author by Professor Aleksandr Slinko of Voronezh State University, a local expert and, not inconsequentially, campaign consultant to Kulakov.
12. See, for instance, "Voronezh Administration Linked to Misuse of Funds," *EWI Russian Regional Report* 5 (8 November 2000), online at www.ewi.org.
13. Although analysts of Russian politics (the author included) consider Unity a centrist party, the left-leaning segment of Russia's electorate considers Unity and most other parties to be reformist.
14. For more on the issue of Russia's ethnic homelands and their status within the Russian Federation, see James W. Warhola, *Politicized Ethnicity in the Russian Federation: Dilemmas of State Formation* (Lewiston, N.Y.: Mellen Press, 1996).
15. For an excellent account of this process and its dynamics, see Jeff Kahn, "The Parade of Sovereignties: Establishing the Vocabulary of the New Russian Federalism," *Post-Soviet Affairs* 16 (2000): 58–89.
16. Nikolai Petrov and Aleksei Titkov, "Rossiiskoe Obschestvo v 1998 g.," in *Regiony Rossii v 1998 g.,* ed. Nikolai Petrov (Moscow: Moscow Carnegie Center, 1999), 35.
17. Svetlana Zaslonkina, "Ethnic Vote Key in Mari El Elections," *EWI Russian Regional Report* 5 (18 December 2000), online at www.ewi.org. In this article Markelov is incorrectly referred to as Markov.
18. Luzhkov's intention to run for the presidency was made public as early as October 1998, when he declared it as he and other political figures urged Yeltsin to call early presidential elections. Yuri Nevskii, "Luzhkov's Tired of Waiting," *Kommersant-Daily,* October 6, 1998, 2.
19. Grigorii Golosov, "From Adygeya to Yaroslavl: Factors of Party Development in the Regions of Russia, 1995–1998," *Europe-Asia Studies* 51 (1999): 1334.

20. Darrell Slider, "Elections to Russia's Regional Assemblies," *Post-Soviet Affairs* 12 (1996): 251–52.
21. Ibid., 259.
22. Ibid., 244.
23. Golosov, "Factors of Party Development in the Regions of Russia, 1995–1998," 1336.
24. Ibid.
25. This account draws largely from the excellent analysis of the elections provided in Vladimir Kozlov, "Vybory v Zakonodatel'noe Sobranie S.-Peterburga," in *Regiony Rossii v 1998 g.*, ed. Petrov, 233–238.
26. Viktoria Voloshina, "Preelection Dealmaking," *Moskovskiye Novosti,* November 29–December 6, 1998, 2–3.
27. Celestine Bohlen, "Liberals Prevail over Violence, Dirty Tricks in St. Petersburg Voting," *New York Times,* December 8, 1998.
28. "Dirty Tricks and Democrats," *Economist,* December 5, 1998, 58.
29. Aleksandr Lvov, "They're on Their Way," *Novaya Gazeta,* November 30–December 6, 1998, 7.
30. Kozlov, "Vybory v Zakonodatel'noe Sobranie S.-Peterburga," 234.

8

Conclusion:
Elections and Voting in the New Russia

In the preceding pages we have explored Russia's rich electoral tradition and looked in detail at every major election in modern Russia, from the Duma elections of 1906 to the presidential and gubernatorial elections of 2000. As this analysis has shown, elections form just one part of the larger political system, which itself may rest anywhere along the continuum from totalitarianism to consolidated democracy. Russia's political system has occupied just about every possible position along that continuum at some time in its history, save that of consolidated democracy. The task now at hand is to assess the ways in which the process of holding elections may help Russia develop into just such a consolidated democracy—or possibly hinder its development. Although the country's future hinges on many things—not the least of which are the whims of its leaders—the ballot box will play an important role and has the potential both to foster democracy and to subvert it.

This conclusion explores several issues that could be obstacles to Russia's transition from a democratizing state to a genuine democracy. Among them is the compatibility between Russia's political culture and historical traditions, on the one hand, and modern politics, on the other. The institutional structures currently in place also present a challenge. There are problems in the electoral system that must be worked out, and the electorate must learn to adapt effectively to the system's incentives and disincentives. Political parties, if they can further develop and perform effectively, should prove critical in the latter regard. A greater degree of civic engagement is also vital to strengthening the country's nascent democracy. Finally, for Russia to become a consolidated democracy the system must be considered legitimate—by both the elite and the masses—and the ballot box must be regarded as the only legitimate means for the transfer of political power.

Cultural Traditions

Although there are several institutional obstacles to the further development of democracy in Russia, culture influences the way in which institutions function, so it makes sense to consider culture first. The primary question we need to be concerned with is, Are Russia's political culture and historical traditions compatible with democratic politics?

The Russian cultural trait with the greatest significance to this question is that of *sobornost*. The term sobornost, which is often loosely translated as "conciliarism" or "togetherness," refers to a desire that the various segments of society function and interact in harmony with each other. In the modern period, sobornost has been understood in terms of building consensus. In contrast to the Western concept of pluralism, which evolved to protect the rights of dissenters, sobornost emphasizes the right of different communities to exist and manifest their distinctive qualities within an overall framework of unity. What is developing in Russia can be defined as "managed pluralism," whereby the state, although imposing no one ideology, nevertheless takes steps to limit the number of options available.[1]

The trait of sobornost influences the political process in several ways. Some scholars have argued that sobornost compels elected leaders such as legislative deputies to view themselves first and foremost as representatives of the people.[2] The trait may explain the behavior of candidates and the electorate as well. For instance, it may compel some candidates to drop out of electoral races or to join forces with movements that have widespread support, in order to work toward unity and consensus. It also may lead the electorate to vote for moderate candidates and parties who prove to be less divisive than radical alternatives. The evidence to support this latter idea is supported by the electorate's move toward the center in recent elections.

The highest expression of the ideal of the harmony that is at the center of sobornost would be to have a leader everyone supports. President Vladimir Putin has come closer by far than any other leader in post-Soviet Russia to fulfilling this ideal, and it appears that Putin himself aspires to it, as indicated in his inaugural address: "I appeal also to those who voted for other candidates. I am convinced that you voted for our common future, for a better life, for a flourishing and strong Russia. Each one of us has his own experience, his own views, but we must be together. We have to do a great many things together."[3] Such accommodationist and non-confrontational values may go a long way toward smoothing the potentially conflictual and disintegrative transition from Communism.

Unfortunately, the ideal of sobornost also has a negative side. Sometimes the cost of achieving unity is suppressing deviant views, and in some situations unity can be achieved only through violent means. Historical and contemporary examples abound, from the practice of beating the opposition into submission in medieval Russia to forced unanimity during the Soviet period. As pointed out in an analysis of the noncompetitive elections of the Soviet Union, "first and foremost among the socializing functions of the elections is the theme of political and social unanimity of the Soviet People."[4] Electoral campaigns emphasized the themes of unity, harmony, and unanimity, which were expressed in speeches, banners, and newspaper headlines. This approach was not simply a trait of the Soviet totalitarian model, moreover, but was congruent with deep-seated elements of Russian political culture.

Harmony and accord are among the most prominent themes in today's campaigns as well. These ideals not only provide political parties with catchy names, such as Unity and Accord, Unity, Spiritual Heritage, and Our Home Is Russia, but also manifest themselves in various other ways. Again, the Putin presidency provides a good illustration. During Putin's electoral campaign in winter 2000, he received the support of many of the country's regional governors and republic presidents despite the fact that he was seeking to reel in their privileges as part of his policy of strengthening vertical power. These very same leaders who would be forced to relinquish special perquisites rallied their populations behind Putin and, although this is unconfirmed, may even have stuffed a few ballot boxes along the way. As strange as it may sound, vote manipulation itself is perhaps another manifestation of the ideal of sobornost—albeit one that stands in the way of the country's development as a democracy.

Making Russians' Votes Count

Although culture certainly affects the way in which institutions function, institutions themselves provide incentives and disincentives for people to act in various ways, and thus they can also present significant obstacles to the development of democracy in Russia. The foremost problem involving the interaction of culture and institutions in Russia today probably is the problem of electoral coordination. We often think of voting as a simple process of casting ballots, but in practice the electoral system serves as a set of mediating institutions through which voter preferences are translated into leadership selection. As in the U.S. presidential election in 2000, this process can be very controversial and divisive.

There have been several persistent problems, illustrated in the preceding chapters, associated with electoral coordination in Russia. The first involves the electorate's failure to make its votes count by voting in large numbers for parties that fail to surpass the minimum threshold in proportional representation contests, such as those for the State Duma. This was not a problem in 1993, as there was only time for a small number of parties to qualify for the ballot, but in the 1995 Duma elections nearly half of the electorate had thus wasted their votes. It seemed likely that this problem could potentially have eroded the legitimacy of the new system. The 1999 Duma elections, however, showed that the electorate could learn from its mistakes, as less than 19 percent of votes, in reaction to this disincentive, went to parties that failed to garner 5 percent.

There have been problems of coordination in single-member district races as well. Distinct segments of the electorate often, instead of voting as a bloc, split their votes among several candidates. Thus the segment that splits the least most often wins. Again, this situation should improve with time, as voters learn to assess which candidates have a realistic chance of winning and cast their ballots accordingly. Additionally, as voters begin to associate with parties, the parties themselves can help ameliorate some of these problems of coordination, in particular by attracting and backing the most promising candidates of their particular political persuasion. It will take time for the institutional design to structure electoral behavior, however, both among candidates and among voters.

Political Parties and Interest Aggregation

Political parties perform the critical role of aggregating mass interests into party platforms as they seek to win political power. By establishing programs that allow voters to identify the party's positions on key issues, they help voters make informed decisions at the polls. Parties are also critical in helping to overcome problems in electoral coordination, as they can unite voters behind a particular slate of candidates. Instead of competing among a large field of candidates at the polls, aspiring politicians can compete within the party before facing the electorate, a process that eventually puts the full support of the party and its voter base behind the party's selected candidates.

Parties also help candidates in other ways. First, half of the seats in the State Duma are allocated on the basis of proportional representation—an incentive for parties to form if there ever was one. Prior to 2001, these seats can only be contested through a party apparatus of some type, including the more loosely organized entity of a political "movement." Since only parties that reach the 5 percent threshold can share in the spoils, the strength of a party and its appeal to voters also matter considerably when voters make decisions about which party to support. Most voters will choose from among the parties that have the best chances of winning—which further contributes to the formation of strong parties.

In the single-member district races, parties also play an important role, as party-supported candidates have a greater chance of winning than independents. In the 1999 Duma elections, party-supported candidates won almost 55 percent of the races they contested, and almost all of these seats were won by candidates supported by one of Russia's seven largest parties. These facts should induce those with political ambitions to seek the backing of a major party, one with a strong support base and organizational depth.

Also encouraging party consolidation are punitive provisions in the electoral laws that force losers to pay for their electoral failures. Parties that fail to reach a certain vote total can, for example, forfeit the monetary deposits that are required to register, be forced to repay the Central Electoral Commission for funds allocated during the campaign, and be forced to compensate the media for the coverage and free advertisement it provides. If these penalties do not actually bankrupt these small parties, they will at least discourage them from running on their own in the future and will likely compel them to join forces with other parties. Either way, the number of parties will be reduced, and voters will be given a more reasonable number of parties to choose from. As with Russia's economy in general, however, getting people to actually pay what they owe is a different story altogether. The Central Electoral Commission successfully sued the twelve organizations that failed to garner 2 percent of the vote in the 1999 Duma elections, but a year after the election more than half had still not paid back the money they owed.[5]

To further promote party development, the Russian government is attempting to provide greater incentives for parties to form and to erect obstacles to their competitors. In May 2001 a new law on political parties proposed by Vladimir Putin was passed by the Duma. The law prohibits all political organizations except duly registered parties from participating in elections, institutes strict rules and procedures for organizations seeking party status, and requires parties to file regular reports on their activities, including fiscal affairs.[6] Although these provisions will limit both party and non-party organizations in various ways, the law also provides support for parties, as it will provide an annual subsidy of twenty kopeks per vote received to parties that garner more than 3 percent of the vote.[7] The changes in the law are positive in many ways, particularly in reducing the number of party and non-party organizations (which numbered almost 200 when the law was enacted), but they also have the potential to diminish the autonomy of political parties and could be used to undermine democracy in the long run.

Civic Engagement

In addition to political parties and institutions, a great deal of the responsibility for the success of democracy rests with the people themselves. To serve as an effective check on the power of the state, Russia's citizenry needs to be interested, active, and politically efficacious. Engaged citizens would not only follow events and participate in formal political and informal civic activities but also make informed choices about the country's future. In developing such a citizenry, Russia today faces formidable obstacles, not the least of which are voter apathy and misunderstanding of the rules of electoral politics. Government agencies and domestic and foreign civic organizations sponsor numerous programs that attempt to increase citizen participation in the political process, such as NGO-sponsored civic awareness initiatives and government-run "get out the vote" promotions. Perhaps the most innovative approach has been the use of voting "lotteries" in several districts, where drawings are held and some voters win prizes. Although such programs may effectively increase voter turnout, they cannot substitute for a genuine civil society, which in the end is a prerequisite for a successful democracy.

The percentage of Russia's eligible citizenry that participates in elections is quite high in most places, which is one indicator that the degree of civic engagement is strong. Electoral turnout in Russia has been consistently high since the introduction of competitive elections in 1989, when it was almost 90 percent for the elections to the Congress of People's Deputies. Although turnout has declined since then, it has remained near 60 percent in all subsequent national elections, except for a dip to slightly more than 50 percent in the 1993 Duma elections, which were conducted hastily in the wake of the extralegal, forcible dissolution of the Supreme Soviet. For presidential elections, which are arguably the most significant, turnout has consistently been near 70 percent. The high level of political participation is not limited to national elections, moreover, as turnout for local and regional elections is high as well, although in certain districts it does drop substantially below the national average.

One of the most crucial ways civil society can check the power of the state is by organizing rapidly in defense of a cause, in the form of spontaneous demonstrations, public outcry, and even strikes.[8] Civil society may lie dormant until such activity is necessary, which makes any determination of its strength highly problematical, but evidence of civic engagement is readily apparent in contemporary Russian society. Cooperative efforts at managing social problems include activities such as the Spring Beautification Day and citizen street patrols for high-crime areas in various cities. Collective efforts by local trade unions and the residents of Vorkuta and Anzhero-Sudzhensk, which blocked the trans-Siberian railroad several times in 1998 in protest of the non-payment of wages, also attest to the ability of Russian citizens to place demands on the government for better treatment instead of just sitting idly by as deferential subjects. Even if it appears that there is no efficacious civil society, therefore, one may emerge in times of need.

A more mundane, but just as important, function of civil society is participation in voluntary associations, such as fraternal organizations, sporting clubs, and cultural associations. Although the absolute number of clubs and cultural associations in Russia has declined slightly since the Soviet period (from 66,000 in 1992 to 58,600 in 1996), the decline reflects the change from regimented participation under the Soviet regime to genuine voluntary participation in the new Russia.[9] Considering that during this conversion regime-sponsored associations lost funding and died off, and truly voluntary associations sprang forth in their place, the continuing high levels of participation attest to the vibrancy of associational life in Russia. It is more vibrant in some regions than in others, with regions such as Novgorod, Smolensk, and Voronezh having some of the highest levels of associational activity, whereas other regions are less favorably endowed.[10]

Finally, survey data, which can lend insight into the actual practices, values, and attitudes of Russian citizens, indicate that nearly one-third belong to voluntary associations.[11] And although politics may rank last in their hierarchy of values, fully 38 percent of Russians say that politics is important to them—more than one-third of the population. So, although only one-third of Russians have strong feelings of political efficacy and can be labeled as civically engaged, this percentage provides a substantial basis for the future growth of civil society in Russia.

Legitimization and Consolidation

Besides the cultural and institutional obstacles to the consolidation of Russia's fledgling democratic system, an additional obstacle, which has perhaps received the least attention, is that some may not consider the system itself to be legitimate. After all, the success of democracy does not simply depend on whether elections are held according to schedule. For Russia to develop into a genuine democracy, the people must consider the institutions and the government it chooses to be legitimate. The system's legitimacy must derive from the citizens' willing cession of political authority to the government, which makes authoritative decisions in the polity.

All indicators suggest that the vast majority of Russians consider the government and its institutions legitimate. Unlike the Soviet regime, which took several years to consolidate its power and whose legitimacy was perhaps always in question, the Russian Federation today is generally accepted as the legitimate political authority over the territory it claims to govern. Although the war in Chechnya may seem to cast doubt on the country's legitimacy, the conflict has remained territorially confined, and that most of Russia's citizens have chosen not to follow a similar path attests to their support for the status quo. Moreover, unlike in the early years of the Bolshevik regime, there is no government in exile or band of forces waiting to seize the moment and overthrow the regime. Absent such irredentist forces, the matter of the system's legitimacy is one that will be determined by the relationship between the government and the governed.

In modern political systems, of course, citizens cede political authority through the ballot box. That more than 50 percent of eligible Russian citizens consistently take part in the electoral process, and that the overwhelming majority vote for parties that do not seek to overthrow the system, are thus important positive signs. There are several parties that question various aspects of the new system, but they receive little support and have become more moderate over the years. In fact, no organized group with a significant support base currently advocates that the system be overthrown, and no party that contested a seat in the 1999 Duma elections proposed reversing any critical component of the current system.

Just as ordinary citizens must consider the electoral process a legitimate means of selecting leaders and replacing political elites, the elites, for their part, must consider the ballot box to be the only legitimate means of gaining political power. As long as they do, political competition will continue to take place according to established procedures, and elections will continue to be held on a regular basis. Of course, some groups will attempt to bend the rules in their favor or gain preferential access. This is to be expected and happens even in consolidated democracies. It is simply a part of the process of fine-tuning that democracy requires, a process that is perhaps never finished.

Finally, Russians now have great faith in their leader and the country's key institutions. A full year after his election, 75 percent of Russians express faith in Vladimir Putin.[12] This stands in sharp contrast to the Yeltsin years, when the president's approval rating hovered in the single digits. Russians not only trust their chosen leader but also trust the system itself, as evidenced by the percentage who express faith in key governmental institutions. Despite its checkered past, almost 51 percent of Russians have faith in the Federal Security Bureau (the successor to the KGB), and 68 percent have faith in the army.[13] Russians thus seem to have great trust in the new system, but the consolidation of democracy in Russia also depends on one other factor—whether the country's leaders have faith in the people and will continue to promote democracy.

Looking toward the Future

Numerous obstacles stand in the way of Russia's effort to develop into a consolidated democracy. Institutional structures remain limited in their ability to affect electoral politics, political parties are developing slowly, and civic apathy is perhaps as prevalent as civic engagement. None of these obstacles should prove insurmountable, however. As the preceding analyses have documented, Russia's experience with democratic elections is no brief flirtation, and considerable progress has been made in the past few years. Although there is no guarantee that Russia will continue along the same path, if democracy does fail to take root in Russia, it is very likely that the blame for this will rest elsewhere than with the electoral system.

For Further Reading

Colton, Timothy. *Transitional Citizens: Voters and What Influences Them in the New Russia*. Cambridge: Harvard Univ. Press, 2000.

Cox, Gary. *Making Votes Count: Strategic Coordination in the World's Electoral Systems*. Cambridge: Cambridge Univ. Press, 1997.

Golosov, Gregory. *Partiinye Sistemy Rossii i Stran Vostochnoi Evropy*. Moscow: Ves Mir, 1999.

Lowenhardt, John, ed. *Party Politics in Post-Communist Russia*. London: Frank Cass, 1998.

Marsh, Christopher. *Making Russian Democracy Work: Social Capital, Economic Development, and Democratization*. Lewiston, N.Y.: Edwin Mellen Press, 2000.

McFaul, Michael, Nikolai Petrov, and Andrei Ryabov, eds. *Rossiya v Izbiratel'nom Tsikle 1999–2000 godov*. Moscow: Moscow Carnegie Center, 2000.

Miller, Arthur, Gwyn Erb, William Reisinger, and Vicki Hesli. "Emerging Party Systems in Post-Soviet Societies: Fact or Fiction?" *Journal of Politics* 62 (2000): 455–90.

Petro, Nicolai, *The Rebirth of Russian Democracy: An Interpretation of Political Culture*. Cambridge: Harvard Univ. Press, 1995.

Sergeyev, Victor, and Nikolai Biryukov. *Russia's Road to Democracy*. Aldershot: Edward Elgar, 1993.

Notes

1. Nikolas Gvosdev, "Tolerance versus Pluralism: The Eurasian Dilemma," *Analysis of Current Events* 12 (2000): 7–10. See also Nikolas Gvosdev, "Constitutional Loopholes, Managed Pluralism, and Freedom of Religion," *Religion, State, and Society*, forthcoming in 2001.
2. Victor Sergeyev and Nikolai Biryukov, *Russia's Road to Democracy* (Aldershot: Edward Elgar, 1993), 130.

3. "Putin's Inaugural Address: 'We Believe in Our Strength,'" *New York Times,* May 8, 2000.
4. Theodore Friedgut, *Political Participation in the USSR* (Princeton: Princeton Univ. Press, 1974), 138.
5. Olga Tropkina, "Losers Don't Want to Pay Up," *Nezavisimaya Gazeta,* January 20, 2001, 3.
6. Andrei Stepanov, "Playing for Money," *Moskovskiye Novosti,* February 6–12, 2001, 6; and Ana Uzelac, "Putin Wins Vote to Limit Parties," *Moscow Times,* May 25–27, 2001.
7. Svetlana Lolayeva, "Count Off by Twos!" *Vremya Novostei,* February 8, 2001, 2.
8. For more on Russian civil society, see Christopher Marsh and Nikolas Gvosdev, eds., *Civil Society and the Search for Justice in Russia* (Lanham, Md.: Lexington Books, forthcoming in 2002).
9. Goskomstat Rossii, *Rossiia v Tsifrakh, 1998* (Moscow: Goskomstat Rossii, 1998), 170.
10. Christopher Marsh, "Social Capital and Democracy in Russia," *Communist and Post-Communist Studies* (June 2000): 183–99.
11. Data from Elena Bashkirova, *Value Change and Survival of Democracy in Russia, 1995–2000* (Moscow: ROMIR, 2001). Available online at www.romir.ru, May 15, 2001.
12. ROMIR, "Sotsial'no-Politicheskaya Zhizn' Rossii v Zerkale Obschestvennogo Mneniya," *Informatsionno-analiticheskii Ezhemesyachnii Biulleten',* March 2001. Available online at www.romir.ru, May 15, 2001.
13. Ibid.

Chronology of Elections and Important Political Events

988	Prince Vladimir converts to Christianity
Before 1500	Veche falls into decline
1549	First convocation of Zemskii Sobor
1598	Death of Tsar Theodore and extinction of the Riurik dynasty; Boris Godunov elected tsar; Time of Troubles begins
1613	Zemskii sobor elects Mikhail Romanov tsar
Mid-1600s	Zemskii sobor falls into decline
Early 1700s	Duma dies out
1711	Peter the Great creates Governing Senate
1766	Catherine the Great convenes Legislative Commission
1825	Decembrist uprising
1861	Abolition of serfdom
1864	Zemstvo reforms
1870	Municipal reforms enacted; popularly elected town councils introduced
January 1905	Bloody Sunday massacre
October 1905	Nicholas II issues October Manifesto
January 1906	Elections to the First Duma
February 1907	Elections to the Second Duma
June 1907	Nicholas II dissolves Second Duma
Fall 1907	Elections to the Third Duma
1912	Elections to the Fourth Duma
March 1917	Nicholas II abdicates
November 1917	Bolshevik Revolution; elections to Constituent Assembly
January 1924	Vladimir Lenin dies
March 1953	Joseph Stalin dies
1956	Nikita Khrushchev delivers Twentieth Party Congress speech; beginning of de-Stalinization

April 1985	Mikhail Gorbachev becomes general secretary of the Communist Party
June 1987	Local Soviet elections; limited competition
March 1989	Elections to the USSR Congress of People's Deputies
February 1990	Article 6 of Soviet Constitution is rescinded
March 1990	Gorbachev elected president of the Soviet Union
March 1990	Elections to the RSFSR Congress of People's Deputies
March 1991	Referendum on the fate of the Soviet Union and creation of Russian presidency
June 1991	Russian presidential election; Boris Yeltsin elected president of Russia
August 1991	August coup
December 25, 1991	Gorbachev resigns as president of the Soviet Union
April 1993	April referendum
October 1993	Stand-off between Yeltsin and the Supreme Soviet
December 1993	December elections and constitutional plebiscite
December 1995	Elections to the State Duma
June 1996	Round one of presidential elections
July 1996	Round two of presidential elections; Yeltsin reelected president
December 1999	Elections to the State Duma
December 31, 1999	Boris Yeltsin resigns the presidency of the Russian Federation; Vladimir Putin becomes acting president
March 2000	Russian presidential election held; Putin elected president

Index

RUSSIA AT
THE POLLS